Computer-Based
Problem Solving Process

Computer-Based
Problem Solving Process

Teodor Rus
The University of Iowa, USA

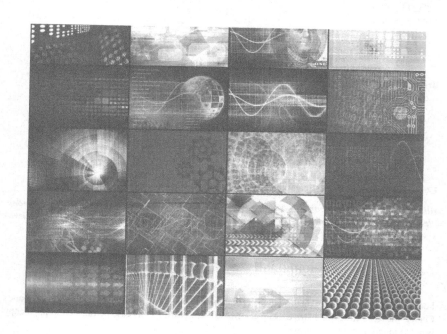

 **World Scientific**

NEW JERSEY · LONDON · SINGAPORE · BEIJING · SHANGHAI · HONG KONG · TAIPEI · CHENNAI

Published by

World Scientific Publishing Co. Pte. Ltd.

5 Toh Tuck Link, Singapore 596224

USA office: 27 Warren Street, Suite 401-402, Hackensack, NJ 07601

UK office: 57 Shelton Street, Covent Garden, London WC2H 9HE

Library of Congress Cataloging-in-Publication Data
Rus, Teodor.
    Computer-based problem solving process / Teodor Rus, The University of Iowa, USA.
        pages cm
    Includes bibliographical references.
    ISBN 978-9814663731 (hardcover : alk. paper)
    1. Computer-aided engineering. 2. Problem solving--Data processing. 3. Mathematics--Data
processing. I. Title.
    TA345.R87 2015
    006.3'33--dc23
                                2014047544

British Library Cataloguing-in-Publication Data
A catalogue record for this book is available from the British Library.

Printed in Singapore

To Elena, my wife, Daniela, our daughter
Isabella and Jacqueline, our granddaughters.

Preface

Computer-Based Problem Solving Process is a work intended to offer a systematic treatment to the theory and practice of designing, implementing, and using software tools during problem solving process. This work is meant to crown my 22 years of experience in designing and implementing system software and 30 years of teaching a variety of courses in computer science curricula.

Teaching a course on "Introduction to System Software" in early 1980, I observed that there were no books providing a comprehensive treatment of system software as a whole. People used books on assembly language programming or introductory books on operating system as textbooks for this course. Based on my previous 20 years of experience with the design, implementation, and use of system software tools during problem solving process, I ventured to fill out this gap in computer science curricula. So, helped by my daughter Daniela Rus, now a Professor of EECS MIT and Director of CSAIL, a PhD Student at Cornell University in 1980s, we started the development of a textbook for "Introduction to System Software" course under the title *System Software and Software Systems: Concepts and Methodology*. Soon it became obvious that this was not to be an easy job. To make it feasible we split the system software tools into two categories: tools helping people to develop computer programs and tools helping people to execute programs on a given computer platform. Hence, the book became a two-volume book, a volume on programming support environment, and a volume on program execution environment. But the tools in the two environments are not independent of each other. To be executed programs need to be first developed and programmers need to execute software tools in order to develop programs. So, how do we present them: programming first and then program execution or vice versa? In addition, software tools presentation and learning requires a specific algorithmic language that handles computer concepts as well as other abstractions specific to the computer architecture and functionality during program development and program execution. Consequently, the plan for the book development has shown us that we need first a book on the algorithmic language we need to use to present the subject matter. Since "system" was used in computer science from its very beginning in conjunction with the computer architecture and computer functionality, the concept of a system became the basic brick in the development of the system software language to be used in our book. And the system software and software systems became a three-volume book: *Systems Methodology for Software* (Volume I), *Execution Support Environment* (Volume II), and *Programming Support Environment* (Volume III).

While Volume I and Volume II have been developed and published by World Scientific in 1990s, our enthusiasm for the completion of the entire project diminished. The books we published were not received by computer community with the enthusiasm we expected. Moreover, during the last 15 years programming support environments of computer platforms evolved towards a collection of tools that support computer-based problem solving process which include programming, but are not limited to programming only. So, we were straggling with the development of Volume III. While Daniela moved into a totally different direction, my determination to complete the project diminished and in 2007 I abandoned the project altogether. However, using Volume I to teach "Introduction to System Software" I realized three important things for computer professional education and computer science evolution:

(1) **System software is dedicated to computer experts.** System software evolved as the theory and practice of the design and implementation of program development and program execution tools, from assemblers, loaders, compilers, operating systems, to domain dedicated software tools and APIs. Hence, system software, as developed so far, is dedicated to the computer experts in particular, instead of being dedicated to computer users in general.

(2) **Complexity of software tools grows uncontrollably.** Software complexity is due to the contradiction between the universal nature of problem domain and the specific nature of computer as a problem solving tool. This contradiction is resolved by making the computer a universal problem solving tool. This means that in order to be solved by a computer, irrespective of problem domain, the problem and its

solution algorithm must be expressed in terms of the machine language, which in fact *embeds problem domain within computer environment.* That is, programming is provided as the "one-size-fits-all" solution to computer use as a problem solving tool. The increasing diversity of problem domains grows uncontrollably with computer applications and makes the complexity of the software tools supporting problem solving growing uncontrollably. Hence, complexity of software tools involved in problem solving process threatens the software technology itself.

(3) **Computer education weakens with software complexity.** The efforts to simplify computer-based problem solving process fail due to programming as the one-size-fits-all solution. As an example consider the Web technology. Though it expands ubiquitously computer utilization, it also requires computer user to learn computer networks, in addition to the language of system software, which complicates the methodology, rather then simplifying it.

This situation convinced me that Volume III of the book *System Software and Software Systems: Concepts and Methodology* should not be dedicated to the programming support environment. Instead, I should roll back the history of computer software development identifying the cornerstones of its evolution and the changes needed to redirect the software tools towards assisting the computer-based problem solving process, including program development and execution. Hence, the new book should be titled: *Computer-Based Problem Solving Process.* System software is treated in this book as an illustration of tool development assisting the problems raised by computer use for computer programming and program execution. Therefore this book will give its readers opportunities to make contributions towards the development of a software technology that will free non-expert computer users from the requirement to be computer experts. Distinguishing between people in charge of software development (computer experts) and people in charge of using computer to solve domain specific problems, provides new solutions to the problems raised by the contradiction between universality of problem domain and specificity of the computer as a problem solving tool. In particular, this provides viable solutions for controlling software complexity and enabling appropriate computer education. In these solutions computer education is split between computer programming and program execution, carried out in computer science as *computational thinking*, and computer use, carried out as the computational emancipation of problem domain or *thinking computationally.*

Looking carefully at the cornerstones of the software technology one may observe that for each system software tool approached, such as operating systems, programming languages, file systems, etc., as well as for each software system used by applications, such as Databases, GUI, Web, etc., the development of the software component treating it relies on the development of a *Domain Algorithmic Language* (DAL) and of dedicated tools handling this language. DAL of a software component was used by computer experts as a thinking computationally tool (that is, using the computer as a "brain assistant") to automate the component implementation and use. Thus, assembly language is the DAL of machine language program development, high-level programming languages are the DALs of compilers and interpreters, virtual monitors are DALs of various operating systems, information organization and storage are DALs of file systems, etc. Furthermore, through the education process the DAL of each system software component is used as a fragment of natural language of computer experts manipulating that software component. This in fact embeds the language of the software tools within the natural language of computer experts. Question we are asking now is: can we develop software that would allow the language of software tools to be embedded within the natural language of problem domain experts? Various researches on domain dedicated software provide various flavors of answers to this question. But all these answers keep asking computer user to be computer science educated.

The idea for a software technology promoted by this book is the *development of software tools that embed computer platform within the problem domain approached*. By this embedding the computer platform becomes part of the natural language employed by computer user during problem solving process, exactly as a software tool becomes part of the natural language of software implementer through the appropriate DAL. Therefore a computer user can use his computer as a *brain assistant* integrated within his natural language. That is, during the problem solving process, a computer user uses his computer at the level of his natural language, assisted by the brain assistant, thus "thinking computationally". Consequently, this releases computer user from the requirement of being computer educated, thus simplifying the process of computer education. The implementation of this idea is based on the approach called "Computational Emancipation of the Application Domain" (CEAD) which consists of:

- Conceptual formalization of problem domain using an ontology where concepts are associated with computer artifacts implementing them.

- Development of a Domain Algorithmic Language (DAL) to be used by domain experts during their problem solving process. DAL algorithms represent solutions to the problems raised by domain experts.
- Providing the problem domain with a virtual machine whose instructions are the computer artifacts associate with domain concepts in the domain ontology.
- Developing DAL interpreters that execute DAL algorithms (programs) developed by DAL experts during problem solving process.

This idea is practically used by all human dedicated technologies developed so far. Since software became part of human problem solving process, to sustain further development of computer technology we need to develop software tools whose usability transcend the computer expert and can be used by every problem solver at the level of her problem domain, without requiring computer user to be computer educated. The book *Computer-Based Problem Solving Process* restructures the presentation of system software tools within this framework. That is, this book illustrates the problem solving process using computer as a "brain assistant", thus thinking with the help of the computer or "thinking computationally", by presenting system software tools in the framework discussed above. Hence, each component of the system software discussed in this book will be presented by first computationally emancipating the problem domain that software component approaches using the following pattern:

- Provide a specification of the Problem Domain (PD) approached by the software component;
- Develop the Domain Algorithmic Language (DAL) characteristic to the problem domain to be used by programmers (domain experts) during problem solving process;
- Design a Domain Dedicated Virtual Machine (DDVM) (a scripting language) that executes (interprets) DAL algorithms (programs);
- Implement the DDVM on the computer platform and make it available to the domain experts.

Problem domain discussed in this book is computer program development and execution. To make this approach usable beyond program development and execution we will integrate the material presentation within the Polya's four steps problem solving methodology: (1) formulate the problem, (2) develop a solution algorithm, (3) perform the algorithm on a problem instance, (4) check the solution correctness. Consequently the material presented in the book is organized into five parts:

(1) The language: systems methodology;
(2) The computer: architecture and functionality;
(3) Software tools supporting program execution;
(4) Software tools supporting program development;
(5) Software tools supporting computer operation during problem solving process.

The material is presented using conventional software technology and is structured by the pattern presented above, at each step identifying the PD, DAL, DDVM, and DDVM Interpretation tools. While these components of the software technology dedicated to system software tool development are well understood and easy to identify and implement, their identification and implementation in the framework of another problem domain may raise challenges. We will use at least one other problem domain (possible vector algebra) to show how to use domain ontology as a PD specification tool, how to use the Web to develop DAL distributed implementation, and how to use Cloud Computing to design and implement DDVM, thus transforming problem solving process into a business process manipulating domain services. In other words, the book will show how the evolution of Computer-Based Problem Solving Process leads to Web-Based Problem Solving Process, which characterizes the software we envision.

To whom is this book addressed? The book is addressed to the system software teachers, to the designers and implementers of various parts of the system software, and of course to anybody who would like to use a computer to solve specific problems of his domain of expertise. As described above, we rely on a new kind of software (remember, embedding computer within the problem solving process, not vice versa). Since this software is not yet systematically developed, this book is not a textbook. However, to sustain the ubiquitous computing we need to prepare computer technology for the phase when it will be offered to the people, as any other human dedicated technology, independent of their computer expertise. Hence, the author hopes that this book may contribute to the development of software dedicated to computer user (including computer experts involved in the software development process).

Thanks are due to all my students for "digesting" this material in a time when it was too crude, and to the publisher, particularly Dr. Ng Yan Hong and Linda Kwan, for putting this text in the avant garde of computer science future, where it should be.

Teodor Rus

Contents

Part 3 Software Tools Supporting Program Execution   113

Part 4   Software Tools Supporting Program Development   197

PART 1
Systems Methodology

Chapter 1

Introduction to System Software

System software is a collection of software tools with the goal of making computers convenient and efficient by:

- allowing programmers to develop programs using a human logic;
- allowing hardware to execute programs using a machine logic.

After more that 50 years of computer use during problem solving process the question one may raise is: does the system software really make computers convenient to computer users?

Postponing the answer to the previous question, we say that today goal of system software should be: *allow application domain experts so solve their problems by manipulating concepts and abstractions of their own problem domains using a computer platform.*

This means move the computer process involved within problem solving from the computer environment within the application domain environment. For example, rather than developing a C or Fortran program to solve a second degree equation $ax^2 + bx + x = 0$ a high-school students should do by typing:

`computer: solve equation` $ax^2 + bx + c = 0$

Likewise, a mechanical engineer should be able to solve differential equations without writing (conventional) Fortran programs!

So, how do we develop (engineer) system software? Is this approach amenable to developing software tools that can be used by application domain experts independent of their computer education?

While developing software tools we should use the same approach as for any other engineering activity, that is:

- Define the artifacts (objects) handled by system software;

3

- Develop a methodology for handling system software artifacts;
- Develop tools to perform this activity.

We use systems methodology for system software development. The rationale for using systems methodology for software tool development are:

- Systems describe complex relationship among things and systems abound in computer industry;
- A system can be formally defined in the framework of universal algebra;
- Similarity of the objects manipulated by algebra and computer science, which are abstractions;
- Reuse of the theories developed by algebraic methodology in the framework provided by system software;
- Universality of algebraic methodology for science discovery.

1.1   Abstraction Manipulation

Since software objects are abstractions the first thing we need is a mechanism for abstraction manipulation. This mechanism is provided by the algebraic methodology where:

- Abstract objects are manipulated by their *representations.* The representation of a concrete or abstract object is an item of information that stands for that object.
- Representations are characterized by the tuple $\langle Value, Literal, Type \rangle$:
  - The *Value* is an entity that measures the represented object thus allowing us to relate abstract objects to each other;
  - The *Literal* is a notation allowing us to refer to the object while manipulating it;
  - The *Type* indicates a set of operations we can use while manipulating the object.

Example abstract objects:

- Numbers: values are units of, literals are strings of digits, types are operations with numbers;
- Blue prints (what do blue-prints represent?): values are concrete object represented, literals are graphic designs used to represent the objects, types are operations used to manipulate the objects;
- C-language constructs (what do C language constructs represent?): values are computation entities represented by the C language construct, literals

are string of terminal characters denoting C language constructs, types are operations used to combine C language constructs getting other C language constructs.

System software tools manipulate abstractions obtained by mapping real world objects into computation representations by the mechanism of abstraction manipulation that operates with:

- Mental representations, M;
- Computational representations, C;
- Explanatory representations, E.

That is, system software tools manipulate abstractions represented by the scheme $M \xrightarrow{E} C$. Here we sketch properties *Value, Literal, Type* for each of M, C, and E. $Value(M)$ is a brain representation of the object represented; $Literal(M)$ is the language representation of the object represented; $Type(M)$ is the collection of operation brain can perform on the object represented. Similarly, $Value(C)$ is measured by the intellectual meaning of the object represented; $Literal(C)$ is the language expression of the object represented, such as a natural language expression or a computational language expression, or a musical language expression, etc., depending upon what M is; $Type(C)$ is the collection of operations allowed by the language used to represent C. The tuple $\langle Value, Literal, Type \rangle$ applied to E can be defined within the framework of knowledge manipulation.

The generic approach for abstraction manipulation through system software tools consist of:

- Develop a semantic model for the object you want to represent (one world), W_1.
- Develop a syntactic model for the object you want to represent (another world), W_2.
- Put them together: $R : W_1 \to W_2$.
- Manipulate W_2 as you would do with W_1.

Examples abstraction manipulation in everyday life are:

(1) Handling numbers: represent them, define operations on them i.e, develop the arithmetic as a tuple

$$Arithmetic = \langle Constants \oplus Variables \oplus Expressions; =, :=, +, -, etc \rangle$$

and study properties of expressions with numbers.

(2) Handling logical objects: define the logical values (true, false), constants, variables, and operations on them ($\wedge, \vee, \neg, \ldots$) thus developing the propositional logic as the tuple

$$Logic = \langle \{true, false\} \oplus Variables \oplus Expressions; =, :=, \vee, \wedge, \neg \rangle$$

and study the properties of logic expressions.

(3) Handling lists: define lists, define list notation, define operations for list creation and manipulation, study properties of list expressions.

Challenge: identify in each of the examples above the three elements involved in abstraction manipulation: W_1 (semantics), W_2 (syntax), and $E : W_1 \rightarrow W_2$ their association mechanism.

1.2 Systems Methodology

Informally a methodology is a collection of methods, principles and rules, as those of an art or science (see Webster). Example methodologies are a high school algebra methodology, high school geometry methodology, C language programming methodology, house building methodology, etc. Note that principles and rules of a methodology are determined by:

- the model of the problem to be solved;
- relations between agents manipulating principles and rules while solving problems.

Consequently we need to understand the concept of a problem.

1.2.1 *Problem solving*

Following Polya [Polya (1957)] we say that to have a problem means to search consciously for some action (**solution**) appropriate to attain a given aim (**purpose**). Note that hidden in this phrase are three things that characterize a problem: *unknown, action, purpose*. To solve a problem means to find such an action. Example problem is C programming: unknown is the C program, action is the C program development, and the goal is solving problems by C programming. A problem is thus characterized by three elements :

(1) *unknown*, (what is a C program?);
(2) *data*, (what do we need to know in order to write C programs?);

(3) *purpose*, (what are conditions satisfied by unknown and data according to the goal of C program development) or (how do we or how does the C compiler recognize a valid C program?).

Consequently the process of problem solving involves the actions: identify the *unknown*, find the *action* that leads you from given *data* to the discovery of unknown, and check that the unknown you found satisfies the *condition* that characterizes the problem.

Problems are classified by the kind of actions that lead to solution. The two big classes are:

- Problems to find (construct the solution);
- Problems to prove (infer the solution).

Since programming can be seen as a problem solving activity, this classification is reflected by the two kind of programming languages: procedural languages, such as C, and logic languages, such as Prologue.

1.2.2 *Problem context*

An important concept for problem solving process is the *problem context* which is determined by the problem model and the relations among agents solving problems of that model, i.e., $Context = Model \times Agents$. For example, if the problem is driving a car in a city, then the $Model = Streets \oplus Lights$ and *Agents* are *cars* (mechanical systems), *drivers* (humans or robots), and the *Environment* (other cars and humans or robots). Consequently this problem context is $(Streetss \oplus Lights) \times (Cars \oplus Drivers)$.

Systems methodology [Systems Methodology (2013)], [Checkland (1998); Checkland and Scholes (1990); Wilson (1990)] provides a systematic way of problem characterization depending on the nature of unknown (domain oriented problems), suggests universal methods that can be applied to classes of problems (if you know how to solve one you know how to solve any), and determines the action depending on the problem domain.

1.3 System, Informally

There are many informal and formal definitions of the concept of a system. Using an English language dictionary, for example a Webster, we can enumerate the following such definitions:

Definition 1: *a system is a regular interacting or independent group of objects forming a whole.* In this definition components of a systems are *objects*, relationships among them is *interaction* or *none*, and the behavior is *acts as a whole*.

Definition 2: *a system is an organized set of doctrines, ideas, or principles usually intended to explain the arrangement of a systematic whole.* In this definition components of the system are *doctrine, ideas, principles*, relationships is *organized*, and system behavior is *explain arrangements*.

Definition 3: *a system is an assemblage of things or parts of things forming a complete unit.* In this definition objects are *things and parts of things*, the relationships is *assemblage*, and system behavior is s *complex unit*.

Definition 4: *a system in any set of correlated objects.* In this definition components of the system are *elements of a set*, the relationships are *relations (correlations) in a set*, and system behavior is *properties of the set*.

Challenge: show how can a class of students learning about system software be considered a system.

Conclusions we can draw from definitions 1, 2, 3, 4 above are:

(1) A system is a composed object;
(2) Components of a system are abstract or concrete objects or parts of objects;
(3) Objects of a systems interact with each other;
(4) A system could be a component object of another system;
(5) System's behavior is a functional entity.

Examples of well known systems are: solar system, human body, a C program. System characterization is determined in terms of system components, interaction (among system components and with the environment), and behavior (purpose achieved). In other words, in order to specify a system, we need to identify:

(1) The objects composing the system and their composition laws;
(2) The rules of interaction between objects;
(3) The system's behavior as a whole.

Depending upon the mechanism of system specification we have: *formal systems*, where (1), (2), (3) are formally characterized by mathematical rules, and *ad hoc systems*, where (1), (2), and (3) are not (or not yet) specified by mathematical rules.

Examples of formal systems are solar system, algebraic systems, geometric systems. Examples of ad hoc systems are human body, a C program, communist system, capitalist system.

1.4 The Environment of a System

The environment of a system is the collection of objects that are not elements of the system but may interact with the system. For example, the environment of human body is the collection of external object human body interact with, the environment of a C program is the collection other C programs that may interact with that program, the environment of a machine-language program is the collection of other machine-language programs that my interact with the given program. According to the system interaction with its environment we have:

Closed Systems: systems whose behavior is independent of the interaction with their environments (the environment is embedded (integrated) within the system). Example is a sequential program and its files.

Open Systems: systems whose behavior depends upon the interaction with their environments. Examples are an operating system and a system that controls the flight of a rocket.

1.5 Universe of Discourse

The universe of discourse is considered here as a collection of systems. A system as element of the universe of discourse is a collection of related objects (systems). The structuring of the universe of discourse is a continuum where: at one end are the simplest systems (mechanical systems), and at the other end are the most complex elements, (systemic systems), Figure 1.1.

Mechanical systems are characterized by: small number of elements, few interactions between elements, well defined laws and behavior, lack of interactions with environment, lack of evolution, i.e., static. Example of a mechanical system is a list management system!

Cybernetic systems are characterized by their interaction with the environment and their dynamic evolution by feedback. Therefore one could say that cybernetic are dynamical systems that possess input, state, and

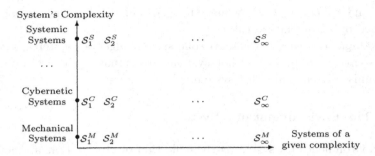

Fig. 1.1   The Universe of Discourse

output, and interact with their environment evolving by the feedback the environment provide at their input.

Systemic systems are characterized by: probabilistic law of behavior, complex interaction with environment, evolve in time, i.e., are dynamic, have purposeful parts. Example of a systemic system is a city driving system.

The relations among agents solving a problem could be: unitary relationships, pluralistic relationships, coercive relationships.

Unitary relationships are characterized by genuine agreement, share common interests, compatible values and beliefs, all agents participate in decision making.

Pluralist relationships are characterized by divergent values and beliefs, different interests and objectives, however, compromise can be reached. Example of pluralist relationship in the driving environment $cars \oplus drivers$ is the rule that determine who goes first!

Coercive relationships are characterized by little common interest, fundamental conflicts, agreement only through power and domination. Example of pluralistic relationships are the relationships that determine political systems!

Our concern while discussing system software tools are the mechanical and cybernetic systems.

Chapter 2

Formal Systems

To understand how can one carry out actions that handle software systems (in software) we examine first how can one handle formal systems (in mathematics). We use set theory [Enderton (1977)] to discuss formal systems.

2.1 Fundamentals of Set Theory

A set is a collection of things (called elements) regarded as single objects (or atoms). We denote sets by capital letters and set elements by lower case letters. Further, if A is a set and t is an element then we write $t \in A$, if t is an element of A and $t \notin A$, if t is not an element of A. Sets are constructed from other sets by the following rules:

- By definition, there is a set that has no elements called the empty set denoted by $\emptyset$.
- A set can be constructed by enumerating its elements. For example, if x_1, x_2, x_3 are given objects (such as $\emptyset$) then $\{x_1, x_2, x_3\}$ is the set of these objects.
- A set can be constructed by giving a property satisfied by its elements. For example, $Evens = \{x | x \in \Omega \wedge x \ modulo \ 2 = 0\}$.
- If A is a set then $B = \{x | x \in A\}$ is a set called a subset, $B \subseteq A$, of A. For example, if $\Omega = \{0, 1, 2, \ldots\}$ is the set on natural numbers then $Evens \subseteq \Omega$.

Two sets A and B are equal if and only if (further denoted by iff) $\forall x \in A$ it follows that $x \in B$ and $\forall y \in B$ it follows $y \in A$. In other words, $A = B$ iff $A \subseteq B$ and $B \subseteq A$.

2.1.1 *Operations with sets*

If A, B are sets then $A \cup B = \{x | x \in A \vee x \in B\}$ is the set union of A and B, $A \cap B = \{x | x \in A \wedge x \in B\}$ is set intersection of A and B, and $A \setminus B = \{x | x \in A \wedge x \notin B\}$ is complement of B relative to A. If A is a set then $\mathcal{P}(A) = \{B | B \subseteq A\}$ is called the power set of A. For example, if $A = \{0, 1\}$ then $\mathcal{P}(A) = \{\emptyset, \{0\}, \{1\}, \{0, 1\}\}$. Using power set operator we can construct the set of natural numbers, Ω:

$$0 = \emptyset$$
$$1 = \{\emptyset\} = \{0\}$$
$$2 = \{\emptyset, \{\emptyset\}\} = \{0, 1\}$$
$$3 = \{\emptyset, \{\emptyset\}, \{\emptyset, \{\emptyset\}\}\} = \{0, 1, 2\}$$
$$\ldots$$

2.1.2 *Ordered pairs*

For x, y set elements, (x, y) is an ordered pair iff (1) $(x, y) = (u, v)$ implies (further denoted by $\Rightarrow$) $x = u, y = v$ and (2) $x = u, y = v \Rightarrow (x, y) = (u, v)$. A definition of the ordered pair as a set that satisfies (1) and (2) is $(x, y) = \{\{x\}, \{x, y\}\}$.

Proof: Let $(x, y) = \{\{x\}, \{x, y\}\}$ and $(u, v) = \{\{u\}, \{u, v\}\}$ be ordered pairs. From set equality, $(x, y) = (u, v)$ as sets, it results that $x = u$ and $y = v$. Vice versa, from the element equality $x = u$ and $y = v$ results the set equality $\{\{x\}, \{x, y\}\} = \{\{u\}, \{u, v\}\}$, i.e., $(x, y) = (u, v)$.

2.1.3 *Relations on a set*

A relation on a set A is a set of ordered pairs of elements of A. For examples, $<$ on natural numbers is defined by: $< \; = \; \{(x, y) | x, y \in \Omega \wedge x < y\}$.

Notation: for R a relation, $(x, y) \in R$ is usually denoted by xRy. For example: $(x, y) \in <$ is denoted $x < y$. The following properties of relations are of interest both in mathematics and system software:

- R is transitive: $xRy \wedge yRz \Rightarrow xRz$.
- R is reflexive: xRx. Note that $x < x$ is not true on Ω, i.e., $<$ is not reflexive.

- R is symmetric: $xRy \Rightarrow yRx$. Example of a symmetric relation is the equality on Ω: $x = y$ imply $y = x$.
- R is antisymmetric: $xRy \wedge yRx \Rightarrow x = y$. For example, $\leq$ on Ω is antisymmetric.

Notation: if R is a relation on A then: $dom(R) = \{x \in A | \exists y \in A \wedge (x, y) \in R\}$, is called the domain of R, and $ran(R) = \{y \in A | \exists x \in A \wedge (x, y) \in R\}$, is called the range of R.

The following relations plays a special role in what follows:

- *Total order:* R is a total order on a set A if R satisfies trichotomy, i.e., $\forall x, y \in A$, $x = y$ or xRy or yRx and R is transitive. For example, $<$ is total on Ω.
- *Partial order:* R is a partial order on a set A if it is transitive, reflexive, and antisymmetric. For example, $\leq$ is partial on Ω.
- *Equivalence:* R is an equivalence on a set A iff it is transitive, symmetric, and reflexive. For example, $\leq$ is an equivalence on Ω

2.2 Formal Systems

A formal system is a non-empty set of objects, denoted D, on which a relationship r is defined. We use the notation $S = \langle D; r \rangle$ to denote this system. Examples of formal systems are:

- $S_1 = \langle \Omega; 0, next \rangle$ where $0 \in \Omega$, and $next : \Omega \rightarrow \Omega : \forall n \in \Omega\ next(n) = n + 1$
- $S_2 = \langle \Omega; \leq \rangle$ where $\leq \subseteq \Omega \times \Omega$ is the usual relation between natural numbers.

2.2.1 *Abstract systems*

An abstract system [Abstract Systems (2010)] is a formal system whose objects D are known only through their relationship in the system. For example, $Stack = \langle Object; Push, Pop, Top, IsEmpty \rangle$ is an abstract system. Essential in an abstract system is the fact that the structure of the system is described by the relationship r defining the system. That is, an abstract system is a model of behavior.

A representation of an abstract system is a system whose objects satisfy the relationship r defining the system. For example, $Stack(\Omega) = \langle \Omega; Push, Pop, Top, IsEmpty \rangle$ is a representation of the *Stack*.

2.2.2 *Homomorphisms and isomorphisms*

Let $S = \langle D; 0, r \rangle$ be an abstract system, where 0 is a constant element of D. Two representations of S, $R_1 = \langle D_1; o_1, r_1 \rangle$ and $R_2 = \langle D_2; o_2, r_2 \rangle$ are homomorphic if there is a function $h : D_1 \rightarrow D_2$ such that: (1) $h(o_1) = o_2$ and (2) if $d'r_1 d''$ then $h(d')r_2 h(d'')$. If the function h is one-to-one then the system R_1 and R_2 are isomorphic.

Let R be the set of real numbers, R_+ be the set of positive reals and R_0 be the set of non-negative reals. Consider the following systems of real numbers:

$$System_1 = \langle R_+, * \rangle, * : R_+ \times R_+ \rightarrow R_+$$
$$System_2 = \langle R_0, * \rangle, * : R_0 \times R_0 \rightarrow R_0$$
$$System_3 = \langle R, + \rangle, + : R \times R \rightarrow R$$
$$System_4 = \langle R, * \rangle, * : R \times R \rightarrow R$$

where $+$ is addition an $*$ is product of real numbers. Then we have:

- Since $log : R_+ \rightarrow R$ is 1-1 and $log(a*b) = log(a)+log(b)$, $log : System_1 \rightarrow System_3$ is an isomorphism.
- Since $abs : R \rightarrow R_0$ defined by

$$abs(x) = \begin{cases} x, & \text{if } x > 0; \\ 0, & \text{if } x = 0; : \\ -x, & \text{if } x < 0. \end{cases}$$

is not 1-1, $abs : System_4 \rightarrow System_2$ is a homomorphism but not an isomorphism.

2.2.3 *Deductive systems (Calculi)*

A deductive system (or a calculi) [Blass and Gurevich (2013)] is a system $S = \langle Q, \Sigma, \Gamma, \Pi \rangle$ where:

- Q is a finite set of states. Each state can be seen as a function that assigns values to variables;
- Σ is a finite input alphabet. Computation data are words in Σ;
- Γ is a finite output alphabet. Result of computations are words in Γ;
- Π is a list of computation rules called inference or construction rules. Each $\pi \in \Pi$ performs a state transition and has the form $w_1, w_2, \ldots, w_m \vdash w_0$,

where w_i, $0 \le i \le m$, are words in $\Sigma \cup \Gamma$, and $\vdash$ is the entailment relation. Sometimes π is referred to as a "computation program" or simply "program".

Common Deductive Systems (Calculi) in system software are: Turing machines [Sipser (2006)], Post systems [Minsky (1967)], Normal algorithms[Markov and Nagorny (1988)], Recursive functions [Malcev (1970)], Grammars (of all sorts) [Hopcroft and Ullman (1979)]. We detail here the Turing Machine and sketch only the definitions of the other deductive systems mentioned here.

2.2.3.1 *Turing Machine*

A Turing Machine T is a tuple $T = \langle Q, \Sigma, \Gamma, \Pi \rangle$ where:

- Q is a finite set of states (called internal alphabet) containing q_0, the initial state of any computation, q_a the accept state, and q_r the reject state.
- Σ is an input alphabet that does not contain the blank symbol $\sqcup$.
- A Turing machine operates on an infinite memory organized on a tape split into cells whose alphabet is Γ. Note, $\sqcup \in \Gamma$ and thus $\Sigma \subseteq \Gamma$.
- Π is a set of operations performed by the Turing machine of the form: $Q \times \Gamma \to Q \times \Gamma \times \{R, L\}$ called computation steps or transitions.

Computations performed by a Turing machine consist of sequences of operations that start in the state q_0, end in either the state q_a or the state q_r, or never end, as explained bellow:

- The instructions performed by a Turing machine T are called computation steps.
- A computation step $(q_1, a) \mapsto (q_2, b, R)$ performs the transition described by: *if T is in the state q_1 and control head is in front of a symbol $a \in \Gamma$, T replaces a with the symbol $b \in \Gamma$ and moves into state $q_2 \in Q$ while moving its control head one symbol to the right, (R).*
- The computation step $(q_1, a) \mapsto (q_2, b, L)$ performs the transition described by: *if T is in the state q_1 and control head is in front of a symbol $a \in \Gamma$, T replaces a with the symbol $b \in \Gamma$ and moves into state $q_2 \in Q$ while moving its control head one symbol to the left, (L).*

One may assume that left-hand side of the tape is the cell 0 and the initial position of the control head H is at the cell 0. Further, assume that the tape contains the input $w = uabv$, $u, v \in \Gamma^*$ and $a, b, c \in \Gamma$. Then the operations performed by the Turing machine can be described by:

(1) If control head is in front of b and the transition function is $\delta(q_i, b) = (q_j, c, L)$ then the computation step is described by: $ua\ q_i\ bv \mapsto u\ q_j acv$

(2) If control head is in front of b and the transition function is $\delta(q_i, b) = (q_j, c, R)$ then the computation step is described by: $ua\ q_i\ bv \mapsto uac\ q_j\ v$

Configuration: as T computes, changes occur in current state, current tape contents, current position of the control head. If current state is q, current tape is uv, and control head is in front of v then the configuration of T is denoted by $u\ q\ v$. Thus, T computes by the rules:

(1) Record the input w on the tape starting with the cell 0 and set control head to that cell, i.e., the initial configuration is $q_0\ w$

(2) At each computation step T performs a transition among configurations, i.e. $u\ q\ v \mapsto u'q'v'$ according to the transition function associated with (q, a) where $v = av_1$

(3) The computation performed by T is a sequence of configurations C_1, $C_2, \ldots, C_n$ such that C_1 is the starting configuration, $C_i \mapsto C_{i+1}$ for $1 \leq i \leq n - 1$, and:

- C_n is an accepting configuration, i.e., $C_n = u\ q_a\ v$, or
- C_n is a rejecting configuration, i.e. $C_n = u\ q_r\ v$, or
- C_n is never $u\ q_a\ v$ or $u\ q_r\ v$, i.e., T never stops.

Example Computation: construct a Turing machine M_1 that tests the membership in the language $B = \{w\#w | w \in \{0, 1\}^*\}$ To understand this problem we simulate the actions performed by M_1 by ourselves. For the input $w \in \{0, 1\}^*$ we can examine w consuming it in any direction, as long as necessary. In addition, we can write to remember anything we want. So, our strategy could be:

- Identify first the character $\#$ in w;
- Zig-zag around $\#$ to determine whether or not the corresponding places on the two sides of $\#$ match;
- We can mark the places we have already visited.

Now we can design M_1 to works following the strategy specified above. That is, M_1 makes multiple passes over the input with the read/write head. On each pass it matches one of the characters on each side of $\#$ symbol. To keep track of which symbols have been checked M_1 crosses off each symbol as it is examined. If M_1 crosses all symbols M_1 accept, otherwise it reject. Informally, M_1 can be described as follows:

On input w:

(1) Scan the input tape to be sure that it contains a single #. If not, *reject*.
(2) Zig-zag across the tape to corresponding positions on either side of # to check whether these positions contain the same symbol. If they do not, *reject*. Cross off the symbols as they are checked.
(3) When all symbols to the left of # have been crossed off, check for the remaining symbols to the right of #. If any symbol remain, *reject*; otherwise *accept*.

Figure 2.1 illusteartes the computation performed by M_1.

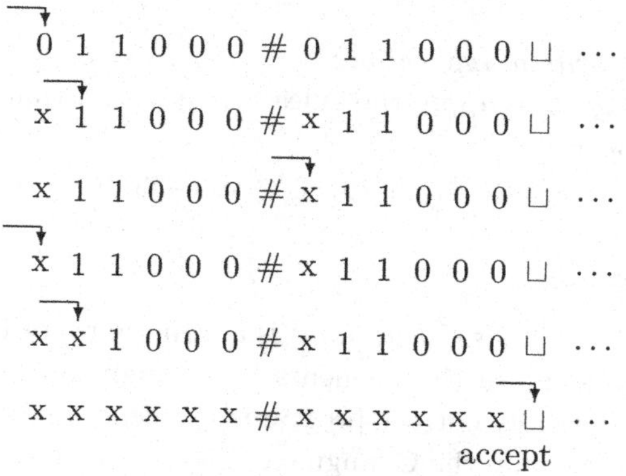

```
→
0 1 1 0 0 0 # 0 1 1 0 0 0 ⊔ · · ·

    →
x 1 1 0 0 0 # x 1 1 0 0 0 ⊔ · · ·

              →
x 1 1 0 0 0 # x 1 1 0 0 0 ⊔ · · ·

→
x 1 1 0 0 0 # x 1 1 0 0 0 ⊔ · · ·

  →
x x 1 0 0 0 # x 1 1 0 0 0 ⊔ · · ·

                          →
x x x x x x # x x x x x x ⊔ · · ·
                      accept
```

Fig. 2.1   Snapshots of M_1 computing

2.2.3.2   *Post Systems*

A Post system is a deductive system $\mathcal{P} = \langle Q, \Sigma, \Gamma, \Pi \rangle$ where

- Q is a set of states
- Σ is the input alphabet
- Γ is the output alphabet
- Π is a set of transitions described by rules of the form: $\alpha \rightarrow \beta$, $\alpha \in \Sigma^*$, $\beta \in (\Sigma \cup \Gamma)^*$.

A computation step performed by P can be described as follows: *if* $w \in \Sigma$ *and computation rule is* $\alpha \rightarrow \beta$ *then* $w = w_1 \alpha w_2 \mapsto w_1 \beta w_2 = w'$.

A Post system computes using an infinite tape, similarly to a Turing machine.

2.2.3.3 *Normal Algorithms*

A Normal Algorithm (also called Markov algorithm) is a Post System whose set of transition $\Pi = \{\alpha \to \beta, \alpha \to .\beta\}$ is applied in the following restrictive form: Let $p = \{r_1, r_2, \ldots, r_i, \ldots, r_n\}$ be a program and $w \in \Sigma^*$. Then p is applied to w by the rules:

(1) Step 1: *rule application:*
   if the rule is $r_i = \alpha_i \to .\beta_i$ than $w = w_1 \alpha_i w_2 \mapsto w_1 \beta_i w_2 = w'$ and computation terminates with the result w'; if the rule is $r_i = \alpha_i \to \beta_i$ (not a final rule) than $w = w_1^1 \alpha_i w_2^1 \mapsto w_1^2 \beta_i w_2^1 \mapsto w_1^2 \beta_i w_2^2 \ldots \mapsto w_1^k \beta_i w_2^k \mapsto \ldots$
(2) Step 2: *algorithm application:*
   for $i = 1, 2, \ldots, n$ apply the rules $r_1; r_2; \ldots; r_i$, that is, a computation has the form:
   $r_1; \; r_1, r_2; \; r_1, r_2, r_3; \; \ldots; \; r_1, r_2, \ldots, r_i; \; \ldots; \; r_1, r_2, \ldots, r_n.$

2.2.3.4 *Grammars*

A grammar $G = \langle TV, NV, P, axiom \rangle$ is another form of Post systems whose computations generate the elements of a language. For example, the C language syntactically correct programs are generated by the context-free grammar that specifies the C language. Look at the end of your C language book to see the grammar specifying the C language.

2.2.4 *Constructing formal systems*

Two major approaches to construct formal systems are: constructive or generating approach, and axiomatic or abstract approach. These approaches correspond to the two classes of problems: *to find*, and *to prove* discussed in Chapter 1.

Constructive Approach: A set of predefined elements and operations of the system are given. These are called system generators. A set of computation rules are also given. A computation rule shows how new objects can be obtained from the defined ones. The example of a constructive formal system is the set of natural numbers Ω: The generators are the element $0, 0 \in \Omega$ and the operation is *next* denoted $' : \Omega \to \Omega$. The computation rule is the operation $'$ defined by: if $n \in \Omega$ then $n' = n + 1 \in \Omega$. hence, $\Omega = \{0, 0', 0'', \ldots\}$. Another example of a constructive formal system is the C language: Primitive (predefined) data and operations on them are given.

Challenges: (1) Find out what are the predefined data/operations in C. Valid type and construct definition rules are also given. (2) Find out what are the construct definition rules in C. (3) Find out what are the type definition rules in C. Note that constructive systems are common in system software.

Axiomatic Approach: A collection of axioms are given. Note that an axiom is a statement expressing an (obvious) property. A set of inference rules are also given. An inference rule is a mechanism that allows us to deduce properties from other properties. Example of axioms in a formal system are the properties of the equivalence relations on a set A: reflexivity, $\forall a \in A(a = a)$, transitivity, $\forall a, b, c \in A(a = b \wedge b = c \Rightarrow a = c)$, symmetry: $\forall a, b \in A(a = b \Rightarrow b = a)$. Examples of Inference Rules in an axiomatic system is the Modus ponens in Logic: $(a \wedge a \Rightarrow b) \Rightarrow b$, and product cancellation in arithmetic $x * y = z * y \Rightarrow x = z$. The two axiomatic systems of interest to us are: integer arithmetic, defined by Peano's axioms and the axiomatic set theory, defined by the 10 axioms known as ZFC-system (Zermelo-Frankel with Choice) [Takeuti and Zaring (1971)]. There are many other axiomatic definitions of set theory. You can find them on the web.

Arithmetic (Peano's Axioms): The set Ω of natural numbers is defined by the following five axions:

(1) $0 \in \Omega$, i.e.., 0 is a natural number.
(2) If $n \in \Omega$ then $n' = n + 1 \in \Omega$.
(3) If $n, m \in \Omega$ and $n = m$ then $n' = m'$.
(4) If $n \in \Omega$ then $n' \neq 0$.
(5) If $P \subseteq \Omega$, $0 \in P$, and $n \in P \Rightarrow n' \in P$ then $P = \Omega$.

Set Theory (ZFC System): Intuitive set theory has come to play the role of a foundation theory in modern mathematics. However, intuitive set theory cannot handle mathematical paradoxes as are Russell's Paradox which states: Let R be "the set of all sets that do not contain themselves as members". Formally this means that A is an element of R if and only if A is not an element of A, i.e. $R = \{A | A \notin A\}$. Is R an element of itself? According to this definition if $R \in R$ then $R \notin R$; if $R \notin R$ then $R \in R$. To address this problem set theory had to be re-constructed, using an axiomatic approach. Axiomatic set theory is a rigorous reformulation of set theory in first-order logic, created to address paradoxes in naive set theory.

The ZFC axioms:

(1) **Axiom of empty set:** There is a set with no elements. We use {} or $\emptyset$ to denote this empty set.

(2) **Axiom of extensionality:** Two sets are the same if and only if they have the same elements.

(3) **Axiom of pairing:** If X, Y are sets, then so is $\{X, Y\}$, a set containing X and Y as its only elements.

(4) **Axiom of union:** Every set has a union. That is, for any set X there is a set Y whose elements are precisely the elements of the elements of X.

(5) **Axiom of infinity:** There exists a set X such that {} is in X and whenever Y is in X, so is the union $Y \cup \{Y\}$.

(6) **Axiom of separation (or subset axiom):** Given any set X and any proposition $P(x), x \in X$, there is a subset of the original set X containing precisely those elements x for which $P(x)$ holds.

(7) **Axiom of replacement:** Given any set and any mapping, formally defined as a proposition $P(X, Y)$ where $P(X, Y)$ and $P(X, Z)$ implies $Y = Z$, there is a set containing precisely the images of the original set's elements.

(8) **Axiom of power set:** Every set has a power set. That is, for any set X there exists a set Y, such that the elements of Y are precisely the subsets of X.

(9) **Axiom of regularity (or axiom of foundation):** Every non-empty set X contains some element Y such that X and Y are disjoint sets. (Remember, elements of a set are sets).**A more intuitive formulation:** Every nonempty set is disjoint from one of its elements.

(10) **Axiom of choice: (Zermelo's version)** Given a set X of mutually disjoint nonempty sets, there is a set Y (a choice set for X) containing exactly one element from each member of X.

2.3 Characterizing a Formal System

A formal system is characterized by the four logic principles: completeness, independence, consistency, decidability.

Completeness Principle: *The set of axioms must be complete, i.e., if an object belongs to the system, then it is either an axiom or it can be obtained by inference rules from axioms.* The application of this principle to system software tool is: if an expression is well-defined, then it can be evaluated. For example, if $n \in \Omega$ then $n = 0$ or $n = (\ldots (0')' \ldots)'$.

Independence Principle: *An axiom cannot be expressed in terms of other objects of the system.* For example, 0 cannot be expressed in terms of other $n \in \Omega$ using Peano's axioms. Also, see axiom of parallels in Euclidean geometry.

Consistency Principle: *No contradiction can be deduced (generated) from axioms and inference rules.* That is, if P can be deduced from $Ax_1, \ldots, Ax_n$, denoted by $Ax_1, \ldots, Ax_n \vdash P$ then $Ax_1, \ldots, Ax_n \nvdash \neg(P)$ The application of this principle to system software tools is the *soundness* property which states that the value of an expression is unique and matches the expression type.

Decidability Principle: *A formal system is decidable if there exists an effective method to determine whether a given element belongs to that system or not.* For examples, naive set theory is not decidable because from $S = \{A | A \notin A\}$ (Russell paradox) one cannot decide whether $S \in S$ or $S \notin S$.

Gödel Incompleteness Theorems [Nagel and Hofstadter (2008)] states that *arithmetic is inconsistent.* That is, there is no system of axioms capable of proving all facts about the natural numbers. However, applying this principle to system software tools we should conclude that programming languages must be decidable. The decider in this case is the $Compiler = (Parser, Generator)$ and the following should hold: syntax of a programming language is decided by the parser. A semantic model must be complete, which implies that any programming object has a value. In addition, a semantic model must be sound which implies that the value of a programming object is unique. Limitations of syntax computation can be prevented by semantic computation (see Semantic Web).

2.3.1 *Algebraic systems*

An algebraic system is a tuple

$$\mathcal{A} = \langle A; a_1, \ldots, a_n, f_1, \ldots, f_m, g_1, \ldots, g_p, p_1, \ldots, p_q \rangle$$

where:

- A is a set (a family of sets) also called sort (sorts);
- $a_1, \ldots, a_n \in A$ are constants (null-ary operations), i.e.,$a_i : \to A$ or $a_i \in A$;
- $f_1, \ldots, f_m$ are total operations of arity r_i, $1 \le i \le m$, i.e.,$f_i : A \times \ldots \times A \to A$, r_i times (arguments);
- $g_1, \ldots, g_p$ are partial operations of arity g_j, $1 \le j \le p$, i.e., $g_j : A \times \ldots \times A \to A$, g_j times (arguments);
- $p_1, \ldots, p_q$ are predicates of arity p_k, $1 \le k \le q$, i.e., $p_k : A \times \ldots \times A \to \{T, F\}$, p_k times (arguments).

Note that the arity of an operation is the number of its arguments. An algebraic system is characterized by its *Signature* which is the tuple of numbers defining the arity of its operations, partial operations, and predicates. That is, consider the arity of $a_i = 0$, $a_i : \to A$, $i = 1, 2, \ldots, n$, the arity of $f_j = r_j$, $f_j : A \times \ldots \times A \to A$, $j = 1, 2, \ldots, m$, r_j times, the arity of $g_k = s_k$; $g_k : A \times \ldots \times A \to A$, $k = 1, 2, \ldots, p$, s_k times, the arity of $p_l = t_l$; $p_l : A \times \ldots \times A \to \{true, false\}$, t_l times, $l = 1, 2, \ldots, q$. The sequence of numbers:

$$\langle 0, \ldots, 0, r_1, \ldots, r_m, s_1, \ldots, s_p, t_1, \ldots, t_q \rangle$$

is called the signature (or type) of $\mathcal{A}$. Example of an algebraic system is $\mathcal{A} = \langle \Omega; 0, + \rangle$. Since $0 \in \Omega$, $0 : 0 \to \Omega$, the arity of 0 is 0; Since $+$ is binary, i.e., $+ : \Omega \times \Omega \to \Omega$, the arity of $+$ is 2. That is, the signature of $\mathcal{A}$ is $Signature(\mathcal{A}) = \langle 0, 2 \rangle$.

Two algebraic systems that have the same signature are called *similar* or *of the same type*.

The relationship between algebraic systems are established by mappings called homomorphisms. Let

$$\mathcal{A} = \langle A; a_1, \ldots, a_n, f_1, \ldots, f_m, g_1, \ldots, g_p, p_1, \ldots, p_q \rangle$$
$$\mathcal{B} = \langle B, b_1, \ldots, b_n, F_1, \ldots, F_m, G_1, \ldots, G_p, P_1, \ldots, P_q \rangle$$

be two algebraic systems of the same type (or similar). Then, a function $H : A \to B$ is a homomorphism $H : \mathcal{A} \to \mathcal{B}$ if it preserves the structure of the two algebraic systems, i.e.:

- $H(a_i) = b_i$, $i = 1, 2, \ldots, n$
- $H(f_j(x_1, \ldots, x_{r_j})) = F_j(H(x_1), \ldots, H(x_{r_j}))$, $j = 1, 2, \ldots, m$
- $H(g_k(x_1, \ldots, x_{k_j})) = G_k(H(x_1), \ldots, H(x_{k_j}))$ $k = 1, 2, \ldots, p$
- $H(p_l(x_1, \ldots, x_{t_l})) = P_l(H(x_1), \ldots, H(x_{t_l}))$, $l = 1, 2, \ldots, q$

Example homomorphism is the mapping $log : R_+ \to R$, which is a homomorphism $log : \langle R_+; 1, * \rangle \to \langle R; 0, + \rangle$ because $log : R_+ \to R$ is ono-to-one ($log(x) = y$ implies $y = e^x$), $log(1) = 0$, and $log(x * y) = log(x) + log(y)$.

2.3.2 *Algebraic specification*

An algebraic specification is a tuple $S = \langle \Sigma, E \rangle$ where Σ is the signature of an algebraic system and E is a set of identities of terms generated by Σ and a set of given constants and variables. Term generation with Σ is defines by the following rules:

(1) Constants and variables are terms generated by Σ;
(2) If $t_1, t_2, \ldots, t_k$ are terms generated by Σ and f_k is an operation symbol (denoting a total operation, a partial operation, or a predicate) of arity k then $t = f_k(t_1, t_2, \ldots, t_k)$ is a term generated by Σ.
(3) Nothing else is a term generated by Σ.

For example, consider the algebraic system $\mathcal{A} = \langle \Omega; 0, + \rangle$. Then we have: 0 is a term because it is a constant, x is a term because it is a variable, +(x,0) is a term because x, 0 are terms, and +(+(x, 0),y) is also a term. Algebraic specifications are used in system software tools through the keyword notations where the keywords are:

- **name**, to specify the system name,
- **opns**, to specify the operation symbols,
- **sort**, to specify the domains and range of operation symbols,
- **vars**, to specify the variables, and
- **axms**, to specify the axioms of the system.

Here we use the following notation to specify an algebraic system.

beginSpec

  name: Spec [using $Spec_1, \ldots, Spec_m$] is
  sort: $name_1, name_2, \ldots, name_n$;
  opns: $f_1 : name_{i_1^1} \times \ldots \times name_{i_{n_1}^1} \to name_{j^1}$;

    $\ldots$

    $f_k : name_{i_1^k} \times \ldots \times name_{i_{n_k}^k} \to name_{j^k}$;
  vars: $List_1: type_1, \ldots, List_p: type_p$;
  axms:$t_1^1 = t_2^1, t_1^2 = t_2^2, \ldots, t_1^q = t_2^q$;

endSpec

Example of an algebraic specification is the following specification of boolean algebra:

beginSpec

   name: Bool1 is

   sort: *Bool*;

   opns: $true :\to Bool$;

     $false :\to Bool$;

     $\neg : Bool \to Bool$;

     $\wedge : Bool \times Bool \to Bool$;

     $\vee : Bool \times Bool \to Bool$;

   vars: $p, q : Bool$;

   axms:$true \neq false$,

     $\neg(true) = false$,

     $\neg(false) = true$,

     $true \wedge p = p;\ false \wedge p = false$,

     $false \vee p = p;\ true \vee p = true$,

     $p \vee q = \neg(\neg(p) \wedge \neg(q))$;

endSpec

Another example of an algebraic specification is the specification of an arithmetic using the boolean algebra specified in the previous example:

beginSpec

   name: $Nat1$ using $Bool1$ is

   sort: N;

   opns: $zero :\to N$;

     $next : N \to N$;

     $+ : N \times N \to N$;

     $* : N \times N \to N$;

     $eq : N \times N \to Bool$;

   vars: $x, y : N, p, g : Bool$;

   axms:$zero + x = x$,

     $next(x) + y = next(x + y)$,

     $zero * x = zero$,

     $next(x) * y = y + (x * y)$,

     $eq(zero, zero) = true$,

     $eq(zero, next(x)) = false$,

     $eq(next(x), zero) = false$,

     $eq(next(x), next(y)) = eq(x, y)$;

endSpec

Chapter 3

Ad Hoc Systems

An ad hoc system S is a tuple $S = \langle D; r \rangle$ where D is a collection of objects and r is a relationship in D such that:

- Objects (or elements) of D may not be specified by rules of math (not yet). For example, C programs are not specified by the rules of math.
- Rules r of interaction in S may not be defined mathematically. For example, relations between functions making up a C program are not formally defined.
- Behavior of the system may not be specified by mathematical functions. For example, the behavior of a process executing a program is in general not a function.

However, we handle ad hoc systems. For a complete specification, ad hoc systems should be characterized by the rules of math. Unfortunately, ad hoc systems are not constructed from ideal (mathematical) objects. Rather, ad hoc systems are models of behavior (representations) of real and very heterogeneous objects — sometimes expensive.

Mathematical construction of formal system provides the approach to dealing with utilitarian ad hoc systems. Keeping an open eye on formal system construction we develop a systematic approach for handling ad hoc systems. We apply the systematic approach for ad hoc systems construction to the structuring of software systems as ad hoc systems.

3.1 Systematic Approach for Ad Hoc System Construction

Systematic approach for ad hoc system construction consists of a sequence of four steps that are repeatedly applied until the system we construct satisfies the given requirements. Pictorial these is shown in Figure 3.1.

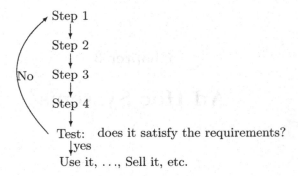

Fig. 3.1   Systematic approach for Ad Hoc System Construction

Step 1: (requirement specification) *Understand and define the major behavior of the systems as a whole.* This implies understanding the interaction of the system with its environment. Therefore, system and its environment need to be well specified. The environment of a system may be another system.

Challenge: how does this apply to programming activity?

Step 2: (system components) *Identify the functional components (generators) of the system.* Examples of functional components making up a program are: modules, computing units such as statements, functions, procedures, blocks, expressions. While defining components, we should minimize the mutual interaction between them.

Challenge: why should we minimize the mutual interaction between a program components?

Step 3: (component specification) *Define the input-output behavior of the components by specifying their environments and actions within the system.* Questions to be answered here are: What is the environment of a system component? Example: what is the *environment* of a function in a C program? (Suggestion for a C program development: design C function components of your program once you understand their behavior.)

Challenges: How should components communicate to achieve their functions? What if components of a program are not all C constructs? What is component integration? What is component interoperability?

Step 4: (system specification) *Define an algorithm (or a procedure) expressed in terms of the components (defined in Step 2 and Step 3) which performs the action expected from the system (defined in Step 1).*

The systematic approach defined by Step 1, Step 2, Step 3, Step 4 above needs to be iterated over the resulting system:

$Env \Rightarrow Step\ 1 \rightarrow Step\ 2 \rightarrow Step\ 3 \rightarrow Step\ 4 \Rightarrow S$
$S \quad \Rightarrow Step\ 1 \rightarrow Step\ 2 \rightarrow Step\ 3 \rightarrow Step\ 4 \Rightarrow S'$
$S' \quad \Rightarrow Step\ 1 \rightarrow Step\ 2 \rightarrow Step\ 3 \rightarrow Step\ 4 \Rightarrow S''$
...

Example of application is the development (writing) of a correct program.

3.2 Ad Hoc System Formalization

We use three languages for ad hoc system formalization:

(1) System Specification Language, SSL: we will use algebraic and transition systems for this purpose. We use algebraic specifications ($\langle \Sigma, E \rangle$) to specify syntax (terms) and we use transition systems (to be seen) to specify semantics (behavior).
(2) System Implementation Language, SIL: we use C language for this purpose. Scala is a valid alternative.
(3) System Validation Language, SVL: we don't have a specific language for this purpose.

First exercise in ad hoc system formalization is the formalization of a software system as the pair: $\langle Specification, Behavior \rangle$. The *Specification* is given by the usual algebraic specification as a pair $\langle Signature, Identities \rangle$ where the *Signature* defines terms representing objects of the system and the *Identities* define the properties satisfied by system components. The *Behavior* (i.e., the action performed by the system) is specified in terms of states and transitions. A state of the system is a mappings of system variables to their values. A transition is a mapping of a system state into other system states by changing variable values or by checking some properties.

3.3 Software System Specification

Software systems are ad hoc systems specified by the language of algebraic specification and their behavior is specified by the language of actions.

Algebraic specification allows us to express computing objects as terms. The language of actions is a pseudo programming language inspired by [Manna and Pnueli (1992)], that allows us to express transition actions on terms thus expressing system behavior. Since the algebraic specifications have been defined in Chapter 2, we focus here on the language of actions which is build in terms of two concepts: primitive actions and composed actions. Depending upon the problem domain, primitive actions are simple, well understood operations, performed by any problem domain user. In programming such primitive actions are *assignment* which allow programmers to initialize and change states. The composed actions are expressions of primitive and composed actions. The composition rules used, again, depend upon the problem domain. However, in programming they are: sequencing (sequential and parallel execution), branching, looping, blocking, and other. Formally composed actions are operators mapping states into states. In conclusion, a system's behavior (or action) is a program in the language used to express transition systems as reactive systems (to be seen further). For completeness, the behavior (action) performed by a software system is added to the algebraic specification of that system using the keyword *action*, abbreviated **actn**. Thus, the software system specification in SSL becomes:

beginSpec
> **name:** expression of system name **is**
> **sort:** data carriers of the system
> **opns:** operations performed by system
> **vars:** typed variables
> **axms:** identities specifying properties
> **actn:** program specifying system's behavior

endSpec

3.4   Software System Implementation

Software system Implementation Language, (SIL) is a language that allows the system to be implemented, i.e., make system behavior be performed by a machine. Since computers are usually machines on which systems are implemented, SIL is usually a programming language. We use C-Language as a software system implementation language. Scala is a newer alternative!

3.5   Software System Validation

The validation is a process that allows us to show that a system accomplish its function. Formally the system validation should be a mathematical proof. In reality software systems are validated by running them on battery of tests covering all cases! The language of these tests is called a software system validation language. We use C-Language as the software system validation language.

3.6   Ad Hoc System Characterization

Formal systems are characterized by logical principles (completeness, consistency, independence, decidability). Ad hoc systems are characterized by doctrines, which are (changeable) agreements (conventions). Common doctrines used in software system characterization are: functionality, reliability, efficiency, simplicity, and maintenance.

Functionality Doctrine: *an ad hoc system should achieve the function for which it has been designed.* A larger function may be performed; for example, hardware performs a larger function than the one we can verify (completeness).

Reliability Doctrine: *an ad hoc system should be reliable, i.e., while achieving its function an ad hoc system should be error free.* System reliability cannot be proved by rules of mathematics. System's reliability means *error tolerance*, i.e., the system should accept erroneous behavior, which means the system should tolerate error by providing means to: discover errors, isolate errors to restrict their malfunction, recover or tell system user. Hence, the concepts used for handling software system reliability are:

Fault: a mechanical or algorithmic action (a defect) that generates errors. Example fault is "undefined operation".

Error: an item of information which when processed by an algorithm generates a failure. For example division is defined but dividing by 0 is not, so its execution generates an error.

Failure: an event at which a system violates its specification and generates errors. For example a call to the function f that takes as an argument an expression that contain a division by zero, $f(a/0)$, fails to run. Note that in a physical system we have:

$$defect \xrightarrow{generate} information \xrightarrow{generate} event$$

Similarly, in a software system we have:

$$fault \xrightarrow{generate} error \xrightarrow{generate} failure$$

Example reliability: For a given hardware system

- a/o is undefined, i.e., it generates an overflow (fault);
- A fault used as an operand generates an error, i.e., $e = a/o + 6$ generate an error;
- A function applied on a error generates a failure, i.e., $f = f(a/0 + 6)$ generate a failure.

Efficiency Doctrine: *an ad hoc system must be efficient, otherwise users don't buy it.* Note on efficiency: computer systems are constructed from expensive components, hence efficiency is achieved by tradeoff cost and performance. This is achieved by designing concurrent functional components, i.e., *memory||processor||devices* and by providing support for component integration and interaction, i.e., modularity (integration and interaction) and sharing resources (memory, processors, devices, information, code, etc).

Simplicity Doctrine: *an ad hoc system must be simple, so simple that for its ignorant user it must be easily understood and easily used.* Popular characterization is "push button".

Maintenance Doctrine: *an ad hoc system must be easily maintained.* Software systems are complex, heterogeneous, and usually not proven (mathematically) correct. Systems evolve with problem domain and their functions need to be updated; this is done by *system maintenance.* System constructor may not be the system maintainer. Errors might occur when designer is not available.

3.7   List Management System

List Management System, (LMS) is an example of an ad hoc system that is used here to illustrate the theory and practice of ad ho system construction. However, LMS has a very special role in this book because it is used as a generic-tool employed for the specification and implementation of all major software tools discussed further. Using the systematic approach for ad hoc system construction we get:

- **LMS major behavior:** allows dynamic creation, organization, accessing, and updating of information.

- **Components:** components of a LMS are data objects and operations.

  – Data objects are list pointers, list headers and tails, list objects, and values recorded by list objects.
  – Operations (functions) on data objects are:
  list(H,T) which takes as arguments a list head H and a list tail T, constructs an empty list, and returns a pointer L to H;
  append(L,obj) which appends the object obj to the list L;
  insert(L,obj1,obj2) which inserts the object obj1 after the object obj2 in the list L;
  update(L,obj,Value) updates the value of the object obj in the list L with the Value;

- **Functional behavior of components:** A list pointer is the address of a list head. A list header specifies the beginning of a list and the list tail specifies the end of a list. The head and the tail of a list must be distinguishable in the LMS and distinguishable between them. A list object is a tuple (Link, Value). When Value has a fixed size it can be embedded in the list object. Otherwise it should be a pointer to the object Value.

Thus, a List is a sequence of linked list objects identified by a list pointer. The graphic representation of this kind of a list in in Figure 3.2. Since we use this LMS as a generic type for the specification and implementation of other software tools we define here a double-linked list that may be easily instantiated into the lists we need and allows its traversal from the head to the tail and and from the tail to the head as situation requires.

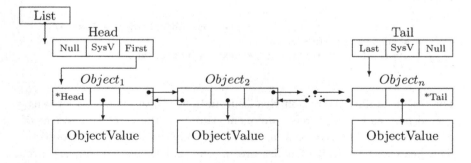

Fig. 3.2 List management system

Since list pointers, list heads, list tails, and list objects are composed, in order to define operations on them we need to show their composition rules. Operations will be expressed as composed operations; their components are operations defined on object components. However, the relationship between these list components are:

(1) A list is determined by a pointer to an object of the type HeadTail;
(2) The head of a list is an object H of type HeadTail whose components have the values: H.First=Null, H.Reserved is a system reserved value (SysV in Figure 3.2), and H.Last = first object of the list.
(3) The tail of a list is an object T of type HeadTail whose components have the values: T.First = last object of the list, T.Reserved is a system value (SysV in Figure 3.2), and T.Last = Null.

Notice that H and T have the same structure and are distinguished by the property H.First = Null and T.Last = Null. A list L is thus empty if it is determined by a head H and a tail T related by the equalities: H.Last = T and T.Fist = H. Consequently, the C pseudocode of the generic elements making up a list management system are:

```
struct Value "To be defined by the application"
typedef struct HeadTail
        {
          struct Object *First;
          int Reserved; /* This is SysV in Figure 3.2 */
          struct Object *Last;
        } Head, Tail, *List;

typedef struct Object
        {
          struct Object *p_Link ; /* previous object of the list */
          struct value *ObjValue;
          struct Object *n_Link ; /* next object of the list */
        } ListObject;
```

For design uniformity reason HeadTail and list object structures are suggested here as having three component. However, the three component of a HeadTail are not the same as the three component of the list objects. The head and the tail of a list are unique and their elements are predefined with regard to a list. The LMS system as an SSL expression becomes:

```
beginSpec
  name: LMS using Integer, Boolean, String is
  sort: integer, boolean, HeadTail, Object, Value, List;
  opns: list: HeadTail x HeadTail -> List,
        isEmpty:List -> boolean, length: List -> integer,
        append:List x Object -> List, Update:List x Object -> List,
        access:List x Object -> Object,delete:List x Object -> List,
        test:List x Object -> boolean,catenate:List x List -> List,
        split:List x Object -> List x List,
        insert:List x Object x Object -> List;
  vars: obj: Object; L: List; H, T: HeadTail;
  axms: isEempty(append(list(H,T),obj)) = false,
        isEmpty(delete(list(h,t), obj)) = true ,
        length(list(H,T)) = 0 ,
        length(append(L, obj)) = length(L) + 1,
        length(delete(L,obj)) = length(L) - 1,
        append(delete(L,obj),obj)=delete(append(L,ob),obj),
        test(L,obj) = if obj in L then true else false;
  actn: Null
endSpec
```

Challenge: develop a C implementation of a generic list management system specified above.

Observations:

- Not all software systems can be formalized so nicely;
- Sometimes we do not know system's axioms and so we cannot formally describe system's behavior;
- This does not mean that system behavior should not be described, an informal approach may be used;
- Another alternative is to describe formally an approximation of the system and try to make it as close as possible to the system it approximates.

Chapter 4

Common Systems in Software Development

The most common systems in computer science are probably the state transition systems related to the finite automata theory [Hopcroft and Ullman (1979)]. However, while state transition systems are used as models of computation in general, transition systems are more appropriate as model of computations as performed by a computer. We follow Manna and Pnueli [Manna and Pnueli (1992)] to discuss this concept in the framework of system software.

4.1 Transition Systems

A transition system is a tuple $\mathcal{T}_s = \langle \Pi, \Sigma, T, \Theta \rangle$ where:

- Π is a set of typed symbols called the state variables. In a program $\Pi = DataVariables \cup ControlVariables$. Data variables are denoted by identifiers while Control variable are denoted by "labels".
- Σ is a set of states. If $s \in \Sigma$ then s is a function that assigns variables in Π to values in their domains, $s : \Pi \to D_\Pi$ where D_Π is the domain of values.
- T is a finite set of transitions. A transition $\tau \in T$ maps states in Σ to the subsets of states in Σ, i.e., $\tau : \Sigma \to \mathcal{P}(\Sigma)$. This means that mathematically transitions are operators mapping functions (states) into functions (states).
- Θ is a predicate called initial condition. When this predicate is true the transition system starts its computation.

This definition shows that any kind of machine-computation can be seen as a transitions system. For an example, consider the transition system provided by following C program called swap.c:

```
#include <stdio.h>
main()
    {
    int x, y, t=0;
    scanf("%d,%d", &x, &y);
    t = x;
    x = y;
    y = t;
    printf("%d,%d\n", x,y);
    }
```

Note: one can compile this program by `cc swap.c` and then run it by `a.out i1 i2` where `i1,i2` are integers. The transition system of `swap.c` is the tuple $TS(swap.c) = \langle \Pi_{swap}, \Sigma_{swap}, T_{swap}, \Theta_{swap} \rangle$ where:

$\Pi_{swap} = \{PC, x, y, t, Input, Output\}$, $D_\Pi = Labels \cup Integers \cup \{Keyboard, Screen\}$, where PC stands for program counter.
$\Sigma_{swap} = \{s_0, s_1, s_2, s_3, s_4, s_5\}$ where: $s_0 : x \mapsto UND, y \mapsto UND, t \mapsto 0, Input \mapsto UND, Output \mapsto UND$.

$T_{swap} = \{\tau_0, \tau_1, \tau_2, \tau_3, \tau_4\}$ where:

τ_0 performs the statement `scanf`, i.e., PC=[scanf]
τ_1 performs the statement `t = x`, i.e., PC=[t=x]
τ_2 performs the statement `x = y`, i.e., PC=[x=y]
τ_3 performs the statement `y = t`, i.e., PC=[y=t]
τ_4 performs the statement `printf`, i.e., PC=[printf].

State transitions performed by $\tau_0, \tau_1, \tau_2, \tau_3, \tau_4$ are:

$\tau_0 : s_0 \overset{scanf}{\mapsto} s_1 : x \mapsto i1, y \mapsto i2, t \mapsto 0, Input \mapsto i1, i2, Output \mapsto UND;$
$\tau_1 : s_1 \overset{t=x}{\mapsto} s_2 : x \mapsto i1, y \mapsto i2, t \mapsto i1, Input \mapsto i1, i2, Output \mapsto UND;$
$\tau_2 : s_2 \overset{x=y}{\mapsto} s_3 : x \mapsto i2, y \mapsto i2, t \mapsto i1, Input \mapsto i1, i2, Output \mapsto UND;$
$\tau_3 : s_3 \overset{y=t}{\mapsto} s_4 : x \mapsto i2, y \mapsto i1, t \mapsto i1, Input \mapsto i1, i2, Output \mapsto UND;$
$\tau_4 : s_4 \overset{printf}{\mapsto} s_5 : x \mapsto i2, y \mapsto i1, t \mapsto i1, Input \mapsto i1, i2, Output \mapsto i2, i1;$

One can continue transitions $\tau_4 : s_4 \overset{nop}{\mapsto} s_5, \ldots, \tau_i : s_i \overset{nop}{\mapsto} s_{i+1}$ for $i+1, i+2, , \ldots, \infty$. However, note that $s_4 = s_5 = \ldots$. That is, s_4 is stationary and can be interpreted as final. Therefore, a stationary state is further called a *terminal state*. To simplify presentation we further rely on the following notation:

- For $u \in \Pi$, $s(u)$ is the value of u in state s, i.e. $s(u) \in D_\Pi$. For example, $t \in \Pi_{swap}$ and $s_0(t) = 0$.

  Challenge: compute the value of variable t in the state 3, that is, compute $s_3(t)$.

- If e is an expression containing variables $u_1, \ldots, u_n$, then the value of e in state s is $s(e) = e(s(u_1), \ldots, s(u_n))$. For example, $x, y \in \Pi_{swap}$, $s_1(x) = i1, s_1(y) = i2$, $s_1(x + y) = i1 + i2$.

- If p is a predicate containing variables $u_1, \ldots, u_n$ then value of p in state s is $s(p) = p(s(u_1), \ldots, s(u_n))$. For example, $x, y \in \Pi_{swap}$, $s_1(x) = i1, s_1(y) = i2$, $s_1(x > y) = i1 > i2$.

- If $s \in \Sigma$ and $\tau(s) \neq \emptyset$, i.e., $\exists s' \in \tau(s)$, then s' is a successor of s and is written $s \xrightarrow{\tau} s'$. For example, $s_0, s_1 \in \Sigma_{swap}$, $\tau_0(s_0) = \{s_1\}$, i.e., s_1 is a successor of s_0.

4.1.1 *Transition characterization*

Each transition $\tau \in T$, $s \xrightarrow{\tau} s'$, is characterized by an assertion relating values of variables in $s : \Pi \to D_\Pi$ and variables in $s' : \Pi \to D_\Pi$, where $s' \in \tau(s)$, denoted ρ_τ. This assertion is thus denoted by $\forall u \in \Pi$, $s(u)\rho_\tau s'(u)$, which can be represented by the following table:

s			τ	s'			ρ_τ
x_1	$\rightarrow$	v_1		x_1	$\rightarrow$	v_1'	$v_1 \rho_\tau v_1'$
x_2	$\rightarrow$	v_2		x_2	$\rightarrow$	v_2'	$v_2 \rho_\tau v_2'$
...			$\xrightarrow{\tau}$	...			...
x_n	$\rightarrow$	v_n		x_n	$\rightarrow$	v_n'	$v_n \rho_\tau v_n'$

For all variable $x \in \Pi$, for all states $s \in \Sigma$ and for all $\tau : s \mapsto s' \in T$ let x' be the copy of x in s'. Then one of the following two alternatives is true:

(1) The value of x in s is the same as the value of x' in s', i.e., $s'(x') = s(x)$, which means: τ does not change the value of x in s', or

(2) the value of x in s is not the same with the value of x' in s', i.e., $s'(x') = s'(x)$, which means τ changes the value of x in s'.

Putting (1) and (2) together we get $s(x)\rho_\tau s'(x) \Leftrightarrow (s'(x') = s(x)) \vee (s'(x') = s'(x))$. For example, consider $s_0 \xrightarrow{scanf} s_1$. The discussion above is synthesized in the following table:

s_0			τ	s_1			ρ_{scan}
x	$\rightarrow$	UND		x	$\rightarrow$	$i1$	$UND\rho_{scan}i1$
y	$\rightarrow$	UND		y	$\rightarrow$	$i2$	$UND\rho_{scan}i2$
t	$\rightarrow$	0	$\overset{scanf}{\longmapsto}$	t	$\rightarrow$	0	$0\rho_{scan}0$
$Input$	$\rightarrow$	UND		$Input$	$\rightarrow$	$i1, i2$	$UND\rho_{scan}i1, i2$
$Output$	$\rightarrow$	UND		$Output$	$\rightarrow$	UND	$UND\rho_{scan}UND$

Note that the following relations hold: $s_0(x) = UND \wedge s_1(x) = i1$, $s_0(y) = UND \wedge s_1(y) = i2$, $s_0(t) = 0 \wedge s_1(t) = 0$, $s_0(Input) = UND \wedge s_1(Input) =$ "$i1\ i2$", $s_0(Output) = UND \wedge s_1(Output) = UND$. Now, we remember that we have two copies of variables, Π and Π'. Transition τ is thus characterized by a predicate $\rho_\tau(\Pi, \Pi')$ whose expression is $\rho_\tau = C_\tau(\Pi) \wedge (x_1' = e_1) \wedge \ldots \wedge (x_n' = e_n)$ where:

- $C_\tau(\Pi)$ is the *enabling condition*. It depends only on values in Π. That is $C_\tau(\Pi)$ states the condition on which $\tau(s) \neq \emptyset$.
- $(x_1' = e_1) \wedge \ldots \wedge (x_n' = e_n)$ is the conjunction of modifications performed by τ.

Every program expresses a transition system. For example, consider the pseudo program

```
begin int x = 1, y = 2, z = 0; z := x+y end
```

Transition system expressed by this program is $\langle \Pi, \Sigma, T, \Theta \rangle$ where:

- $\Pi = \{PC, x, y, z\}$, $D_\Pi = Labels \cup Integers$, PC is a fictive control variable denoting program location counter;
- $\Sigma = \{s_0 = \{x \mapsto 1, y \mapsto 2, z \mapsto 0\}, s_1 = \{x \mapsto 1, y \mapsto 2, z \mapsto 3\}\}$;
- $T = \{\tau_0 : s_0 \rightarrow s_1\}$, i.e., $\tau_0 : \{x \mapsto 1, y \mapsto 2, z \mapsto 0\} \rightarrow \tau_1 : \{x \mapsto 1, y \mapsto 2, z \mapsto 3\}$;
- $C_\tau = x > 0$, i.e., $\Theta = x > 0$.

Values taken by PC are statements defined by program control flow; to simplify examples we disregard them.

Observations:

- $\rho_\tau(\Pi, \Pi') = (x > 0) \wedge (z\prime = x + y)$;

- $s_0(x) > 0 \land \tau_0(s_0)(z) = s_1(x) + s_1(y)$;
- Transitions in the transition system defined by a program are represented by program statements;
- Control variables in the transition system defined by a program are "program counters" and their values are target transitions.

Since transitions are represented by program statements, control variables (i.e., program counters) take as values statement labels.

4.1.2 *Computation*

Let $\mathcal{T} = \langle \Pi, \Sigma, T, \Theta \rangle$ be a transition system. A computation σ of $\mathcal{T}$ is an infinite sequence of states: $\sigma : s_0, s_1, \ldots$ that satisfies the following requirements

- *Initiation:* s_0 is initial, that is $\Theta(s_0(\Pi)) = true$, ie., s_0 satisfies Θ;
- *Consecution:* $\forall i.[i \geq 0]\ s_{i+1} \in \tau(s_i)$ for some $\tau \in T$; $s_i \xrightarrow{\tau} s_{i+1}$ is called an execution step;
- *Diligence:* either σ contains infinitely many diligent steps ($s_i \xrightarrow{\tau} s_{i+1}$, $s_i \neq s_{i+1}$) or it contains a terminal state, s_i, $s_i \mapsto s_i \mapsto s_i \ldots$.

If s_i is terminal, i.e., $\forall j \geq i \land \forall \tau \in T\ s(j) \xrightarrow{\tau} s(j)$, then $\forall u \in \Pi$, $s_i(u)$ is the resulting value of u; if there is no terminal state then computation is not terminating. For example, the computation performed by the `swap.c` program is: $\tau_0, \tau_1, \tau_2, \tau_3, \tau_4$ since s_4 is a terminal state. For another example consider the following C function `copy.c`:

```c
int copy (FILE *F1, *F2)
   {
   int C;
   C = getchar (F1);
   while (C != EOF)
        {
        putchar(C, F2);
        C = getchar(F1);
        }
   return(1);
   }
```

Transition system expressing the computation performed by copy.c is
$T(copy.c) = \langle \Pi_{copy}, \Sigma_{copy}, T_{copy}, \Theta_{copy} \rangle$ where:

- $\Pi_{copy} = \{PC, F1, F2, C, EOF\}$
- Σ_{copy} is:

```
s_0:  PC = [C = getchar(F1)], F1 := {a,b,c}, F2 = empty, C = 0
s_1:  PC = [while(C!=EOF){...}], F1= {a,b,c}, F2 = empty, C = a
s_2:  PC = [putchar(C,F2)], F1= {a,b,c}, F2 = empty, C = a
s_3:  PC = [C = gewtchar(F1)], F1= {a,b,c}, F2 = {a}, C = a
s_4:  PC = [while(C!=EOF){...}], F1= {a,b,c}, F2 = {a}, C = b
s_5:  PC = [putchar(C,F2)], F1= {a,b,c}, F2 = {a} C = b
s_6:  PC = [C = gewtchar(F1)], F1= {a,b,c}, F2 = {a,b}, C = b
s_7:  PC = [while(C!=EOF){...}], F1= {a,b,c}, F2 = {a,b}, C = c
s_8:  PC = [putchar(C,F2)], F1= {a,b,c}, F2 = {a,b} C = c
s_9:  PC = [C = gewtchar(F1)], F1= {a,b,c}, F2 = {a,b,c}, C = c
s_10: PC = [while(C!=EOF){...}], F1= {a,b,c}, F2 = {a,b,c}, C = EOF
s_11: PC = nextCopyCall
```

- T_{copy} is left as an exercise;
- Θ_{copy} is also left as an exercise.

As a hint for the above exercise we note that some transitions change state
while other may only test it, leaving it unchanged.

4.2 Language of Actions

Primitive Action: A primitive action in the language of actions is an
expressions of the form $l : S : \hat{l}$ where $l, \hat{l}$ are labels and S is a statement (simple or composed). Primitive actions expressing program statements are:

(1) $l : skip : \hat{l}$ (do nothing, go to next statement);
(2) $l : await(e) : \hat{l}$ (evaluate e; if true go to next, else repeat l);
(3) $l : (x_1, \ldots, x_n) := (e_1, \ldots, e_n) : \hat{l}$ (multiple assignment).

Composed Actions: Composed actions are represented by composed
statements and are:

(1) Concatenation $l : S_1; S_2 : \hat{l}$;
(2) Deterministic choice: $l : if(e)$ *then* S_1 *else* $S_2 : \hat{l}$;

(3) Loop: $l : while(e)$ *do* $S : \hat{l}$;

(4) Nondeterministic choice: $l : S_1$ *or* $S_2 : \hat{l}$;

(5) Parallel composition $S_1 || S_2$;

(6) Block: $[D; S]$ where D is a list of variable declarations and S is a statement representing a primitive or a composed action.

Linguistic expression of an action A is: $A :: [D][A_1 || A_2 || \ldots || A_n]$ where:

- A is the name of the action performed by the system;
- D is the list of variable declarations on which the action is performed; a declaration in D has the form:

$$\textbf{mode } \text{List: type } \textbf{where } \texttt{predicate};$$

  where $\textbf{mode} \in \{in, out, inout, local\}$ and $\texttt{predicate}$ is a property of variables in List.

- $A_1, A_2, \ldots, A_n$ are the actions in terms of which the action A is specified; each A_i, $1 \leq i \leq n$, is of the form $[D_i] \, S_i$ where S_i is a statement representing an action or an action call.
- $||$ denotes the parallel composition of actions.

4.2.1 *Process*

Actions are represented by linguistic expressions. When they are executed by an appropriate agent they become processes. Hence, a process is an abstraction defined by an agent that performs the action specified by a system. We use the following notation to handle processes: *Process* = $\langle Agent, Action, Status \rangle$ where:

- Agent could be an abstract processor such as the C processors that performs C statements, or a physical processor such as NS32000 or Intel 8088, etc.
- Action is the linguistic expression of the action performed by the process (such as a program).
- Status is the state of process execution, such as executing, suspended, etc.

Example process could be a program execution on a computer platform. The Agent in this case is the physical processor performing machine language instructions, Action is the transition system of the program, the Status could be *running, interrupted, terminated, etc.*. The example of an action performed by a process is the Greatest Common Divisor, GCD, that computes the greatest common divisor of two numbers.

GCD:: in n1, n2: integer where $n1 > 0 \wedge n2 > 0$;
    local a, b: integer where $a = n1 \wedge b = n2$;
    out gcd: integer;
        l_1:while (a $\neq b$) do
            l_2: when $a > b$ do a := a - b : $\hat{l}_2$
                or
            l_3: when $b > a$ do b := b - a : $\hat{l}_3$;
        $:\hat{l}_1$
        l_4: gcd := a: $\hat{l}_4$

This action can be performed by a human process, where the Agent is a human brain, or by a computer process, where Agent is the processor of the computer platform on which the action is computed.

Conclusions on ad hoc system formalization are:

- An ad hoc system will be a tuple $AS = \langle TS, A \rangle$ where TS is an algebraic specification of a transition system and A is an action performed by TS.
- The language of actions can be freely extended to express various computations. Its purpose is to express the behavior of ad hoc systems.
- The reader is encouraged to use this language to express the actions performed by the systems which we will develop further.

Example Ad Hoc System: Consider the set of integers $I = \{ \dots -3, -2, -1, 0, 1, 2, 3, \dots \}$ where ... represents the operation *previous number plus 1*. INT1 is a system that performs the computation of GCD of two integer numbers and is formally specified by:

```
beginSpec
  name INT1 using NAT1 and Bool1 is
  sort: N, I, Bool;
  opns:neg:I->I, +:I x I -> I, -:I x I -> I,
      eg:IxI->Bool, ge:IxI->Bool;
  vars:x,y: I; z: N; p,q: Bool;
  axms:neg(x) = 0-x, neg(neg(x)) = x, x+0=x, x+y=y+x,
      x+neg(x) = 0, neg(x+y)=neg(x)+neg(y), x-y = x + neg(y),
      eq(x,x) = true, eq(x,neg(x))=false,
      ge(z,0)=true, ge(x,y)=ge((x-y),0);
```

```
actn:GCD:: in x1, x2:I where ge(x1,0) and ge(x2,0);
    local a,b:N where a=x1 and b=x2;
    out gcd: N;
        l_1: while (a <> b) do
                    l_2: when ge(a,b) do a:=a-b:^l_2
                    l_3: when ge(b,a) do b:=b-a:^l_3
        :^l_1
        l_4:gsd := a :^l_4
endSpec
```

Challenge: is INT1 a process? Justify your answer!

4.3   Computing Systems

The term "computing system" evolved as a linguistic expression of the actions performed by computer programmers while developing software tools[Donovan (1972)]. Recognizing its grass roots basis, here we present informally this term, starting with the following definition: *A computing system is a collection of computing facilities (resources) together with a set of services offered to computer users.* Example computing facilities: C language and a C language compiler. Services provided by these resources are: allow computer users to solve problems using C language programming. Further, a collection of actions that can be performed on a computer platform while using services provides by a computing system acting on that platform defines a new computing system. Example of a new computing system is a List Management System (LMS). LMS can be implemented on a computer platform using C language and C compiler. Computer users can use services provided by LMS to develop software tools that manipulate computer resources, such as memory, processors, files, etc. Other examples of computing systems are:

- Machine language programming: Computing facilities are computer resources (memory, processor, devices), machine language instruction set, instruction execution cycles. Services: allows programmers to write and execute machine language programs.
- Assembly language programming: Computing facilities are assembly language and the assembler. Services: allows programmers to use mnemonic notations while developing machine language programs.

- C-Language programming: Computing facilities are C language, C compiler, and the Debugger dbx. Services: allows programmers to use C language while developing machine language programs.

4.3.1   *Constructing a computing system*

The following is a generic procedure used to construct computing systems based on a given computer platform:

(1) A collection of (predefined) data types is provided. Example: `int`, `float`, `char` in C.
(2) A collection of type constructors allowing new data types to be constructed in terms of those already constructed (inherited).Example: `struct`, `[ ]`, `*`, `typedef`, `FILE` in C.
(3) A collection of predefined operations are given. Example: `+`, `-`, `*`, variables, constants, expressions in C.
(4) A collection of constructors allowing new operations to be defined in terms of the existing ones. Example: `statement`, `function`, `program` in C.

A computing system is characterized by: data processed, operations performed, services provided.

System methodology allows computing systems structuring in a hierarchy. The first level of the hierarchy is given. Usually the hardware of a computer platform is the first level of a computing system hierarchy. A new system level in a hierarchy (example level $i+1$) is defined by inheriting components from previous levels (levels 0, 1, ..., i) which then may be enriched with new data and operations. Formally, given the levels $0, 1, \ldots, i$, of a system hierarchy, i.e., $S(i) = \langle PrdefData(i), Data(i), PrdefOp(i), Op(i) \rangle$, $i = 0, \ldots,$ to construct the level $S(i + 1)$ one proceeds as follows:

(1) Define $PredefData(i + 1)$ as a subset of $\cup_i Data(i)$;
(2) Enrich $PredefData(i + 1)$ and provide new type constructors thus defining $Data(i + 1)$;
(3) Define $PredefOp(i + 1)$ as a subset of $\cup_i Op(i)$;
(4) Enrich $PredefOp(i + 1)$ and provide new composition rules thus defining $Op(i + 1)$;
(5) Select among $Data(i + 1)$ and $Op(i + 1)$ those that are provided (exported) as services to computer users.

This construction is illustrated by software system hierarchy in Figure 4.1.

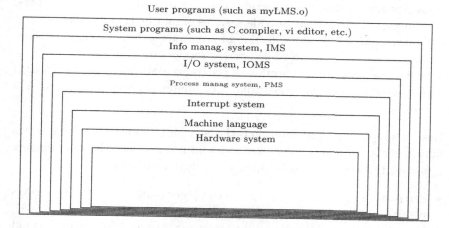

Fig. 4.1   Software system hierarchy

4.4   Overview on Systems Methodology

- The system has been discussed both as a mathematical and as an ad hoc concept.
- A systematic approach for constructing ad hoc systems has been specified.
- Manipulation of ad hoc systems through System Specification Language (SSL), System Implementation Language (SIL), and System Validation Language (SVL) has been presented.
- Doctrines of the ad hoc systems have been discussed (functionality, reliability, efficiency, easy to use, easy to maintain).
- Ad hoc systems have been formalized as tuple $\langle TS, Action \rangle$ where TS is an algebraic specification of a transition system and $Action$ is the action performed by the system. $Action$ is a linguistic expression in the language of the processor that performs the transitions. We use the *action specification language* to express actions.
- The concept of a computing system has been introduced and a methodology for ad hoc system construction has been provided using a hierarchy of computing systems.

4.4.1   *Terminology*

The term system is further used with the meaning of an *ad hoc system*. Essential ad hoc systems discussed in this book are:

- **Hardware system:** a collection of hardware components (processors, memories, devices) that provide services of information processing.
- **System software:** the collection of programs and documents that controls a hardware system while offering services to its users.
- **Software system:** a collection of programs, data, and documents used to solve classes of problems using a computer platform, organized as a system.

Basic concept in our presentation is the concept of a software system which informally is a software structured as an ad hoc systems. Using systematic approach this concept can be further specified as follows:

- **Purpose:** solves problems on given computer platforms. Example, solves systems of linear equations.
- **Components:** programs and documents determined by the problem at hand.
- **Functional behavior:** according to given specifications.
- **Expression:** package of programs and data, see LMS.

Software system structuring is provided by layering its components on levels, according to the services provided by them to their users and the architecture of user applications.

Employing the concept of a software system as basis, we can define the term *system software* as the software system designed to manipulate computer resources thus providing services to computer users. Using the systematic approach this definition becomes:

- **Purpose:** makes computer platform manageable by computer users. Example, solves systems of linear equations.
- **Components:** hardware, software, and programs and data that manipulate them.
- **Functional behavior:** according to given specifications.
- **Expression:** package of programs and data, see C compiler.

System software structuring is obtained by layering its components on levels according to the services they provide based on the following facts:

(1) Each component of the system software is a user of computer resources (hardware and software).
(2) Each component of the system software is a server of some computer resources (hardware and software).

(1) and (2) above imply that components of the system software can be organized into a hierarchy defined as follows:

- **Layer 0:** system software components that do not use services provided by other components. Example, machine language program execution, which, as we will see in Part 2 of this book, can be defined by the following C language pseudo-function:

```
ProgramExecution:
{
    while ((PC.opcode)<>Halt)
        { Execute(PC); PC:= Next(PC) }
}
```

Data processed by this function are machine language instructions. Operations performed are instruction analysis and execution. Services provided are the machine language programming.
- **Layer 1:** system software components that use only services provided by the components in Layer 0. Examples are the machine language programs.
- **Layer i:** system software components that use services provided by Layer 0, Layer 1, ..., Layer i-1. Example is a C-Compiler.

4.4.2 *Users of a computer platform*

The users of a computer platform are the programs executed by hardware system and the programmers developing these programs. The action performed by this system is expressed by the machine language codes. Services provided by this system are the processes $\langle Processor, Code, Status \rangle$. Looking at the programmers as "systems" interacting with the hardware we observe that the action they perform is the development of programs (programming). The language expressing this action depend upon the resources they can use. However, the processor performing this action is the programmer's brain. Thus, the services provided is performing brain rules for program development by the process $\langle Brain, Tools, Status \rangle$. *Tool*-s are editors, compilers, assemblers, interpreter, etc. Since programmers use tools that are programs, this define a hierarchy relationship between hardware and users. In view with this relationship we structure the system software in two layers: **Execution Support Environment (ESE)** which is the component of the system software that provides services for program executions, and **Programming Support Environment (PSE)** which is the component of the system software that provide services for program development. ESE is a collection of tools that handle hardware and software resources required by process execution, and interrupts and exceptions, which are events that occur during program execution. Example ESE is the Run-Time Environment (RTE). PSE is the component of the system software that provides services for program development. Example tools that belong to PSE are compilers, assemblers, editors, applications. Tools provided in PSE handle user requests. Since user requests imply process execution, protection and security requirements imply that tools execution be provided as services by the ESE.

Observation: computer based problem solving process (CBPSP) consists of using software tools to solve problems employing a computer platform. The consequence is that the acronym PSE is also used to stand for Problem Solving Environment.

PART 2
Computer Architecture and Functionality

Chapter 5

Hardware System

This part of the book presents the architecture and functionality of the hardware of a computer platform as an ad-hoc system. We do this using the systematic approach for ah-hoc system construction developed in the Chapter3, which iterates the following actions:

(1) Define the major behavior of the system;
(2) Identify system components performing the system behavior;
(3) Specify the functional behavior of system components;
(4) Develop an (algorithmic) expression of the system in terms of components at (2) performing the actions specified t (3);

until system performs according to its major behavior specified at (1).

5.1 Major Behavior of a Hardware System

A hardware system is seen here as an information processing tool that performs the following operations: receive information from the environment, store information for later use, process information stored in the system, transmit information into the environment. The components of a hardware system that perform these operations are:

- Memory which performs the storing operations;
- Processing processors which perform information processing operations;
- I/O devices which perform information exchange operations with the environment;
- Control processors (CPU) that controls the flaw of information among other components.

The formal expression of a hardware system using SSL is:

```
beginSpec
  name Hardware System is
  sort Memory, Processor, Device, Control;
  opns receive:Device x Control -> Memory,
       transmit:Memory x Control -> Device,
       store:Processor x Control -> Memory,
       fetch:Memory x Control -> Processor,
       process:Memory x Processor x Control -> Processor,
               Memory x Processor x Control -> Memory,
               Processor x Control -> Processor;
  vars PC: Control;
  axms: Value(PC.operation) in the set
              {receive, transmit, store, fetch, process};
  actn Run: while PluggedIn and PowerOn do
              1_0: Perform (PC); PC := Next(PC) :^1_0
endSpec
```

The environments of a hardware system consists of all information carriers (supports) to which hardware components may react (receive information from and transmit information to) and are called here Input-Output Devices that are further referred either by IO devices or simple IO or devices.

Example of information carriers that may belong to a hardware system environment are: a package of punched cards, a disk pack or a diskette, a magnetic tape, a paper tape, the screen of a terminal, the keyboard of a terminal, etc. Hardware interaction with its environment is performed by receiving information from the environment and transmitting information into the environment.

5.2 Memory

The memory of a hardware system allows information to be received, processed, stored, and preserved for later use. For this purpose the memory is composed of an array (usually of size a power of 2) of two (stable) state elements such as: semi-conductors, flip-flops, magnetic cores, etc. The information in memory is encoded in terms of the state of memory elements. The state of one memory element is called a bit of information and is denoted by Bit, $Bit = 0$ or $Bit = 1$ (two states). Hence, information in memory is a long string of bits. The elements making up a memory are organized into an array of bits grouped in units of addressable fields called locations. A memory location is a group of successive memory bits in memory array whose contents can be accessed as an information unit. Hence, each memory location is characterized by: address, i.e., position in memory array, size, i.e., the number of bits components, and type, i.e., the information it may contain. In other words, the type of the information stored in a memory location coincides with the interpretation of this information by the processor accessing it. Examples of memory locations are byte, half-word, word, long-word, double-word, etc.

5.2.1 *The byte*

The byte is the smallest location in memory. The size of other memory locations is measured in bytes. Byte size is an architectural characteristic of the hardware system and could be any number of bits that is suitable for information codification. Knuth[Knuth (1968)] discusses a computer architecture where byte size is 6 bits. We assume here that a byte is composed of $2^3 = 8$ bits. Hence, a memory of 2^{23} bits contains $2^{23}/2^3 = 2^{20}$ bytes.

Byte Address: since a byte is the smallest location, memory is also seen as an array of bytes. In the example above, $0 \leq ByteAddress \leq 2^{20} = 1M$.

Byte Type: the contents of a byte B could be any configuration $b_0 b_1 \ldots b_7$, $b_i \in \{0,1\}$ of 8-bits. Therefore the byte type is the byte interpretation by the processor accessing it and the operations defined on that interpretation. If we interpret $b_0 b_1 \ldots b_7$ as a binary number then we have $0 \leq b_0 b_1 \ldots b_7 \leq 2^8 - 1$; hence, the byte type is a number b, $0 \leq b \leq 255$.

Byte Value: the value encoded on these bits depends upon the processor accessing it. Usually a byte B can be interpreted as representing a character code, a short positive integer, $0 \leq B \leq 255$, a short integer, $-128 \leq B \leq 127$.

The processor that accesses a byte (or any other memory location) interprets it according to its own type, i.e. *a processor sees in a memory location the information it (the processor) was designed to process.*

5.2.2 *The half-word*

The half-word is a memory location composed of two successive bytes. Hence:

- half-word size is 2 *Bytes* = 16 *bits*;

- half-word address is $2 \times ByteAdrress$. In the above example any even number in the range $0 \leq Addr \leq 2^{20}$, such that $Addr\ modulo\ 2 = 0$, is a half-word address;
- half-word values are the binary codes $0 \leq n \leq 2^{16} - 1$ that can be interpreted as short integers, instructions, etc. Hence, the half-word type is determined by the processor operations defined on the respective interpretation.

5.2.3   *The word*

The word is a memory locations composed of two successive half-words. Hence:

- word size is $2\ HalfWords = 32\ bits$;
- word address is $2 \times HalfWordAdrress$. In the above example, any number $0 \leq Addr \leq 2^{20}$ such that $Addr\ modulo\ 4 = 0$
- word values are the binary codes $0 \leq n \leq 2^{32} - 1$ that can be interpreted as integers, reals, instructions, etc. Further, the word type is determined by the processor operations defined on the respective interpretation.

5.2.4   *The long-word*

The long-word, also called double-word, is a memory locations composed of two successive words. Hence:

- long-word size is $2\ Words = 64\ bits$
- long-word address is $2 \times WordAdrress$. In the above example, any number $0 \leq Addr \leq 2^{20}$ such that $Addr\ modulo\ 8 = 0$
- long-word values are the codes $0 \leq n \leq 2^{64} - 1$ that can be interpreted as long integers, double-precision reals, machine instructions, program-status words, etc. The long-word type is determined by the processor operations defined on the respective interpretation.

Other useful terms are:

Memory Cycle: is the time necessary to a processor to access the information stored in a memory location.

RAM: random access memory, is the collection of memory locations that can be directly accessed by a processor. While accessing a memory location, a processor can write (store) information in that location, or it can read (fetch) information from that location.

ROM: read-only memory, is a memory that allows only read (fetch) operations.

Main Memory: (internal memory) is the memory directly accessible to the processors.

Secondary Memory: (storage) is the memory that is not directly accessible to processors. To access information in the storage it (the information) must be moved first in the main memory.

Cache Memory: is a direct and very fast accessible internal memory.

5.3 Processor Components

Processor performs information preprocessing. Example processors in a conventional computer platform are:

- CPU (Central Processing Unit) composed of ALU (Arithmetic and Logic Unit) and instruction execution unit.
- Processing processor, performs data processing operations;
- Control processor, controls processing operations i.e., control processor performs program execution. In a conventional computer platform control processor is "part of CPU".
- I/O devices performing information exchange with the environment.

We simplify this classification considering only two type of processors:

- Data Processor (Processor) is a processor that performs operations on data. Example of data processors are ALU, FPU, I/O devices, etc.
- Control Processor (Controller) is the processor that controls the operations performed by processors. That is, a control processor performs program execution.

Each processor is completely determined by:

- Type of information it processes. Example char, int, float, I/O records, instructions, etc.
- Operations it performs on its information type. For example, if type is *char* then `compareC`; if type is *int* then `+`, `-`, `*`, `/`, `compareI`; if type is *float* the `+f`, `-f`, `*f`, `/f`, `compareF`; if type is *DiskSector* then `read`, `write`; if type is *instructions* then `fetch`, `execute`.

The architecture of a processor is shown in Figure 5.1.

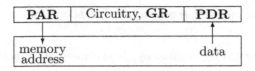

Fig. 5.1   Structure of a data processor

Note that if processor processes char data, address is a byte, if processor processes int data, address may be a byte, a half-word, a word, etc., if processor processes instruction, address is an instruction word, if processor performs I/O operations, address is an I/O record.

Notation:

(1) Processor Address Register (PAR) is the register that points to the memory location that holds the data on which processor performs.
(2) Processor Data Register (PDR) is the register that holds the data on which processor performs.
(3) General Registers (GR) are registers interface to memory and circuitry to carry out the operation.

5.3.1   *Special data processors*

I/O devices are considered in this book as special data processors. They are grouped in classes characterized by:

(1) Information carrier, such as magnetic tapes, disks, screens, etc.
(2) Record on the Information Carrier (RIC). RIC is the part of the information carrier that can hold the unit of information exchange that the I/O device performs within one operation. For example, if the information carrier is the screen of a terminal the RIC may be character or line; for a card-reader or a card-puncher the RIC can be 80 column or 60 column card; for a disk the RIC may be a sector of 128 or 512 bytes or 1K bytes or others; for tapes the RIC may be block of 512 or 1024 (1K) bytes, or others.
(3) Operations performed by the devices of a class are $Read : RIC \rightarrow I/ORegister \rightarrow Memory, Write : Memory \rightarrow I/ORegister \rightarrow RIC, Control : StateOfDevice \rightarrow \{Busy, Free, Error\}$.
(4) Physical link of the device class in the system, also referred to as the interface to the memory, which can be direct, channel, or bus.

Theoretically the information carriers of IO devices are physical media of potentially infinite length. For example, one can pack a potential infinite number of cards in a card reader; one can type a potential infinite number of characters on a keyboard; one can use a potential infinite disk size (disk pack) to store/retrieve information, etc. The actual sizes of information carriers for a given computer platform are limited by the implementation restrictions imposed by computer architecture. Note that $Read, Write$ operations perform information exchange between RIC-s of I/O devices, which are standards of fixed length and structure, and memory using I/O registers, i.e. $Read : RIC \rightarrow I/Oregister \rightarrow Memory$ and $Write : Memory \rightarrow I/Oregister \rightarrow RIC$.

5.4 Communication Channels

Memory, Controller, Processors, and I/O devices communicate using communication channels that are referred here as direct link, channel link, and bus link. To simplify presentation Processors and I/O deceives are further referred to as Devices.

5.4.1 *Direct link*

With direct link the Devices operate under direct control of the controller, Figure 5.2, using programmed operations.

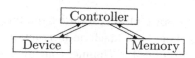

Fig. 5.2   Device operates under direct control

The Device operations are encoded in the program as machine language instructions. Thus, a Device performs operations (in particular I/O operations) under the direct control of the controller by the following protocol:

- The program initiates an operation using a machine language instruction interpreted by the Controller.
- After the operation initiation, the Device performs while Controller (in particular CPU) waits for the operation termination.

- When the Device terminates the operation the Controller continues interpreting the next program instruction.

Essential for programmed Device operations is the manner in which Controller waits for the Device operation termination. The Controller may wait the operation termination during the operation cycle doing nothing (busy-waiting loop) or it may suspend the execution of the current program and perform the execution of another program during the time taken by the Device operation.

5.4.2 *Channel link*

The I/O devices operating on channel link are controlled by a dedicated controller called the *channel*, Figure 5.3. Devices perform I/O operations

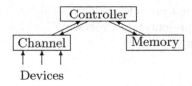

Fig. 5.3   Device operates under Channel control

under the control of the channel by the protocol:

- The program initiates an I/O operation by sending an I/O program to the channel. This is done by a machine instruction which is interpreted by the Controller by telling the channel that an I/O program waits its attentions.
- Controller (i.e., the CPU) continues to operate in parallel with I/O device.
- Channel and Controller synchronize their actions by interrupts or polling. Interrupts are signals send by the Channel to the Controller, while polling is a mechanism that allows Controller to test the device status.

Channel, Controller Synchronization: while performing in parallel, the Controller (executing machine language instructions) and the Channel (executing I/O operations) synchronize by the following mechanism:

- Controller may find device status by the mechanism of polling.

- Channel may inform CPU about I/O program termination by sending an interrupt signal which tell the Controller the status of its operation.
- According to the Channel, Controller dialog during I/O operations, the channels could be selective or multiplexer. With selective channels only one device can operate at once under the Channel control. Selective channels are suitable for high speed devices. With multiplexer channels all I/O devices under the Channel control can transmit at once. This is suitable for slow devices.

5.4.3 *Bus interface*

The Bus is a processor that provides a communication link on which addresses of processors, I/O devices, and memory as well as data contained in these addresses circulate between processors and memory. Figure 5.4 shows a simplified picture of this kind of an component interface. The I/O

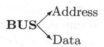

Fig. 5.4   Hardware components under bus control

devices perform under bus link by the protocol:

- I/O operations are encoded in the program as I/O requests. An I/O request is a tuple (Operation, RIC, MemoryAddr);
- During program execution Controller sends an I/O request on the bus;
- Bus identifies the processor and memory involved and initiates the I/O operation: $Write : Memory \rightarrow I/O \ device, \ Read : IO \ device \rightarrow Memory$.
- Operation termination is signaled by the Bus to the Controller by interrupts or Controller polls the Bus for the device status.

Observations

(1) All hardware components may be connected with each other using a high speed bus;
(2) All hardware components may operate simultaneously by sending/receiving requests, i.e. tuples $(Operation, Data, Aaddress)$ on the bus;

(3) An example of a bus is the [Schanin (1986)] Encore Multimax bus called *nanobus* transmitting 100 MB/second. The name *nanobus* come from the fact that the bus is 1 foot long which is the distance traveled by light in one nanosecond i.e., $1/10^9$ second.

5.5   Control Processor (CPU)

Control processor (Controller) is the hardware component in charge of program execution. This is achieved by standardizing the operations performed by the hardware as *machine instructions* and by structuring the computation performed by the hardware as a sequence of machine instructions called the *program*. Operations composing a program usually involve more hardware components. For example,

```
LDR, Adr: Processor x Memory ==> Processor
STR, Adr: Processor x Memory ==> Memory
```

Operations performed by hardware are initiated and controlled by the Control Processor. Pertinent components of the Controller are shown in Figure 5.5. Since the Controller is a processor its components are

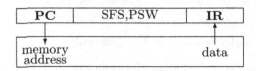

Fig. 5.5   Structure of a data processor

the same as the components of any other processor. However, due to its special task, namely *program execution*, its components have special names:

- Store/Fetch Switch (SFS) is an arbiter (usually implemented as a 2 bit register) that controls the information movement *Memory → Controller* or *Controller → Memory*, (PSW) is the process status word.
- Processor Address Register (PAR) is called the Program Counter (PC);
- Processor Data Register (PDA) is called the Instruction Register (IR);

- Processor Status Word (PSW) is a collection of registers that contain info about status of operations performed by the CPU. Example of processor status word is the tuple $PSW = (cc, ov, PC, prioritytLevel, etc)$, where cc stands for condition codes, ov stands for overflow toggle, PC is the program counter, priorityLevel is the priority of program currently executed, etc. Notice that though PSW is a collection of registers it is usually accessed as a single register, by a single instruction.

In conclusion observe that Controller processor operates on data that represent encoded machine operations. These data are usually called instructions. A sequence of instructions representing the operations of an algorithm is called a program. In order to be executed, a program needs to be stored in a sequence of memory locations. This is what controller executes!

5.5.1 *Machine instructions*

Since instructions are data processed by control processor we also call them the *Control Data Type*, (CDT). In other words, in order to be executed by computers, algorithms need to be encoded as programs. Consequently, the algorithm operations must be codified and stored in memory as *instructions*. The codes used to encode operations must specify: the operation law (such as addition, subtraction, etc), processor performing the operation, operands and results. By convention, usually the operation law and the processor performing it are both identified by the operation code. A memory location that contains an instruction is called an *instruction word*. By convention, usually various pieces of info that compose an instruction have fixed places in an instruction word as seen in Figure 5.6.

Opcode	Operands	Result

Fig. 5.6   Structure of an instruction word

For example, the instruction word codifying the C assignment $c = a + b$ is in Figure 5.7.

Code(+)	Addr(a)	Addr(b)	Addr(c)

Fig. 5.7   Instruction word for addition

To get the feeling of what this encoding implies we consider the following problem:

Develop a program that represents the following fragment of a C algorithm:

```
int x, y := 10;
if (x > y)
  x :=  x - y
else
  y := y + x
```

How many operation codes do we need here?

Solution: assume that data are allocated to memory as follows: x is in the location 1000, y is in the location 1001, 10 is in location 1002, and 0 is in location 1003. Then the sketch of a machine language program, using three-address instructions, that encode this C code is in the table in Figure 5.8.

Location	Code	Addr1	Addr2	Addr3
1004	Load	1001	1002	1001
1005	Cmp	1000	1001	
1006	JLES	1009		
1007	SUB	1000	1001	1000
1008	JMP	1010		
1009	ADD	1000	1001	1001
1010	Done			

Fig. 5.8   Machine language program

5.5.2   *Address expressions*

The operands and the result in an instruction word are specified by expressions called Address Expressions (AE). Usual elements composing an AE are: processor registers, addresses of memory locations, codes interpreted as effective data (such as integers), modifiers that tell the Controller how to interpret data in an instruction field. Example modifiers are immediate addressing, which is a bit that tells the processor whether AE represents the data itself or the address of the data, direct and indirect addressing, which is a bit that tells the processor whether AE represent the address of the data (direct) or the address of the address of data (indirect), indexed addressing, which is a bit that tells the processor how to compute the value of AE. Example, using C language assignments as algorithm operations, the AE-s used in the instruction fields are:

- If the operation is c = a + b then the instruction is:

  `Code(+) Location(a) Location(b) Location(c)`

- If the operation is c = a[i] + b[i] then the instruction is:

  `Code(+) Index[i] Location(a) Location(b) Location(c)`

- If the operation is c = *a + *b then the instruction is:

  `Code(+) Indirection Location(a) Location(b) Location(c)`

Note that index and indirection can refer to a location, to both locations, or to all locations used in the instruction. This depends on computer architecture.

5.5.3 *Instruction set architecture*

The collection of all instructions performed by a Controller characterizes a computer platform and is called Instruction Set Architecture (ISA). Instructions of an ISA are codified on a given number of patterns designed to hold AE-s composing the instructions. Instruction execution is performed by algorithms that evaluate address expressions recorded in these patterns and perform the operations encoded by instruction patterns. The algorithms that interpret instruction patterns are wired in hardware and thus characterize the ISA. This allows architectural classification of computer platforms.

5.6 Computer Architecture Classification

According to the size and structure of the instruction word computers are classified as: fixed-format instruction word, multiple-format instruction word, variable-size instruction word, Reduced Instruction Set Computer (RISC), Complex Instruction Set Computer (CISC), etc.

5.6.1   *Fixed-format instruction word computers*

All instructions performed by the control processor have the same size and format. Example of a fixed-format instruction word computer is the MIX machine [Knuth (1968)] whose instruction word is in Figure 5.9.

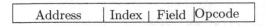

| Address | | Index | Field | Opcode |

Fig. 5.9   Mix machine instruction word

MIX machine is a theoretical computer developed by D E Knuth in 1960s to evaluate the complexity of algorithms discussed in his book.The controller of the Mix machine has two general registers A (arithmetic) and X (extension of A), 6 index registers, and an operation toggle. Each MIX machine operation is a two-operand operation. The arithmetic register (A), possible extended with X register, stores the first operand. The second operand is in the memory location at the address **Address**. MIX machine controller fetches in the IR the instruction whose address is in the PC register and interpret IR by the formula:

$$A, X := (A, X) \ Opcode \ (Field) \ Address(Index)$$

Notice, here $(Field) \ Address \ (Index)$ is an address expression.

5.6.2   *Multiple-format instruction word computers*

A given number of instruction formats are designed where operation code, among other, also specifies the instruction format. Each format is used for the representation of a specific kind of operation. Instruction interpretation is a case-statement determined by the operation code. Example of a multiple format instruction word computer is the IBM 360/370. The IBM 360/370 controller has 16 32-bit general registers, denoted here by $R_0, R_1, \ldots, R_{15}$ that can be used to store operands and indexes, 4 64-bit floating point registers, and a 64-bit Processor Status Word (PSW), that contains the contents of the Program Counter, protection information, and interrupt status. IBM 360/370 has has 6 instruction word formats:

(1) RR format, encoded on 2 bytes, Figure 5.10. Controller interprets this format by performing $R_1 := R_1 \ Opcode \ R_2$.
(2) RX format, encoded on 4 bytes, Figure 5.11: Controller interprets this format by performing $R := R \ Opcode((Base + Opnd) + Index)$.

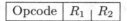

Fig. 5.10   IBM-360/370 RR instruction word

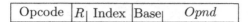

Fig. 5.11   IBM-360/370 RX instruction word

(3) RS format (used for 3-arg operations, such as shifts) encoded on 4 bytes, Figure 5.12. Controller interprets this format by performing $(Bases + Opnd) = Opcode(R_1, R_3)$

Opcode	R_1	R_3	Base|	$Opnd$

Fig. 5.12   IBM-360/370 RS instruction word

(4) SI (used for operations on immediate data) encoded on 4 bytes, Figure 5.13.

Opcode	I	Base|	$Opnd_2$

Fig. 5.13   IBM-360/370 SI instruction word

Controller interprets this format by performing

$$(Base + Opnd_2) := I \; Opcode \; (Base + Opnd_2)$$

(5) SS format 1, used for storage to storage operations with operands of the different lengths, encoded on 6 bytes, Figure 5.14. Controller interprets

Opcode	L_1	L_2	B_1	$Opnd_1$	B_2	$Opnd_2$

Fig. 5.14   IBM-360/370 SS instruction word

this format by performing:

$$\langle B_1 + Opnd_1, L_1 \rangle := (\langle B_1 + Opnd_1, L_1 \rangle) \; Opcode \; (\langle B_2 + Opnd_2, L_2 \rangle)$$

Here the notation $(\langle A, L \rangle)$ is used to indicate the contents of the operand of address A and length L.

(6) SS format 2, used for storage to storage operations with operands of the same length, encoded on 6 bytes, Figure 5.15. Controller interprets

Opcode	L	B_1	$Opnd_1$	B_2	$Opnd_2$

Fig. 5.15   IBM-360/370 SS instruction word

this format by performing:

$$\langle B_1 + Opnd_1, L \rangle := (\langle B_1 + Opnd_1, L \rangle) \; Opcode \; (\langle B_2 + Opnd_2, L \rangle).$$

5.6.3   *Variable size instruction word computers*

Instruction word pattern is fixed while the size of memory locations holding instructions depend upon the number of operands and operand type. The instruction is composed of a *head* and a *body*. Instruction head has a fixed length that specifies the operation law and the length of the body (number of operands). Each operand is specified by an address expression whose value has one of the modes *immediate, direct, indirect*, and occupies a fixed-size location in instruction body. Controller interprets the instructions by the following procedure:

- Processor fetches first the instruction head and determine the number of operands.
- For each operand the processor determines its type and performs: if operand is immediate than its value is either in a machine register specified by the operand or the operand itself; if operand is direct its value is in the memory location specified by the address expression on the operand; if operand is indirect then its value is in the memory location whose address is in the memory location specified by the address expression on the operand.

Example of a variable size instruction computer is the VAX-11/780 microprocessor [Levy and Eckhouse (1980)], whose instruction pattern is given in Figure 5.16.

5.6.4   *Reduced-instruction-set computer*

A RISC computer uses a relative simple load-and-store instruction set allowing the user to load and store registers. Instructions may perform

Opcode
Length, #operands
Operand specifier
. . .
Operand specifier

Fig. 5.16   VAX-11/780 instruction word

Register-to-Register, Register-to-Memory, and Register-to-Instruction operations. Typically a RISC machine has a large number of registers, multiple functional units, and pipelined instruction execution.

RISC machines instruction word uses a fixed size memory location to codify instructions. However, this location may accommodate many formats. Example of a RISC computer is the IBM RS-6000[IBM (1992)] which uses eleven instruction formats, all codified on 32-bits word. Most common is D-format. Controller of RS-6000 is called a *branch processor* and performs instruction fetch, instruction execution, and interrupt actions. There are three classes of instructions in RS-6000: branch, which transfer control (i.e., load PC with the address of the next instruction), fixed-point arithmetic operations, and floating-point arithmetic operations. The RS-6000 processor is both word-oriented and fixed-point, and double-word oriented and floating-point. It uses 32-bit-word-aligned instructions and provides for byte, half-word, word, and double-word operand fetches and stores between memory and a set of 32 general purpose registers, (GPR)-s, and memory and 32 floating-point registers (FPR)-s. The architecture of IBM RS-6000 is shown in Figure 5.17

Branch Processor: RS-6000 branch processor registers are: Condition Register (CR), Link Register (LR), Count Register (CTR), and Machine State Register (MSR). CR is a 32-bit register that reflects the result of certain operations and provides a mechanism for testing and branching. LR is a 32-bit register that holds the target for branch conditional register instructions. It also holds the return address for branch and link type instructions and supervisory call, SVC. CTR is a 32-bit register designed to hold a loop count and is automatically decremented during the execution of a branch and count instruction. CTR also holds the target address for the branch to count register instruction. MSR is a 32-bit register that defines the state of the machine. When a return from interrupt instruction is executed $MSR[16..31] := SRR1[16..31]$. MSR can be modified by *move*

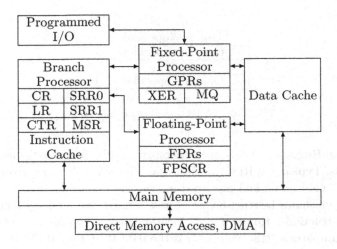

Fig. 5.17   RS-6000 processor architecture

to machine state register instruction. The bits definitions of MSR are:

$$MSR[16] = \begin{cases} 0, & \text{when external interrupts are disabled;} \\ 1, & \text{when external interrupts are enabled.} \end{cases}$$

$MSR[17]$ is the *mode bit* called Problem State (PS), and is defined by:

$$MSR[17] = \begin{cases} 0, & \text{when any instruction can be executed;} \\ 1, & \text{only non-privileged instructions are executed.} \end{cases}$$

$MSR[18]$ is called Floating-Point, FP, available and is defined by

$$MSR[18] = \begin{cases} 0, & \text{floating-point instructions cannot be executed;} \\ 1, & \text{floating-point instructions can be executed.} \end{cases}$$

$MSR[19]$ is called Machine Check Enable, ME, and is defined by

$$MSR[19] = \begin{cases} 0, & \text{machine check interrupts are disabled;} \\ 1, & \text{machine check interrupts are enabled.} \end{cases}$$

$MSR[20]$ is called Floating-Point Exception Interrupt Enable, FE, and is defined by

$$MSR[20] = \begin{cases} 0, & \text{interrupts on floating-point exceptions are disabled;} \\ 1, & \text{interrupts on floating-point exceptions are enabled.} \end{cases}$$

$MSR[24]$ is called Alignment Check, AL, and is defined by

$$MSR[24] = \begin{cases} 0, & \text{alignment check is off, low order bits of address are} \\ & \text{ignored;} \\ 1, & \text{alignment check is on, low order bits are checked.} \end{cases}$$

$MSR[25]$ is called Interrupt Prefix, IP, and is defined in terms of the interrupt offset 'xxxxx' by

$$MSR[25] = \begin{cases} 0, & \text{interrupts vectored to X'000xxxxx';} \\ 1, & \text{interrupts vectored to X'FFFxxxxx'.} \end{cases}$$

$MSR[26]$ is called Instruction Relocate, IR, and is defined by

$$MSR[26] = \begin{cases} 0, & \text{instruction address translation is off;} \\ 1, & \text{instruction address translation is on.} \end{cases}$$

$MSR[27]$ is called Data Relocate, DR, and is defined by

$$MSR[27] = \begin{cases} 0, & \text{data address translation is off;} \\ 1, & \text{data address translation is on.} \end{cases}$$

Fixed-Point Processor: The fixed-point processor operates using 32 32-bits general purpose registers denoted by GPR_{00}, $GPR_{01},\ldots$, GPR_{31}, a 32-bits fixed-point exception register, XER, and a 32-bits multiply quotient register, MQ. The Fixed-point exception register (XER) is a 32 bit register whose bits $XER[3..15]$ and $XER[24]$ are reserved. The other bits are defined as follows: $XER[0]$ is called the *summary overflow (SO)* and is set to 1 whenever an instruction sets the overflow bit, OV. It remains set until software resets it. $XER[1]$ is called the *overflow (OV) bit*. It is set to indicate that an overflow has occurred during an instruction operation. OV is not altered by compare instructions. $XER[2]$ is called the *carry (CA) bit*. It is set to indicate a carry from the bit 0 of the computed result. CA is not altered by compare instructions. $XER[16..23]$ is used by the Load String and Compare Byte Indexed instruction; the byte being compared against is stored in $XER[16..23]$. $XER[25..31]$ is used by the Load String Indexed, Load String and Compare Byte Indexed, and Store String Indexed instructions to indicate the number of bytes loaded or stored. Multiply-quotient register (MQ) MQ is a 32 bit register which provides a register extension to accommodate the product for the multiply instructions, the dividend for the divide instructions, an operand for the long rotate and shift instructions. It is also used as a temporary storage for store string instructions.

Floating-Point Processor: The floating-point processor uses 32 64-bits floating point registers denoted FPR_{00}, $FPR_{01}, \ldots$, FRP_{31}, and a floating-point status and control register denoted by $FPSCR$. FPSCR contains the status and control flags for floating-point operations. The field $FPSCR[0..19]$ contains status bits and the the field $FPSCR[20..31]$ contains control bits. $FPSCR[0]$ is called floating-point exception summary (FX). It is set when a floating-point instruction causes any of the floating-point exceptions or when the floating-point exception bits in FPSCR are explicitly set by instructions. $FPSCR[1]$ is called floating-point enabled exception summary (FEX). It is set when an enabled exception condition occurs. $FPSCR[2..14]$ are set by floating-point exception conditions. $FPSCR[15..19]$ contains the floating-point result flags defined as: $FPSCR[15]$ is the result class descriptor, $FPSCR[16]$ is the floating-point negative indicator, $FPSCR[17]$ is the floating-point positive indicator, $FPSCR[18]$ is zero result indicator, and $FPSCR[19]$ is the *not a number*, NaN, result indicator. $FPSCR[20..23]$ and $FPSCR[29]$ are reserved. $FPSCR[24..28]$ are set by other floating-point exception conditions. $FPSCR[30..31]$ controls the rounding result conditions:

$$FPSCR[30..31] = \begin{cases} 00, & \text{determines rounding to nearest,} \\ 01, & \text{determines rounding towards zero,} \\ 10, & \text{determines rounding towards plus infinity,} \\ 11, & \text{determines rounding towards minus infinity.} \end{cases}$$

RS-6000 Instruction Formats: IBM RS-6000 uses eleven instruction formats, all codified on 32-bits words. The only fixed field of an instruction word (IW), for all instruction formats is the field defined by the bits $IW[0..5]$ where the operation code, *Opcode*, is represented. We describe here only the D Format which is most often used.

D Format: This format is used to codify two operand operations of the form *Opcode Op1 Op2* that perform *Op1 := Op1 Opcode Op2*, i.e., *Op1* is both the source and the target operand and *Op2* is a source operand. The *Op1* is codified on the bits $IW[6..10]$ and could be one of:

- A general fixed-point or floating-point register, R.

- The TO bit used to be AND-ed with a condition where: $IW[6]$ compares less than, $IW[7]$ compares greater than, $IW[8]$ compares equal, $IW[9]$ compares logically less than, and $IW[10]$ compares logically greater than.
- The specifier BF of a field i of the condition register CR or one of the FPSCR fields as a target. If $i = IW[6..8]$ then the field i refers to bits $i*4..i*4+3$ of the CR register.

The $Op2$ of D Format is composed of a register, R, used as a source operand, and a displacement D. The register R used as a source operand is codified on the bits $IW[11..15]$ The displacement is codified on the bits $IW[16..31]$ and it could be one of: a 16 bit two's complement integer, D, sign extended to 32 bits, a 16 bit signed integer, a 16 bit unsigned integer. The structure of the D-format instruction word is in Figure 5.18.

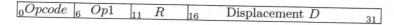

Fig. 5.18   D format instruction

Chapter 6

Functional Behavior of Hardware Components

6.1 Functional Behavior of Memory

Memory operates under Controller and performs two main operations:

- Fetch: *Processor* × *Memory* → *Processor*, which takes the contents of a given memory location and sends it into a register in the Processor.
- Store: *Processor* × *Memory* → *Memory*, which takes the contents of a given register in the Processor and stores it into a memory location.

The memory location and processor register involved in fetch and store operations are specified by the instruction word.

For performance reasons memory and processors operating on it are designed such that they can perform their operations in parallel. However, memory is shared by all processors. This means that all processors components operate on memory while each processor perceives the structure of memory according to its own type. For examples, a processor operating on bytes must be able to fetch and store bytes; a processor operating on half-words must be able to fetch and store half-words; a processor operating on words must be able to fetch and store words; a processor operating on double-words must be able to fetch and store double words. Therefore the memory must be organized as a generic type. That is, operations fetch and store must perform information exchange of type the type of processor requesting them. This implies that operation on memory are actually performed by a Memory Control Units (MCU) that receive generic operations and customize them to the type of operations requested by the processor.

73

6.1.1 *Memory control unit*

MCU allows memory sharing and operation synchronization and consists of:

- A Store Fetch Switch, SFS, a two-bit register defined by:

$$SFS = \begin{cases} 00, & \text{if a } store \text{ operation is being executed;} \\ 01, & \text{if a } fetch \text{ operation is being executed;} \\ 10, & \text{if no operation is being executed;} \\ 11, & \text{if the memory is in an erroneous state.} \end{cases}$$

- A Memory Address Register, MAR loaded with the address of the memory location involved in the operation.
- A Memory Data Register, MDR loaded with the data involved in the operation.

We assume here that MCU performs automatically $SFS := 10$ when an operation completes and $SFS := 11$ when an operation fails. The type of the processor is determined by the operation code (opcode) and is denoted here by `sizeof(R)`, where R is the register involved in the operation.

In order to simulate the memory through a program, independent of other hardware components, here MCU is seen as a data type specified by a Processor Memory Interface Register (PMIR), described by the C structure:

```
struct PMIR
     {
        int        SFS;
        location *MAR;
        register  MDR;
     };
```

Notice that since MAR and MDR are generic, they are described by the `location` and `register` types respectively, which are hardware dependent and therefore not described here. To simulate the actions performed by memory and other hardware components we use the language of actions defined in Section 4.2.

Now, to simulating the `store` operation we assume that the instruction format is `Store R, A` where R is the register whose contents needs to be stored in the memory location of address A. The processor initiates the `store` operation by setting $SFS := 00$ at which MCU performs the action:

```
Store::
    inout R: register, A: address;
    local B: PMIR; i: integer;
        l_0:B.MAR:=A; B.MDR:= R; i:=sizeof(R):^l_0
        l_1:while(i>0) do *B.MAR+i:=MDR+i; i:=i-1:^l_1
        l_2:B.SFS := 10 :^l_2;
```

In the simulation implementation, R and A should be in the limits provided by the architecture.

For the `fetch` operation simulation we assume that the instruction format is `Load R, A`, where R is the register to receive the contents stored in the memory location of address A. A processor initiates a `fetch` by setting $SFS := 01$ at which MCU performs the action:

```
Fetch::
    inout R: register, A: address;
    local B: PMIR, i: integer;
        l_0:B.MAR:= A; i:= sizeof(R):^l_0
        l_1:while(i>0) do B.MDR+i:=*B.MAR+i; i:=i-1:^l_1
        l_2:R:=B.MDR; B.SFS:=10:^l_2
```

Again, in the simulation implementation R and A should be in the limits provided by the architecture. Since MAR and MDR are implemented by arrays of bits, the actual Store and Fetch are operations on bits. To speed-up memory operations a larger number of bits may be transmitted at once. The number of bits that memory can receive/transmit in a time-unit, such as a second, is sometime referred to as the *memory bandwidth*. Therefore in the implementation of the simulation one should use the memory bandwidth of the particular hardware. Here, the abstraction level of the term *bandwidth* is raised to mean: *memory bandwidth measures the rate of information exchange among hardware components.* Further, *memory bandwidth measures the rate of information exchange at the level of application.*

6.1.2 *Memory simulation*

As observed above, memory locations and *fetch* and *store* operations are generic. At any call, MCU instantiates *fetch* and *store* operations into the actual *Fetch* and *Store*. Therefore the functional behaviour of the MCU is specified by the following `StoreFetch` action:

```
StoreFetch::
    inout alpha: channel;
    local B: PMIR where B.SFS = 10;
        l_0: repeat
                l_1:while(SFS=10) do Receive(alpha,B):^l_1
                l_2:case B.SFS
                    when B.SFS=00 then Store(B.MAR,B.MDR);
                    when B.SFS=01 then Fetch(B.MAR,B.MDR):^l_2
                l_3: if B.SFS=11 then Error:^l_3
            forever:^l_0
```

Here *alpha* is a communication channel whose records are tuples of the form $\langle Register, Address, Code \rangle$. When a processor requests an operation on memory, it executes Send(alpha,message), where message is the tuple $\langle R, A, C \rangle$ with C = 00 or C = 01. MCU performs a non-blocking Receive(alpha,B). If there is no message on the channel then B.SFS = 10 and thus Receive(alpha,B) is repeated. When a message appears on alpha then B.SFS is set to the operation code and MCU executes the operation. Upon operation termination if B.SFS=10 the while loop is repeated; if B.SFS=11 the action Error is performed.

In conclusion, a computer memory is a data type that can be represented by the tuple **Memory** $= \langle LocationSet; Store, Fetch, StoreFetch \rangle$. This means that one can experiment the memory properties of a new computer by simulating it on an available hardware. For that one only has to design a memory data structure as an array of memory locations of the type of interest and implement the memory data type using an appropriate simulation language, such as C. Then one can measure the quality of the memory designed as a function of memory size measured in Killo-bytes ($K=2^{10}$ bytes), and number of location types, size of location type, and operation frequency.

6.1.3 *Memory hierarchy*

The memory hierarchy and its input/output relationship with a processor are depicted in Figure 6.1.

6.1.4 *Sharing memory*

StoreFetch action allows memory sharing, but only one processor can operate on memory at a given time. Since the fetch operation does not change

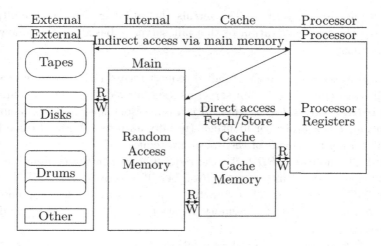

Fig. 6.1   Memory hierarchy

the contents of the memory, all processors could `fetch` concurrently. The `store` operation however does change memory contents, and thus only one processor at a time should be allowed to execute it. To increase the efficiency of memory operations the MCU should allow `fetch` operations to be executed concurrently and `store` operations to be executed in mutual exclusion and in mutual exclusion with `fetch`-s. In addition, MCU should implement a criteria that allow the priority between `store` and `fetch` to be defined. This is achieved by designing the MCU as a *fair server*.

6.1.5   *Fair server for memory simulation*

A fair server provides services (in our case `fetch, store`) to a given number of customers, in our case processors $P_1, P_2, \ldots, P_n$. Here the fair server will be provided by a Memory Control Unit, in charge of executing `store` operations and a Processor Control Unit (PCU) in charge of executing the `fetch` operations. All customers are serviced in parallel by a fair server. In our case PCU will allow all processors $P_1, P_2, \ldots, P_n$ to fetch info in parallel. Only one customer requesting a given service (in our case `store`) is serviced at a given time (in our case by the MCU). PCU and MCU operate in mutual exclusion and MCU has priority over PCU. Hence, the fair server is a tuple $FairServer = (PCU, MCU)$ where PCU and MCU operate on memory in mutual exclusion. PCU controls the parallel execution of multiple `fetch`-s and MCU controls the serial execution of multiple `store`-s. The implementation of this fair server is based on the following assumptions:

- Each processor has a register called request record (RR) . The processor sends this register to the fair server as a service request. The structure of RR is $RR = \langle R, A, I, Fl \rangle$, where R is a processor register, A is a memory location, I is a processor identifier (usually an integer), and Fl is a flag representing the status of the operation requested.
- The PCU interprets RR to be the request to `fetch` the contents of the memory address A into register R on behalf of processor I.
- The MCU interprets RR to be the request to `store` the contents of the register R into the memory location of address A on behalf of processor I.
- $Fl = T$ initially and after the initiation of the service; $Fl = F$ when a service has been requested and not yet initiated.
- Both, PCU and MCU have access to RR.

The assumptions here are: Processors are identified by $I \neq 0$; Records RR from different processors are organized as two arrays, $FR[1..n]$ for `fetch` requests, and $SR[1..n]$ for `store` requests, where n is the number of processors in the system. A request from P_i is signaled by the field $RR[i].I \neq 0$. The behavior of the processor P_i is specified by the action `Process[i]`:

```
Process[i]::
inout FR:array[1..n] of RR where FR[i].Fl=T,i=1,2,...,n;
      SR:array[1..n] of RR where SR[i].Fl=T,i=1,2,...,n;

local RR: request, Serv: char;
      l_0:repeat
          l_1: RR := MakeRequest; Set(Serv):^l_1
          l_2:if Serv='s' then SR[i]:=RR; await(SR[i].I=0);
              else if Serv = 'f' then FR[i]:=RR;
              else System error:^l_2
      forever:^l_0
```

Here the action `MakeRequest` constructs the record $\langle R, A, I, F \rangle$ where $RR.R$ is the Processor register implied, $RR.A$ is the memory location implied, $RR.I$ is the processor id, and $RR.Fl = F$ to indicate an unserviced request. Communication protocol:

- **MakeRequest** is the computation action performed by the processor.
- When a processor needs to exchange information with the memory it constructs a request record, **RR**, sets the variable **Serv** to 's' if store is requested, or to 'f' if fetch is requested.
- Updates store requests array, **SR**, or fetch requests array, **FR**, and then waits for the service to be provided.

6.1.5.1 *Processor Control Unit, PCU*

PCU examines cyclically the fetch requests array, **FR**; When a new request is discovered in **FR** its service is started and the next record is examined without waiting for the service completion. The action performed by PCU is the **FetchServer**:

```
FetchServer::
    inout FR:array[1..n] of RR where FR[i].Fl=T,i=1,...,n;
    local i: integer where i = 0;
        1_0:repeat
            1_1:if (FR[i].I not= 0 and FR[i].Fl=T) then
                Fetch(FR[i]);
            else
                i:=i+1(modulo n):^1_1
        forever:^1_0
```

To synchronize the actions where all processors may perform fetch in parallel while only one processor stores in mutual exclusion, the fair server uses three variables:

(1) AF (active fetches), a counter which counts the number of processors fetching info in parallel; AF is set by PCU and is tested by MCU;
(2) FetchLock, a lock-variable used by PCU to increase/decrease AF in mutual exclusion.
(3) StoreLock, a lock-variable used by MCU to perform store actions in mutual exclusion, and by PCU to synchronize fetch and store.

The action **Fetch** is executed by PCU when a processor requires a fetch operation:

```
Fetch::
inout B:request; StoreLock, FetchLock:lock; AF: integer;
local PDR:Register; PAR:Address; i:integer where i=sizeof(B.I);
    1_0: await(not(StoreLock));
```

```
1_1:lock(FetchLock); AF:=AF+1; unlock(FetchLock):^1_1
1_2:PAR := B.A:^12
1_3:while(i>0) do PDR+i:=*PAR+i; i:=i-1:^1_3
1_4:B.R:=PDR; B.I:=0:^1_4
1_5:lock(FetchLock); AF=AF-1;unlock(FetchLock):^1_5
:^1_0
```

Notice that *Fetch* is enabled only if no store operation is performed by the *StoreServer* but all processors can perform fetch operations in parallel. The action `ProcFetch` below simulates the behavior of the PCU:

```
ProcFetch::
local FR:array[1..n] of RR where FR[i].Fl=T,i=1,...,n;
     1_0:FetchServer || Process[1] || ... || Process[n]:^1_0
```

Note that *Process*[*i*] is the action of setting the RR by processor *i*. Since each processor has its own RR, all processor can set their RRs in parallel.

6.1.5.2   *The Memory Control Unit, MCU*

The MCU implements the store services and it is similar with fetch server. However, it operates on the array SR and only one store operation is carried out at once. The actual store operation is performed atomically. The action `StoreServer` interacts with the action `FetchServer` by a protocol characteristic to the computer architecture. In this interaction protocol the `AF` is the number of active fetch in progress; a store operation is enabled only when `AF=0`. AF is updated by `Fetch[i]`, for i=1,2,...,n, and is tested by `Store`. StoreLock is locked by the `Store` action when it starts operating and is unlocked when it terminates. `Fetch[i]` is enabled only when `StoreLock` is unlocked.

```
StoreServer::
inout SR: array[1..n] of RR where SR[i].Fl=T,i=1,2,...,n;
local i: integer; StoreLock: lock where StoreLock=unlocked;
  1_0:repeat
    1_1:if (SR[i].I not= 0 and SR[i].Fl=F) then
          1_2:lock(StoreLock);Store(SR[i]);unlock(StoreLock):^1_2
          1_3: SR[i].Fl:=T:^1_3
        else i:= i+1(modulo n):^1_1
  forever:^1_0
```

The action `Store` is performed by the MCU when a processor requires a store operation. `Store` sets `SR[i].I=0` upon completion.

```
Store::
    in B: request; AF: integer;
    local MDR: Register; MAR: Address; i: integer;
        1_0: await (AF=0);
            1_1: i:=sizeof(B.I); PDR:=B.R; PAR:=B.A :^1_1
            1_2: while (i>0) do
                    1_3:*PAR+i:=PDR+i; i:=i-1:^1_3
                B.I := 0:^1_2
        :^1_0
```

The action `ProcStore` below simulates the behavior of MCU:

```
ProcStore::
local SR:array[1..n] of RR where SR[i].Fl=T,for i=1,2,...,n;
    1_0: StoreServer || Process[1] || ... || Process[n]:^1_0
```

Here *Process[i]* is the action of setting the RR by processor *i*. Since each processor has its own RR, all processor can set their RRs in parallel.

The actions `ProcStore` and `ProcFetch` are integrated into the unique action *StoreFetch* specified as follows:

```
StoreFetch::
local SR:array[1..n] of RR where SR[i].Fl=T,i=1,2,...,n;
    FR:array[1..n] of RR where FR[i].Fl=T,i=1,2,...,n;
    1_0:ProcStore ||ProcFetch :^1_0
```

In conclusion, we have designed a system that allows the concurrent execution of *fetch* operations and the exclusive execution of only one *store* operation. Figure 6.2 shows the relation between a MCU and a PCU that share a memory operating in parallel using the fair server approach. This allows us to design a system where all processors operate on the memory in parallel, by implementing a package of programs that simulates parallel memory access using the fair server approach presented here. We can measure the quality of this memory system in function of number of parallel operations executed by the memory on time unit compared with the number of sequential operations executed by the memory on the same time unit.

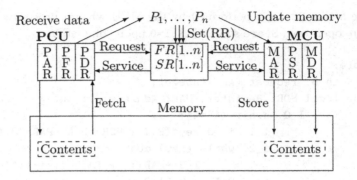

Fig. 6.2   Memory sharing

6.2   Functional Behavior of Processor Components

We have identified two kind of processor components: data processors and control processors. Data processors perform data processing operations. Examples of data processors are ALU, FPU, IO/devices. Control processors control the execution of operations performed by other processors. Example control processor is the CPU. We have already examined the functionality of processing processors such as ALU, FPU, etc. in the context of memory sharing. We examine here the functionality of control processor and I/O devices.

6.3   Functional Behavior of Control Processors

The role of control processors is to execute programs. Informally the functional behavior of a control processor can be described by the following action:

```
repeat
  Fetch the instruction whose address is in PC in IR;
  Decode IR; Let the contents of IR be:
        Opcode, AE_1,...,AE_k
  Evaluate AE_1, ..., AE_k to a_1,...,a_k
  Fetch the contents of a_1,...,a_k in registers R_1,...,R_k;
  Perform R:=Opcode(R_1,..,R_k);
  Update the PC accordingly, i.e., PC:=Next(PC);
forever
```

This action is performed by the Controller and consists of a repeated instruction execution. The assumption here is that the Controller is provided with a function (called Next(PC) above), which determines the location containing the next instruction of the program from the location containing the current instruction of the program. Hence, if the first instruction of the program is given, program execution by the Controller is well defined.

The execution of an instruction by the CPU is called the instruction cycle and it is a built-in hardware function of the CPU. The algorithm solving a problem must be codified as a sequence of instruction words called a *machine language program*. Program execution is formally specified by the action *Exec*:

```
Exec::
in Interrupt, Halt: boolean where Interrupt = F and Halt = F;
local IR: instruction;
     PC: pointer to instruction  where PC = FirstInstruction;
     1_0: while (not(Interrupt) and not(Halt)) do
             1_1: IR := *PC; Analyze(IR):^1_1
             1_2: if Opcode(IR) = End then
                     Halt = T;
                  else
                     Perform(IR);
             PC := Next(PC):^1_2
     :^1_0
```

This action terminates explicitly by the instruction whose operation code is "End", or it terminates implicitly by various events that may occur during program execution which are specified here by the register called Interrupt.

6.4   I/O Devices

The I/O devices perform the operations: Input: informationCarrier → mainMemory and Output:mainMemory → informationCarriers. The I/O device structure allowing these operations to be performed is given in Figure 6.3.

The input operations, also called read operations, are executed in two steps: $Step_1$:informationCarrier→internalRegister and $Step_2$:internalRegister→ mainMemory. The output operations, also

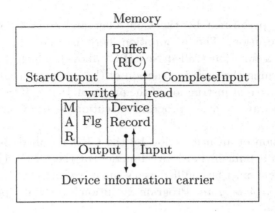

Fig. 6.3   Device functional structure

called `write`, are executed in two steps:

$Step_1$: `mainMemory`→`sinternalRegister` and

$Step_2$: `internalRegister`→ `informationCarrier`.

The Internal-Register is the Device Record in Figure 6.3 which was also called Record on Information Carrier, RIC. The two components of I/O devices that perform these operations are *an electronic component* and, depending upon the physical properties of the information carrier, a *mechanical, magnetic, optical* component. The electronic component performs info exchange between memory and the internal registers of the I/O device and its execution speed is of the same magnitude as other memory operations. The mechanical, magnetic, optic component, that performs the actual transfer of info between the internal registers of the I/O device and information carrier of the I/O device usually has an execution speed of two or more orders of magnitude smaller than memory speed. This difference in speed between the two components of the I/O device provides the bsis for many optimizations of program execution by the Controller.

Two steps activity of output operations are the `start` of the operation and `complete` of the operation. The `start` is performed by the electronic component of the device and thus, it is a machine language instruction, decribed by the following `StartOutput` action:

```
StartOutput::
inout Buffer: Device Record; Flag: boolean;
local InfoRec: Device Record;
    1_0: await(Flag=T); InfoRec:=Buffer; Flag:=F:^1_0
```

The complete part of the output operation is usually a much slower and is carried out by the action Output.

```
Output::
    out alpha: channel of device information carrier;
    local InfoRec: Device Record; Flag: boolean where Flag=T;
    l_0:repeat
        l_1:await(Flag=F); Send(alpha, InfoRec); Flag:=T:^l_1
    forever:^l_0
```

The assignment Flag := F is performed when the StartOutput instruction is complete. It takes longer time to perform Flag := T.

The two steps activity of input are input and complete input. The input step is carried out by the action Input which is initiated by the device. This action is much slower than the machine language instructions.

```
    Input::
    in alpha: channel of device information carrier;
    local InfoRec: Device Record; Flag: boolean where Flag=T;
    l_0: repeat
        l_1: await(Flag=F); Receive(alpha,InfoRec); Flag:=T:^l_1
        forever :^l_0
```

The assignment Flag := F is performed by a machine language instruction that start the input. It takes longer to perform Flag := T that marks the completion of Input operation. The second step of an input operation is initiated by a machine language instruction and is carried out by the action CompleteInput that executes with the same speed as the other machine language operations.

```
CompleteInput::
    inout Buffer: Device Record; Flag: boolean;
    local InfoRec: Device Record;
        l_0: await(Flag=T); Buffer:=InfoRec; Flag:=F:^l_0
```

Observations:

- The actions StartOutput and CompleteInput are machine language instructions and are carried out by the control processor.
- The actions Output and Input are associated with the device and are performed by the device controller.

- The status of a device is usually accessible to the control processor through an instruction that identifies the device flag. We refer to this operation as the `TestDevice`.
- The interaction between the control processor, in charge of executing machine language instructions, and the I/O devices, depends upon the mechanism used to implement `TestDevice`.

We discuss further program performance as a function of `TestDevice` implementation, which could be one of:

(1) TestDevice is implicit within the I/O operation;
(2) TestDevice is a special instruction initiated by the program, i.e., Test-Device is a machine language instruction;
(3) TestDevice is a special action initiated by the device.

We assume further that the structure of an outputting program is described by the following action:

```
repeat
   1_0: Compute;
        StartOutput(DV); Output(DV);
        forever :^1_0
```

and the structure of an inputting program is described by the following action:

```
repeat
   1_0: DV.Flag:=F;Input(DV); CompleteInput(DV);
        Compute;
        forever: ^1_0
```

6.4.1 *Implicit TestDevice*

I/O operations are executed by the control processor synchronously with the other machine language operations:

```
PC := Address of IO operation;
IR := Opcode Device Memory
   Analyse (Opcode);
   Start Operation;
   while (NotDone) /* The busy-waiting loop */
      ;
```

```
PC := Next(PC);
```

Therefore the speed of program execution is reduced to the speed of the I/O operations.

6.4.2 *Explicit TestDevice*

An I/O operation is started, and while device is busy, the control processor executes other instructions in parallel with I/O device. I/O devices and processors overlap their activities while performing for a given program. The structure of an outputting program is described by the action OverlapOutput.

```
OverlapOutput::
local DvRecord: Device Record;
    l_0: repeat
            l_1: Compute; /* Generate(DvRecord) */
                    l_2: while (TestDevice(DV)=F) do
                            OtherComputations;
                    :^l_2
                    StartOutput(DV,DvRecord);
            :^l_1
            forever:^l_0
```

Notice that here while output device is busy Controller performs other computations rather than remaining in a busy waiting loop. The structure of an inputting program is described by the OverlapInput action, as follows:

```
OverlapInput::
local DvRecord: Device Record;
    l_0: repeat
            l_1: Dv.Flag = F; Input(DV,DvRecord);
                    l_2: while (TestDevice(DV.Flag)=F) do
                            OtherComputations;
                    :^l_2
                    Compute; /* Use(DvRecord) */
            :^l_1
            forever:^l_0
```

Again, while input device is busy Controller perform in parallel other computations.

6.4.2.1   *Alternate Buffering*

Further optimizations of the program execution can be obtained by observing that programs are composed of four actions, `Generate(DvRecord)`, `Use(DvRecord)`, `Input`, and `Output`. The actions `Generate(DvRecord)` and `Use(DvRecord)` are compute-only, i.e., they contain no I/O operations. The actions `Output` and `Input` can be further refined using multiple-buffering, such as alternate buffering which consists of:

- Use three distinct buffers, `Binput`, `Boutput`, `Bcompute` for the three actions `Input`, `Output`, `Compute`, performed in parallel on the three buffers.
- When actions `Input`, `Output`, `Compute`, are complete rotate the buffers on which they are performing by the rules:

    ```
    Binput becomes Bcompute;
    Bcompute becomes Boutput;
    Boutput becomes Binput.
    ```

6.4.3   *Automatic TestDevice*

Control processor starts the I/O operation. Upon termination, the I/O device interrupts the control processor asking to complete the I/O operation. Program structures are shown by the actions `AutomaticOutput` and `AutomaticInput`, respectively.

```
AutomaticOutput::
local DvRecord: Device Record;
1_0: repeat
     1_1: Generate(DvRecord) || StartOutput(DV,DvRecord):^1_1
forever:^1_0
```

```
AutomaticInput::
local DvRecord: Device Record;
1_0: repeat
     1_1: Input(DV,DvRecord) || Use(DvRecord):^1_1
forever:^1_0
```

I/O operations are performed by I/O processors and consequently are not visible here.

6.5 Multi-Programming

With both explicit and automatic `TestDevice` the bottleneck of the system is the use of the control registers to move info to and from memory. The Direct Memory Access (DMA), have been created to allow the I/O devices direct access to the memory. Thus, I/O devices become processing processors operating under the control of the control processor and in parallel with it. When a device is busy, program may be suspended and processor may be preempted and used to execute another program.

Multi-programming was developed as a manner of machine operation where I/O operations performed by some programs are executed by I/O processors in parallel with the computation operations of other programs, performed by the control processor. Anticipating, we observe here that an operating system that supports multi-programming was called a *multi-programming system*.

6.5.1 *Efficiency of a hardware system*

Speed up of computation can be realized by combining system components together to work in parallel on a single problem. There are two issues to be addressed:

(1) decomposition of the data processing algorithms into parallel independent components, and
(2) connection of more processors (or computers) together in order to perform parallel computations in a reliable and economical manner.

Recall that computations are codified as machine language programs executed by the control processor. The structure of programs whose components perform in parallel is the subject of *parallel programming*. The structure of computer systems whose components performs in parallel is the subject of *multiprocessing hardware architectures*.

Chapter 7

Algorithmic Expression of a Hardware System

Step 4 of the systematic approach requires an algorithmic expression for the behavior of the system in terms of its components. The algorithmic expression of a hardware system using SSL is:

```
beginSpec
   name Hardware System is
   sort Memory, Processor, Device, Control;
   opns receive:Device x Control -> Memory,
        transmit:Memory x Control -> Device,
        store:Processor x Control -> Memory,
        fetch:Memory x Control -> Processor,
        process:Memory x Processor x Control -> Processor,
                Memory x Processor x Control -> Memory,
                Processor x Control -> Processor;
   vars PC: Control;
   axms: Value(PC.operation) in the set
                {receive, transmit, store, fetch, process};
   actn Run: while PluggedIn and PowerOn do
                1_0: Perform (PC); PC := Next(PC) :^1_0
endSpec
```

This expression of a hardware system is unique. It is like a blue print of the magic box called computer. Therefore computer expert education should start by understanding the concept of *computer abstraction*, as a term of natural language. It familiarizes the computer user with the meaning of the computer concept through the resources a computer has and the operation it performs, embedded in the Run action. The essence of this action is that as long as the computer is alive it executes forever because each

91

every step of this action contains the definition of its next step. Everyday life example of such an action is the reproduction of the biological systems; mathematical examples of such action are provided by recursive functions, turing machines, markov algorithms. However, while Run action mimics everyone of these concepts of an algorithm it is more general because it allows the computer user to define her own Run action, the program. Even more, through the I/O devices, discussed as components of the computer system, the user can define its interaction with the environment, thus making the computer a *machine interacting with an oracle* which according to Turing, is computationally more powerful than Turing machines (alias algorithms). This justifies the universality of the computer seen as a problem solving tool.

Though the complexity of a hardware system was beyond its phisical constructor's ability to generate such an expression, using systems methodology this became feasible. Moreover, the general expression of the hardware system shows us that a computer is junk if no power or not plugged in. However, to make it alive we need to instantiate it by setting an appropriate system configuring action which allows us to:

- Execute a first program by the "push-button" action. This is a bootstrap program.
- The bootstrap program loads and executes the next program.
- This repeats until the system is completely configured.

Rules of behavior are:

(1) The control processor has complete responsibility for the system's behavior. The other components are initiated by the control processor and when their activities are completed they report to the control processor.
(2) The control processor spends its activity in the infinite loop:
    - fetch instruction from main memory
    - analyze and execute instruction
    - according to the result and the events, determine the address of the next instruction.

    This loop is wired as the *Program Execution Loop* (PEL).

Chapter 8

Using Computers to Solve Problems

We need to emphasize the importance of the algorithmic expression of a computer system, developed previously as an ad hoc system, over and over in this text, thus justifying the computer use as a universal problem solving tool. Therefore, though redundantly, we start the discussion of computer based problem solving methodology by the reproduction of this expression:

```
beginSpec
  name Hardware System is
  sort Memory, Processor, Devices, Control;
  opns receive:Device x Control -> Memory,
       transmit:Memory x Control -> Device,
       store:Processor x Control -> Memory,
       fetch:Memory x Control -> Processor,
       process:Memory x Processor x Control -> Processor,
               Memory x Processor x Control -> Memory,
               Processor x Control -> Processor;
  vars PC: Control;
  axms: Value(PC.operation) in the set
               {receive, transmit, store, fetch, process};
  actn Run: while PluggedIn and PowerOn do
               1_0: Perform (PC); PC := Next(PC) :^1_0
endSpec
```

Functional assumptions of the hardware system are:

(1) The computer has a register called Program Counter (PC) which is loaded with the address of a machine instruction.
(2) The only action this system can perform is the repeatedly executing of the instruction whose address is loaded in PC, called Run.

(3) The control processor is provided with the capability to determine the address of the next instruction to execute using the contents of the instruction whose address is currently loaded in the PC. That is, Run is a recursive function.

Though this is a very primitive system it is used to solve spectacular problems that revolutionized science, technology, and business, and currently its use revolutionizes entire foundation of human everyday life. For computer experts this is just an evolutionary matter of our understanding of computer science and computing technology. But for non-experts, i.e., for most people, this is an amazing story which raises a lot of questions. In their hurry to revolutionize people's life using computers, computer experts have no time to spend answering such "trivial" questions as *how is this done?*. Yet, all other technologies developed by humans so far, that were destined to affect human life, ended in tools to be used by humans for their own problem solving purposes at the level of human languages, without asking tool users to be tool masters. But computer-based problem solving is currently based on computer languages whose use requires computer education. This stretches computer technology at a degree where it threaten to kill computer technology itself. [Horn (2001)]. Therefore, among others, the goal of this book is to unravel the mystery behind computer system use during the problem solving process. We hope that this will also show the human face of the computer and how can computer experts transform the computer into a human tool whose use need not require computer expertise. So, the questions we want to ask in this chapter are: how do we (computer experts) really solve problems with a computer and how could we adapt our methodology such that computer can be used by any problem solver to solve her own problems, without asking her to be a computer expert.

8.1 Using Computers to Solve Problems

As seen above, a computer doesn't know what a problem is. So, to solve it with the computer the problem solver needs to know first *how to solve it* [Polya (1957)]. Provided that computer user understand her problem and has developed an algorithm to solve it, in order to use the computer to solve it, she needs to:

(1) represent the solution algorithms as machine language programs;

(2) load programs and data into computer memory and set the PC to point to the first instruction to be executed by the computer;

(3) extract the solution when action Run halts.

The problem understanding and solution development are problem domain specific activities and they can be fun for the problem domain expert. But the actions required to use the computer to solve a problem are tedious, error prone, and are natural for computer experts only. These actions manipulate the computer architecture and functionality and consequently requires problem solver to be both a problem domain expert and a computer expert. Though these actions are natural for computer expert they are still tedious and error prone. So, in order to avoid errors and make computer-based problem solving process fun, computer experts have developed tools that automate the actions (1), (2), (3) above. System software evolved as a collection of tools that assist problem solving process, providing services to the problem solver, which is a priori considered a computer expert. The important question now is what kind of services must system software provide to computer users to make the raw computing power of the hardware convenient and efficient? An obvious answer to this question would be: system software tools should manipulate computer resources and the events that arrive during program execution. Computer resources are computer components and the events arriving during program execution are determined by the behavior of the program representing the problem solving algorithm and the interaction of computer components during program execution. Hence, the system software tools handling processes, resources, and events provide services to program execution. But programs must be written in machine language in order to be executed. Therefore software tools for machine language program development are needed too. However, for a complete answer one needs to analyze the process of problem solving as performed by humans, independent of the computer use. Then we need to look at problem solving process as carried out by people using computers. From this analysis we deduce the service tools provided by the system software to aid computer users in problem solving with a computer.

8.2 Mathematical Methodology

Mathematical methodology for problem solving starts with mathematical concepts of problem and solution. But `problem` is a primitive concept used in all aspects of human life and because of its universality there is little hope that a meaningful formalization can be achieved. Teaching mathematics Polya [Polya (1957)] has developed the four steps methodology for mathematical problem solving process:

(1) Formalize the problem;
(2) Develop an algorithm to solve the problem;
(3) Perform the algorithm on the data characterizing the problem;
(4) Validate the solution.

This is actually valid for mathematical problems as well as for any other kind of problem. Problem formalization means express the three components of the problem, unknown, data and condition, as mathematical objects. The solution algorithm is a sequence of well-coordinated operations starting from the data and ending in the required unknowns. Performing the algorithms means instantiate the problem by appropriate data, conditions, and unknowns and apply the algorithm to the problem thus instantiated. Validation of the solutions means to prove that the solution satisfies the conditions in the instance of the problem. When there is no such a proof (as it is the case for most computer algorithms) test the solution on all configurations of data and conditions.

Real-life problems are not so easy to be solvable following Polya methodology. Though neither of the four steps of Polya's problem solving methodology do refer explicitly to mathematics and the computer is a universal tool, Polya problem solving approach is limited by the contradiction between potential infinite spectrum of real-life problems and limited expression power provided by computer language. Hence, computer use during problem solving process requires special tools that smoothen this contradiction. But unlike the tools required by other technologies, the tools required by computer use handle abstractions rather than concrete tangible things, and are meant as brain assistants, instead of extending user's hands power. So, the major question faced by computer technology is what kind of tools do the computer experts need to develop in order to make the computer a problem solving tool in the hands of all computer potential users? This question is difficult because the only computer users we know so far are the computer experts. Advances on ubiquitous computer use are obtained by ad hoc extensions of the concept of computer user, without following a systematic approach. Hence, looking at computer experts as computer users we can classify the tools so far developed as follows:

- Computer requires the solution algorithm to be encoded in machine language. Since this is tedious and error prone, tools that map algorithms into machine language programs are required.
- In order to be executed, programs and data need to be stored in computer memory and the address of the first instruction to be executed need to be stored in PC. Hence, tools that take information media (careers) and load information they carry out in computer memory are also required.
- Program execution is a process that handles computer resources (processors, memory, devices) as well as events (interruptions and exceptions) that may occur during program execution. Hence, software tools that handle processes, resources, and events are also needed.

8.3 Computer-Based Problem Solving Methodology

Computer-Based Problem Solving Process (CBPSP) is seen here as an adaptation of the Polya four steps methodology to the computer and consists of a well determined sequence of transformations undergone by the expression of the problem and its solution algorithm. Original form of the algorithm is a natural language expressions in the universe of discourse. This expression is mapped toward a machine language program form that can be executed by the computer. Upon execution completion the sequence of transformations is reversed, thus mapping the machine-language result back into the original universe of discourse. Formally this is an eight steps methodology:

(1) **Formulate the problem**, that is, describe the problem as a relationship among data, conditions, and unknowns. Natural language may be used. A mathematical say tells us that *if you can formulate it you can solve it!*

(2) **Formalize the problem**, that is, represent the relationship defining the problem as a well-formed expression of a logic language, which *depends upon the problem domain*. Arithmetic, geometry, statistics, mathematical logic, actuarial science, accounting, etc., are examples of languages that may be used.

(3) **Develop an algorithm that solves the problem.** This means find a sequence of transformations that lead from data to the unknowns while observing the conditions. This sequence can be empirical, i.e., the result of an experimental analysis, or it can be formal (mathematical), i.e., the result of a systematic analysis.

(4) **Program the algorithm.** To program an algorithm means to represent it as a well-formed expression of a machine language. Since the machine language is not natural for humans, high-level notations have been designed in order to handle the machine language. These notations evolved as *high level programming languages*, such as Ada, Algol, Assembly, C, Cobol, Fortran, Lisp, Machine language, Pascal, PL1, etc. [Landin (1966)]. The algorithm's expression in a high-level programming language is called the (source) program of the algorithm.

(5) **Compile the (source) program.** If the language used in Step 4 is different from the machine language then translate the *source program* expression into a machine language expression. The machine language expression thus obtained is called the *target program*.

(6) **Initiate program execution.** This means load the target program into the main memory of the machines, link it with other target programs if necessary, and initiate program execution by loading the program counter with the address of the target program's first instruction.

(7) **Control program execution.** That is, assist the process of program execution providing services required by *computer resource management* and *event handling* during program execution.

(8) **Terminate program execution.** When the execution of the program terminates, send the results of the program back to the original universe of discourse (UoD).

Fact 1: Steps 1, 2, 3 of computer based problem-solving process manipulate problem-domain concepts. Step 4 requires problem solver to encode problem-domain concepts into the language of a machine. That is, Step 4 of computer based problem-solving process actually requires problem solver to be both, a problem domain expert and a programming language expert. Hence, computer-based problem solving methodology developed so far unifies problem solving processes arising from all (very different) problem domains into one single approach: *programming*. That is, programming is offered as the *one-size-fits all* methodology to all very diverse problem solving domains. However, successes of this approach for computer usage in problem solving transformed the computer into a universal tool for problem solving. The consequence is the cognition-process spiral where *computer technology increases the human cognition power which in turn increases the demand for more computer technology*. But, one cannot reasonable expect all people to become computer programmers. In addition, the diversity of problem solving algorithms unified into one single process of running a program on a computer spawn software tool complexity that threatens computer industry itself. In other words, feedback of software tool development, that increase computer power in CBPSP, is the threatening of the CBPSP itself. This requires us to develop a problem solving methodology that do not require problem domain expert to encode solution algorithm into programming language concepts! That is, the feedback of software complexity on computer-based problem solving methodology requires us to develop software tools that allow domain experts to use computers without asking them to be computer experts.

Fact 2: For a $Problem \in UoD$ the sequence of transitions

$$\textbf{Step 1} \xrightarrow{Formulate} \textbf{Step 2} \xrightarrow{Formalize} \textbf{Step 3} \xrightarrow{Algorithm} \textbf{Step 4}$$

regard the creative activity involved in problem-solving. Some computer systems (in particular AI systems) hint at this sequence of transformations but, so far, no machine is capable of automating this activity.

Fact 3: The transformations involved in the transitions

$$\textbf{Step 4} \xrightarrow{Program} \textbf{Step 5} \xrightarrow{Compile} \textbf{Step 6} \xrightarrow{Link} \textbf{Step 7} \xrightarrow{Execute} \textbf{Step 8} \xrightarrow{Result} \textbf{UoD}$$

represent the mechanical activity involved in computer-based problem solving methodology. This is done by the software tools, components of system software, which we classify as follows:

(1) Transitions **Step 4**$\Longrightarrow$ **Step 5** $\Longrightarrow$ **Step 6** $\Longrightarrow$ **Step 7** are translation operations executed by translators. They assist the human programmer for program development.

(2) Transitions **Step 7** $\Longrightarrow$ **Step 8** $\Longrightarrow$UoD involve resource management and event handling and are performed by software tools that handle computer processess and computer resource. They assist the process of program execution.

Depending on the target language, which can be machine language, a virtual machine language, an assembly language, the target program resulting from a translator $T : SL \rightarrow TL$ may need further transformations in order to become an executable program on the machine. These transformations are offered by translators, as special services for program development.

8.4   Services Offered by Translators

Translators allow program development using *human-oriented languages*
while program execution uses *machine-oriented languages*. In addition, a
translator may allow programmers to extend the source languages with
task dedicated constructs, such as macro-operations and function libraries,
which support modular program development and improve programming
efficiency. Macro-operations are programmer defined constructs that allow
programmer to factor out repetitive tasks into a per-program library
of named (parameterized) source language constructs, encapsulating frequently used source language expressions. Then, while developing the source
program the programmer can use the name of this code (called macro-call)
where its expression is needed. A pre-translation step creates a per-program
macro library. At translation time macros are substituted for macro-calls.
The function libraries are collections of prefabricated code developed and
optimized by computer and domain experts. The source program includes
a library identifier, which allows the programmer to use library functions
as required, without asking her to provide the code. Both macro-operations
and function libraries must preserve the conventions of the source language
therefore they are specific to the source language.

8.4.1   *Macro-operations in C*

C macro-operations are defined by the directive **#define**. That is, C macro-
operations are expressions of the form **#define name replacement** where
name is a string and **replacement** is a (parameterized) C code. For examples

```
#define SIZE 1024
foo = (char *) malloc(SIZE);
```

is expanded into

```
foo = (char *) malloc (1024);
```

Similarly,

```
#define NUMBERS 1, /* EOL allows multi-line replacement */
                2,
                3
```

is used to expand the macro-code

```
int x[] = { NUMBERS };
```

into the C code:

```
int x[] = { 1, 2, 3 };
```

Function-like macros are parameterized macro-operations of the form: `#define name(X,Y) replacement(X,Y)`. For example

```
#define max(A,B) ((A)>(B) ? (A) : (B))
x = max(p+q, r+s);
```

is expanded into

```
x = ((p+q) > (r+s) ? (p+q) : (r+s));
```

However, one must understand the meaning of C operators in order to preserves the program correctness by macro-operations. For example, the macro-code

```
y = max(i++, j++);
```

is wrong because i,j are increased two times in the C code obtained by macro-expansion. Also, the macro-definition

```
#define lang_init () c_init()
```

is wrong because no blanc is allowed in a string used as a macro-name. Using this macro, the call

```
lang_init()
```

would be expanded into

```
() c_init()
```

which is not intended.

8.4.2 Controlling the preprocessing

Macro-operations provide a way to include code in a source program selectively, depending on the value of conditions evaluated during the preprocessing process. This is also called conditional programming. A C macro-operation that allow selective code selection during the preprocessing process has one of the forms:

```
#if Expression
Code to be included
#endif

#if Expression1
Code1 to be included
#elif Expression2
Code2 to be included
#else Expression3
Code3 to be included
#endif
```

Using these macros the sections of C code denoted Code1, Code2, Code3, are included in the source program depending upon the value of expressions Expression1, Expression2, Expression3 which can be evaluated by the preprocessor to true or false. The macro-names #ifdef and #ifndef are specialized forms of the following macros:

```
#if Expression1 #define Expression2
Code to be included
#endif
```

and

```
#if !Expression1 #define Expression2
Code to be included
#endif
```

They allow programmers to control the conditional programming. The scope of #if Exp #define Code can be controlled with #undef. For example,

```
#define BUFFER 512
#define SQR(x) ((x) * (x))
```

are nullified by

```
#undef BUFFER
#undef SQR
```

Other services provided by compilers are libraries of subprograms, separate compilation, and libraries of system calls.

8.4.3 *Subprograms*

Subprograms are programs prefabricated by programmers and problem-domain experts, which solve specific kind of problems. For example, all elementary function in numerical analysis can be pre-programmed and optimized by professional programmers and offered to the usual programmer in a library of functions called MathLib. Hence, translators allow programmers to use subprograms developed and stored in libraries called *libraries of functions* or *library of subprograms*. Subprograms of a library could be in various intermediate forms, from source to target. However, subprograms of a library must observe the restrictions imposed by the source language of the compiler.

One or more per-translator libraries of subprograms, written by experienced system programmers, are usually provided in the system software. Subprograms in these libraries can be referenced by user programs. But usually one cannot use a C subprogram in a Fortran program. The translator locates the referenced subprograms and embed them in the source program. If the subprogram is in the target form it is linked with other program components usually called *modules*. If the subprogram is in the source form it is copied in the user program and is further subject to program translation.

The difference between macro and library facilities provided by a translator as services to program development concerns the user they are targeted to. Macro-facility provides services for program development to the individual programmer while library facility provides service for program development to every programmer that uses the compiler's source language. Hence, unlike macros, the text of a subprogram is not necessarily placed where its call occurred.

Example subprogram libraries is the C library `math.h` and `#include` directive supported by C as a library specification mechanism. That is, the subprograms in `math.h` are included in a C program by the directive

```
#include "math.h"
```

Once this directive is provided, a C programmer can refer to a function in math.h by name. For example, one can simple write `y = sqrt(x);` when $\sqrt{x}$ is needed in her program. Further, the subprograms in `math.h` are included in C programs they use and are linked with other C program modules by loader/linker. For that one needs to use the appropriate option of the `cc` command.

8.4.4 *Modular program development*

Some translators allow program development by separately compiling various parts of the source program and then linking the compiled code into an executable program. Separate compilation facility is different from macro and library facilities. It provides the service for program modular development.

For example, C language allow separate compilation of functions composing a program. The command `gcc -c function.c` asks the C compiler to create the target `function.o` that can be later linked with other program components.

8.4.5 *System calls*

One or more per-operating system libraries of functions called *system calls* may also be provided. System calls concern the interface between program execution and processing environment provided by the operating system. That is, system calls allow a program to change its execution environment thus providing services for resource management and event handling. A user program can reference system calls following conventions established by the operating system.

System calls are mapped by the translator into instructions that generate machine language exceptions called `system call` (originally IBM's `svc`) which are usually executed under the control of the operating system. That is, looking at the action `Run` performed by the hardware system, a system call is implemented by making the function `Next()` perform two sub-actions: first it saves the contents of the PC into a dedicated register, say `OldPC`, and then it loads PC with the contents of another dedicated register, say `NewPC`. The `NewPC` allows a program to execute another program which is not part of its address space and `OldPC` allows the original program to be restarted from the place where the system call was originated. Examples system calls in a Unix system are:

(1) I/O operations provided in `stdio.h` library. They are included in the program using `#include ⟨stdio.h⟩` directive.
(2) Memory management functions provided by `malloc()`, `free()`. They are usually provided within the C compiler standard library. Sometimes you need to provide `#include ⟨stdlib.h⟩` in the program in order to use them.

(3) Process creation and process synchronization provided by fork(), sproc(), exec(), wait(), exit(), pipe(), socket(). To use them the programmer needs to include in the source program #include ⟨sys/types.h⟩ and #include ⟨unistd.h⟩ directives.

(4) Sharing computer resources using IPC in Unix 5. These need to be included in the program by using the directives:

```
#include ⟨sys/ipc.h⟩
#include ⟨sys/msg.h⟩
#include ⟨sys/sem.h⟩
#include ⟨sys/shm.h⟩
```

8.5 Kind of Translators

According to the source language and the transformation steps performed towards the machine language program generation we distinguish four kind of translators: compilers, interpreters, assemblers, linker/loaders.

8.5.1 *Compilers*

Compilers are translators that take as input programs written in a high-level programming language and generates as output programs written in a virtual machine language.

The target program obtained as the output of a compiler is loaded into the main memory for execution. The execution of a compiled program can be repeated on various data sets.

8.5.2 *Interpreters*

An interpreter consists of two components: a translator and an executive. The translator takes as data programs written in the source programming language and translates them into an intermediate form that can be easily interpreted. The executive executes the program acting on the intermediate form produced by the translator and on the data supplied by the user.

Each execution of a program by an interpreter requires that the interpreter works directly on the source program. For example, LISP is usually implemented by interpreters.

8.5.3 *Assemblers*

An assembler is a translator which takes as input assembly language programs and generates as output (virtual) machine language programs. Assembly languages are mnemonic notations of machine languages. Assemblers play an important role in system programming.

8.5.4 *Loader/linkers*

A loader/linker inputs virtual machine language modules and output executable programs in the language of the real machine. A loader/linker performs four transformations:

(1) Allocate resources of the real machine to virtual programs to produce executable modules (this is allocation);
(2) Links together a number of executable modules producing an executable program (on the disk) (this is linking);
(3) Loads the executable program into the memory of the real machine (this is loading);
(4) Updates the executable program according to the resources of the target machine (such as address space) available at program execution time. For example, the relocation of a relocatable program on the free address space available at program execution time is such an update.

8.6 Programming Environment

Programming Support Environment (PSE) is the collection of programs and documents that provide services for program development. Recently (mainly in AI community) PSE is also an acronym for Problem Solving Environment. The main objectives of a PSE (while providing services for program development) are to achieve:

(1) System efficiency, by sharing resources and performing concurrent operations.
(2) User convenience, by allowing users to interact with the processes performing on their behalf.
(3) System evolution, by providing software tools allowing system to evolve with problem domains and technology.

Sharing can expand from sharing hardware resources (such as memory, devices, and processors) to sharing data and code. However, sharing requires special mechanisms which ensure the consistency of the shared resource. This is performed by using functions in special library provided by the system. Performing concurrent operations could be done by using the same processor while taking turns, which is termed *interleaving*, versus using true parallelism, which requires multiple processors performing in parallel. Interaction between the executable programs is achieved by messages that programs can exchange among them, or by using shared resources (memory). Interaction between the process executing a program and the computer user is achieved by a command language mechanism which allows the user to receive messages from the running program and to transmit commands to the running programs thus controlling the process. Integration is the mechanism by which program components are put together to interoperate while performing a program. This is done by providing machine language operations which allows the function Next() to switch control from one program to another program in the same address space (by function call) and in different address spaces (by system call). The machine language operation that allows Next() to switch control in the same address space, such as a subroutine call, takes as arguments the address of the called function and the program counter of the place where control needs be returned. Switching control between different address spaces is more sophisticated because it concerns the changing of the rights to the machine resources of the processes involved. We will examine these mechanisms in Part 4 of the book.

8.7   Services for Program Execution

Software services for program execution are provided by a collection of system software tools called the Run-Time Environment (RTE). RTE tools handle processes, resource requirements, program behavior, and events that occur during program execution. These services are offered by RTE to the process of program execution and are organized in libraries of system functions called system calls.

8.7.1   *Abstractions manipulated by RTE*

Tools of the RTE manipulate three kind of abstractions: processes, resources, and events.

A process is a tuple $P = \langle Agent, Action, Status \rangle$, where $Agent$ is the processor, $Action$ is the program, and $Status$ is the status of program execution by processor. Processes are represented as data using data representation of process components.

The resources are memories, processors, I/O devices, information, and are manipulated by their data representations.

Events are messages sent by processes and their environments that characterize system behavior. The events characterizing system behavior are observable during process execution and are classified as:

Exceptions: are the *synchronous events* generated by the process execution.

Interrupts: are the *asynchronous events* generated by agents that belong to the process environment during process execution.

Observations:

- Program behavior during process execution is handled by RTE using functions dedicated to each event that may occur.
- Functions that treat interrupts and exceptions are part of RTE; they are not part of the user program.
- Programs interact with RTE by special calling mechanisms.

RTE provides services to program execution by:

- Synchronous calls issued by the program during its execution through the mechanism of exceptions. Examples of such calls are: supervisory calls, traps, faults, aborts.
- Asynchronous calls issued by agents allowing to interrupt the process through the mechanism of interrupts.Examples of such calls are I/O operation termination, memory violation (segmentation fault), power-off, etc.

Hence, the services provided by RTE for program execution are structured in a hierarchy of subsystems:

(1) *Interrupt system:* a collection of programs handling synchronous and asynchronous events generated during program execution;
(2) *Process management system:* creates, schedules, dispatches, controls, and terminates processes;
(3) *Memory management system:* manages the program's memory requirements;

(4) *I/O management system:* manages the program's I/O device requirements;

(5) *Information management system:* handles the program's information requirements.

8.7.2 Execution Environment

Execution Support Environment (ESE) is the collection of programs and documents that provide services to program execution by handling resources and treating events.

The term ESE has larger connotation than RTE. An ESE may include a Virtual Machine Monitor (VMM) as well as the collection of RTE tools supported by this VMM. ESE parallels the term PSE in both objectives and mechanisms to achieve them. Thus, the major objectives of ESE (while providing services to program execution) are to achieve:

System Efficiency: by sharing and concurrency. That is, system components work concurrently and share info!

User Convenience: by interaction and integration. That is, computer user interacts with ESE using control languages. Also, computer expert develops ESE by integrating stand-alone components.

System and User Evolution: supports portability of old systems on new machines.

Figure 8.1 shows a picture of a system software, seen as a collection of tools used by computer experts during computer-based problem solving process.

8.8 Summary

The main steps of CBPSP are:

(1) Formulate the problem. For example, develop an algorithm for solving second degree equations.

(2) Formalize it. In the example above, express it using problem domain logic, that is, find all numbers $x \in R$ such that for given $a, b, c \in R$ with $a \neq 0$ satisfy the relation: $ax^2 + bx + c = 0$.

(3) Develop a solution algorithm. For the above example, using the properties of real numbers develop the formulas:
$x_1 = -b + \sqrt{b^2 - 4ac}/2a$, $x_2 = -b - \sqrt{b^2 - 4ac}/2a$.

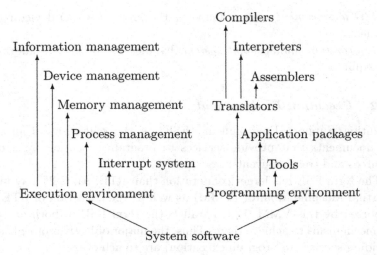

Fig. 8.1   System software structuring

(4) Codify the algorithm as a PL program. For example, using C language, develop the file `solver.c` with the contents:

```
#include <stdio.h>
#include <math.h>
int main(int argc, char *argvc[])
   {
   float a, b, c, x1, x2, d;
   scanf("%f", &a);
   scanf("%f", &b);
   scanf("%f", &c);
   d = b^2 - 4*a*c;
   if (d >= 0)
     {
     x_1 = (-b + sgrt(d)) / 2*a;
     x_2 = (-b - sqrt(d)) / 2*a;
     printf("%f\n", x1);
     printf("%f\n",x_2);
     }
   else
```

```
        printf{"%s Equation has no real solutions\n");
        return();
    }
```

(5) Compile the PL program (i.e., map it into a machine language program). For the above example, while logged in and file `solver.c` in the home directory, give the command `gcc -o solver solver.c`

(6) Load the machine language program in computer memory. For the above example, C compiler generate the executable file `solver`, so no special load and link command is necessary.

(7) Store the address of the first instruction into processor's PC. In the above example, the `main()` function of a C program performs this operation implicitly and automatically.

(8) Provide resources (memory, processor, I/O devices, information) and treat the events (interrupts and exceptions) during program execution. The Unix system perform this actions automatically when the executable is invoked.

Consequently, problem solving methodology using a computer is a terribly tedious activity and errors are hard to avoid. Assistance for program development needs to be provided by the system software. This is offered by translators. Assistance for loading the program in computer memory and for storing the address of the first instruction in PC is also necessary. This is offered by loader-linkers. During its execution, the program requires assistance for resource management and for treating various events that may occur. This is offered by the RTE. All these software tools must be developed by system software programmers as programs (i.e., must be codified using processor's instruction cycle).

To help CBPSP, software tools are organized into a hierarchy. The operation cycle is a generic algorithm for machine language operation execution. This is hardware-instantiated into the list of machine instructions, ISA. Machine instructions provide the interface between hardware and system programmers. Thus, the hardware is viewed as a finite set of operations which define the machine language. System software programmers use the machine language to construct tools to manipulate hardware and software resources. These tools simplify the task of problem solving with the computer. Since tools implemented in system software are programs, system software programmers may use tools already implemented in various stages of their development. The organization of system software tools is done according to their users and services they offer, both horizontally and vertically, as shown in Figure 8.2.

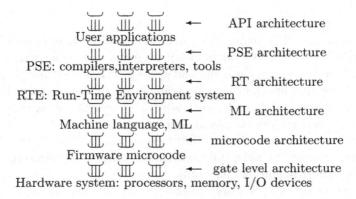

Fig. 8.2   The System Software Vertical Hierarchy

8.8.1   *Vertical structuring*

By vertical structuring software tools are organized into a hierarchy of software levels. Each level of this hierarchy contains tools designed for a specific class of computer users and is characterized by the distance of its users from the bare hardware. The specification of the tools in a level of this hierarchy is given in terms of the interface offered as the architecture by the lower levels; this interface consists of a finite set of data and operations which provide the *generators for the next level*.

Note: For a deeper understanding of software tool vertical structuring you need to review the section *Common systems in software design* (specifically computing systems hierarchy).

8.8.2   *Horizontal structuring*

In the horizontal structuring model, each level of the vertical structure is organized as a collection of software systems. A software system can itself be extended into a vertical hierarchy of layers. The layers of a software system can be organized as collections of software subsystems. For example, PSE is a collection of software tools (editors, compilers, interpreters, etc.) organized as *software systems*.

PART 3

Software Tools Supporting Program Execution

Chapter 9

Computer Process Manipulation by Programs

System software tools are programs which manipulate processes, software resources, hardware resources, and events. Processes are abstractions that represent computations performed by hardware. Software resources are programs written in various PL-s, data, and documents. Hardware resources are processors, memories, devices. Events, are interrupts, exceptions, and messages that occur during program execution. We dedicate this chapter to the software tools used to manipulate processes.

9.1 Process

A process was defined by a tuple $P = \langle Agent, Action, Satus \rangle$ where:

(1) *Agent* is an abstract or concrete object that can perform;
(2) *Action* is an expression in the language of the *Agent*;
(3) *Status* shows the status of the *Action* performed by the *Agent*.

The behavior of a process is observable as the behavior of process components. We are interested here in computer processes whose agents are processors used as components of hardware systems.

A computer process is defined in terms of its observable behavior as the tuple $ComputerProcess = \langle Processor, Program, Status \rangle$. Here *Processor* is the processor component of a hardware system. Processor behavior is expressed in terms of the given number of operations that define the machine language, i.e., (ISA). *Program* is a machine language program describing the action performed by the processor while solving a problem. *Status* is the status of *Processor* performing the *Program*, such as running, suspended, terminated, etc.

For a processor A whose language of operations is L_A, there may be potentially infinite many processes $P_A = \langle A, E_A, S_A \rangle$, where $E_A \in L_A$, in various stages of executions S_A. Usually the status S_A of a process carrying out the action specified by E_A is one of **ready, running, suspended, terminated**. In order to manipulate a process by program, the process needs to be represented as a data. The data representation of P_A is therefore the data representation of its tangible components: A, E_A, S_A.

A computer process $P = \langle Processor, Program, Status \rangle$ is represented by a data structure called Process Control Block (PCB) defined by the tuple $PCB(P) = \langle D(Proc), D(Prog), D(Status) \rangle$. Here $D(Proc)$ is a data structure which accommodates all the processor registers pertinent to program execution. $D(Prog)$ is a data structure which represents the program performed by the processor. $D(Status)$ is a data structure which represents the status of program execution by processor.

9.2 Processor Data Representation

We have identified two classes of processors in the architecture of a computer system: data processors, in charge of executing operations encoded in a programs and control processor, in charge of executing the program. The registers of a data processor are: Address Register (AR), which contains the (memory) address of the operands, Data Register (DR), which receives the operands of the operation, and a set of general registers which define the interface between the processor and the program. Since operations executed by a data processor are encoded in the program as *machine instructions* and are pointed to by the PC, only the general registers used by a data processor are pertinent for program execution.

The data representation of a register is a data structure specifying the type of values it can accommodate. That is, the data representation of a register is the data representation of the information type that register can accommodate. Thus, a register R handling integers can be represented in C by `int R`; a register R handling characters can be represented in C by `char R`; a register R handling a data structure S can be represented in C by `struct S R`; The C declarations used as register data representation provide memory locations to store/load registers by program.

Registers used by a control processor for program execution are the Program Counter (PC) and Instruction Register, (IR). Since the contents of IR is the machine language operation stored in the memory location pointed to by PC, IR is irrelevant for Control Processor Data Representation. Other registers pertinent for program execution are Condition Codes, CC, a set of registers containing the state of the last operation executed by the processor, and a set of registers which record the events encountered during the program execution. These events are classified as *interrupts, exceptions,* and *messages.* When an event occurs, the control processor may be preempted from its current activity, i.e., according to the processing priority of the event, the operations `OldPC := PC; PC := NewPC` may be automatically executed. `OldPC` is a dedicated memory location (or a dedicated register) which allow the interrupted program to be re-started from the instruction executed while the event occurred, and `NewPC` is the memory location where the program that treats the event is located.

Interrupts are events which occur asynchronously with program execution. Example of interrupt events are: power off, an IO device completing its activity, a timer signaling the elapse of a time period. Exceptions are events generated by the program therefore they are synchronous with program execution. That is, exceptions are generated by the operation cycle during the execution of machine instructions. Hence, exceptions may be classified according to the stage of operation execution at which they occur as: *traps, faults, aborts, system calls.* Traps are generated by the result of an operation. Examples of traps are arithmetic overflows or underflows. Faults are generated when data required to complete an operation is not available. Example of a fault is `page fault` in a Unix system. The operation generating a fault is terminated when the data becomes available. Aborts are generated when the operation cannot be executed. Example of an abort is an illegal opcode. System calls are operations which cannot be executed by the hardware, instead, they can be executed by software simulating them. Messages are events generated by process communication with its environment. A process may need to communicate with other processes that belong to its environment during its execution. This communication can be organized by enabling the process to identify other processes and to send (or receive) messages called *signals* to (or from) other processes. This can be achieved by providing the control processor with special purpose registers. Hardware informs operating systems about its behavior setting special bits of these special registers. These bits represent signals. Operating system deliver these signals to the destination process upon process return from operating system mode. Signals are processed by both the operating system and the destination process using appropriate system calls. Various hardware architectures provide dedicated data structures called Processor (or Program) Status Word (PSW), for data representation of a control processor. PSW is manipulated by special instructions, such as: `Store PSW Address`, which collects all components of PSW and store them in memory at the address `Address`; `Load PSW Address`, which interpret the memory location at the address `Address` as the address of PSW and scatter its components into the registers making up PSW. Depending upon the hardware complexity, other operations may also be designed.

By assembling the data processor representation and the control processor representation we obtain the processor data representation called the `Real Processor Control Block`, (RPCB).

9.3   Program Data Representation

A data structure that represents a program in memory may have the following components: Code Address (CA), the address of program code; Data Address (DA), the address of data processed by the program; Stack Address (SA), the address of the program stack, when execution model uses a stack for local data; Priority of the Program (PP), which is a number characterizing the priority of program scheduling for execution; Access Rights (AR), the rights of the program imported from other processes; Exported Rights (XR), the rights exported by the program to other processes. Hence, program representation is a data structure that captures all elements that characterize a program within its execution environment. The data structure collecting the information pertinent for program representation is called here the `Program Process Control Block`, (PPCB).

9.4   Process Status Data Representation

During its execution by the processor, a computer process is characterized by: status, such as created, ready, executing, suspended, terminated; event generating the status transition, such as interrupt, exception, signal, which may be refined further by the mechanism implementing process state transition; process name (usually the program name); process identification in the process data structure, usually called `Pid`; process parent and process children; others, depending upon system complexity. The data structure that collects the information which characterizes the status of a computer process is called here the `Status Process Control Block` (SPCB).

9.5   Process Control Block

The data structure representing a computer process is further called the Process Control Bloc (PCB). The PCB of a process P consists of: RPCB(P) representing the processor component of the process, PPCB(P) representing the program component of the process, and SPCB(P) representing the status component of the process. Assuming that Processor, Program, Status are C structures representing the Processor, Program, Status, respectively, a process can be represented by the C structure:

```
struct Process
     {
       struct Processor RPCB;
       struct Program   PPCB;
       struct Status    SPCB;
       }PCB;
```

For optimization reasons the PCB in various OS-s mixes together process components. The consequence is both faster operations of process management by program and also rigidity in process management. The collection of processes competing to be executed by the processor are maintained into a data structure called Process Data Structure (PDS). Since we are interested here in the logical design of process management rather then the efficiency of process management, here PDS is a linked list of PCB-s, Figure 9.1 For reasons of optimization, usually PDS is not organized as seen in Figure 9.1. Instead, arrays of PCB-s called Process Table are usually used. See process table in a Unix system [Googheart and Cox (1994)]. Among consequences is that system

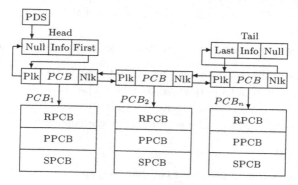

Fig. 9.1   Process Data Structure

evolution is difficult to accomplish. Patching the system to accomplish system evolution results in sloppiness in process management. See U-area structuring in Unix [Googheart and Cox (1994)].

9.6   Process Management System

PMS is the collection of functions that operate on PDS and manipulate processes. Examples of such functions are process execution and process suspensions. When processor registers of the processor are loaded with the contents of a PCB from PDS the processor is instructed to start the execution of the process identified by that PCB. When processor registers characterizing the status of a program execution are stored in the PCB of the active process in PDS, an instance of the computation carried out by the active process is saved and the process is thus suspended. Other functions performed by PMSs are:

- `create(processor, program)` creates a PCB and sends it in the PDS.
- `schedule(PCB)` schedules PCB for execution.
- `dispatch(PCB)` load processor registers with information in PCB.
- `suspend(PCB,event)` suspends the execution of (current) process sending processor registers in its PCB in the PDS for the **event**. For example, $suspend(PCB, IO)$ would suspend the process performing it for the event *IOtermination*.
- `resume(PCB,event)` resumes the execution of PCB for the **event**; i.e., it asks the PMS to resume the execution of process in PCB in the PDS because the *event* occurred. For example, $resume(PCB, IO)$ would resume the process whose PCB is in the PDS queue waiting for the event **IOtermination** occurrence.
- `terminate(PCB)` terminates the execution of **PCB**. This may removes it from PDS.
- Many other operation depending upon the complexity of the hardware.

Formally the PMS is a data type whose data carrier is the PDS and whose operations are functions performed by PMS. That is, PMS = ⟨PDS, create, schedule, dispatch, suspend, resume, terminate, ...⟩. From the implementation viewpoint PMS can be seen as a list management system!

Observations:

- The status of the uniprocessor computers is specified only by the program counter, condition codes, and general registers.

- More advanced uniprocessor architectures use more registers to specify the status of processes carried out by them, organized as a hardware-defined data structure called the *Program Status Word*, PSW.
- The status of a process in a multiprocessor architectures is defined by a larger collection of registers.

9.7   Examples Process Data Representation

9.7.1   *Example 1: Mix machine process*

The Mix machine architecture [Knuth (1968)] is shown in Figure 9.2

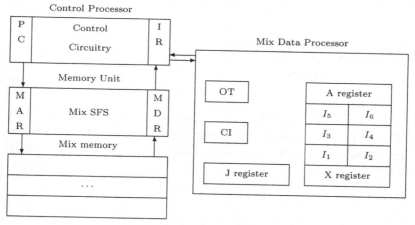

Fig. 9.2   Mix machine architecture

Facts:

(1) PC is the program counter; values PC can hold are addresses of memory locations. Hence $0 \leq Value(PC) \leq Max\#Loc$;

(2) OT is an "Operation Toggle", i.e., a switch that shows the mode of the operation performed by the processor. Example such values are $OT = user$ or $OT = system$;

(3) CI is the condition indicator (condition codes). Example condition codes are $CI = 0$ if result ≥ 0, $CI = 1$ if result < 0.

(4) J register is the "Jump Register" used to implement **return from subroutine**. Hence, it should hold the same range of values as PC;

(5) A, X registers are the general registers used to perform operations;

(6) $I_1, I_2, I_3, I_4. I_5, I_6$ are index registers.

Hence, MixPDS is a double-linked list whose elements are:

```
struct MixProcess
      {
        struct MixProcess *Plink;
        struct MixPCB     *Process;
        struct MixProcess *Nlink;
      };
```

where `Plink` shows the previous process in the MixPDS and `Nlink` shows the next process in the MixPDS. MixPCB is the data structure:

```
struct MixPCB
{
 struct MixRPCB *RPCB;
 struct MixPPCB *PPCB;
 struct MixSPCB *SPCB;
};
```

Looking at the architecture of Mix Machine in figure 9.2 we conclude that MixRPCB can be obtained by packaging J register, OT, and CI, into one memory word. We call this memory word JOTCI. Hence, Mix RPCB becomes:

```
struct MixRPCB
      {
        int PC, ARegister, XRegister;
        short Index[6];
        struct Conditions JOTCI;
      };
```

where the structure `Conditions` is:

```
struct Conditions
      {
        unsigned J : 12;
        unsigned OT :  1;
        unsigned CI :  2;
      };
```

Assuming that a Mix program is represented by the tuple: ⟨CodeAddress, CodeSize, DataAddresss, DataSize⟩ `MixPPCB` is defined by:

```
struct MixPPCB
    {
        int CodeAddr, CodeSize;
        int DataAddr, DataSize;
    };
```

Now, Mix process status can be represented by priority, identity, and status, i.e., MixSPCB is defined by the C structure:

```
struct MixSPCB
    {
        int Priority;
        int ProcId;
        char Status;
    };
```

9.7.2 *Example 2: IBM 360/370 process*

IBM 360/370 is a real and very influential processor. Hence, IBM 360/370 process data representation is not a toy example. The IBM 360/370 data processor consists of 16 32-bit general registers (4 8-bit bytes each) which are addressed by the numbers 0 through 15. The control processor contains a Program Status Word, PSW, that represents both the control processor and the program executed by it. IBM-360/370 PSW is composed of the following registers:

(1) An 8-bit register that records the system masks, SM. SM is used to inhibit some of the interrupt events which can occur during program execution.
(2) A 4-bit register to hold the Program Protection Key (PPK). PPK in conjunction with a Memory Access Key (MAK) determines the process's rights of access to the memory.
(3) A 3-bit register to record the flags defining the Machine Operation State (MOS). MOS records the character mode (ASCII or EBCDIC), the machine check mask, the wait state, and the problem state.
(4) A 1-bit register to record the operation mode called the Mode Bit (MB). Note, Mix architectures calls it Operation Toggle (OT).
(5) A 16-bit register to record the Interrupt Identification Code (IIC). When an interrupt event occurs IIC records the identity of the interrupting agent.

(6) A 2-bit register called the Instruction Length Counter, (LLC). ILC is used by the function Next() performed by the program execution loop, to determine the next instruction of the program.

(7) A 2-bit register called the Condition Codes (CC). At the instruction completion CC is loaded with the condition codes of the operation performed.

(8) A 4-bit register called Program Mask (PM). PM is loaded with the program masks, used to inhibit some of the program exceptions.

(9) A 24-bit register called the Program Counter (PC). PC is loaded with the address of the next instruction to be fetched for execution.

Graphic the IBM-360/370 PSW is in Figure 9.3.

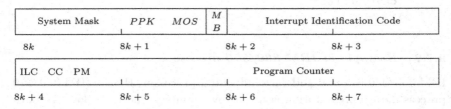

Fig. 9.3   IBM-360/370 PSW

It results that the PSW can be saved in and fetched from a double memory location, i.e., an 8 byte memory location of address a multiple of 8. Consequently the C language expression of IBM-360/370 PSW could be:

```
struct IBMPSW
     {struct ProcessorState PSW1;
     struct ProgramState PSW2;
     };
struct ProcessorState
     {unsigned SM  : 8;
     unsigned PPK : 4;
     unsigned MOS : 3;
     unsigned MB  : 1;
     unsigned IIC : 16;
     };
```

```
struct ProgramState
     {unsigned ILC : 2;
      unsigned PM  : 4;
      unsigned CC  : 2;
      unsigned PC  : 24;
     };
```

Now, the PCB for the IBM-360/370 architecture is:

```
struct IBMPCB
     {
      struct IBMRPCB *RPCB;
      int CodeAddress,DataAddress,Priority;
      char Status;
     };
struct IBMRPCB
     {
      int GR[16], ProcId;
      struct IBMPSW PSW;
     };
```

The IBM-360/370 PDS can be organized as the doubly linked list:

```
struct IBMProcess
     {
      struct IBMProcess *Plink;
      struct IBMPCB *Process;
      struct IBMProcess *Nlink;
     }*PDS;
```

Note that IBMPCB does not have an explicit component for program or status representation. They are packed in PSW.

9.7.3   *Example 3: VAX-11/780*

Vax-11/780 implements a stack model of computation where an executable program consists of a collection of executable functions and a global data area at which all functions in the collection have access. There is a function that starts the computation. This is the main() function in a C program. Each function composing the program is specified by its machine language code and a segment of data called Activation Record (AR). AR collects all function's parameters and data defined/declared in the function body. During program execution all functions can access the program global data area. Thus function components of a program can communicate with each other by sharing the global data area of the program and using the parameters supplied in the call. Hence, an executable program in Vax-11/780 consists of three segments: DataSegment, TextSegment, StackSegment. DataSegment is a memory area that contains the global data accessible to all functions composing the program. TextSegment collects the code of the functions making up the program. Text segment is read-only. StackSegment, is a memory area where AR-s of the functions that make up the program are stored during program execution.

A Vax 11-780 program is executed by Operating System (Unix) by the following rules:

- Main function start the execution by pushing AR(main) on the stack;
- When a function, say f1(), calls another function, say f2(), AR(f2) is pushed on the stack on top of the AR(f1) and control is transferred to the first instruction of f2();
- When function f2() terminates its execution AR(f2) is popped out from the stack and the control is transferred to the function f1() that called f2().
- Process execution terminates when main() terminates.

The data processor in the VAX-11/780 architecture is characterized by 16 32-bit registers, R0, R1, ..., R15, where:

R12 is known as the argument pointer; R12 points to the stack area where function arguments are loaded.
R13 is known as the frame pointer; R13 shows the address of the function's activation record on the program stack.
R14 is known as the stack pointer; R14 points to the memory area where program's stack is allocated.
R15 is known as the program counter.

VAX-11/780 Processor Status Longword, PSL, is defined by two 16 bit registers shown in Figures 9.4 and 9.5 where IOTE stands for Integer Overflow Trap Enabled, FLUTE stands for Floating Underflow Trap Enabled, and DOTE stands for Decimal Overflow Trap Enabled. A bit in PSL is set when its condition occurs after an operation execution. For example, N bit is set if the result of the last operation is negative, otherwise it is cleared, etc.

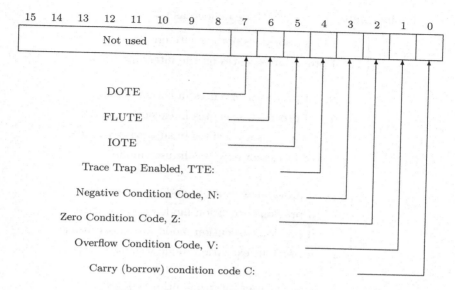

Fig. 9.4   VAX-11/780 Program Status Word

VAX-11/780 Processor Status Word is in Figure 9.5.

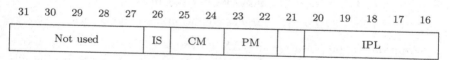

Fig. 9.5   VAX-11/780 Processor Status Word

Notations used in this figure are:

- IS indicates whether the process is executed on program stack or on the interrupt stack.
- CM shows the current mode of the process.
- PM shows the previous mode of the process.
- IPL is the interrupt priority level of the current process.

Processing mode in VAX-11/780 is more complex than in the previous architectures. It allows the operating system to distinguish four execution modes: kernel, executive, supervisory, user. Each one of these modes defines a specific collection of process rights to the machine resources. However, the Virtual Machine Monitors [Popek and Goldberg (1974); Smith and Noir (2005)] may require even further diversification of processor execution modes.

The bits composing the PSW are defined as follows:

$$IS = \begin{cases} 0, & \text{if processor does not execute on interrupt stack;} \\ 1, & \text{if processor executes on the interrupt stack.} \end{cases}$$

$$CM = \begin{cases} 00, & \text{if processor executes in kernel mode;} \\ 01, & \text{if processor executes in executive mode;} \\ 10, & \text{if processor executes in supervisory mode;} \\ 11, & \text{if processor executes in user mode.} \end{cases}$$

$$PM = \begin{cases} 00, & \text{if previous execution mode was kernel;} \\ 01, & \text{if previous execution mode was executive;} \\ 10, & \text{if previous execution mode was supervisory;} \\ 11, & \text{if previous execution mode was user.} \end{cases}$$

$$IPL = \begin{cases} 0, & \text{user interrupt priority level;} \\ 1 \leq IPL \leq 15, & \text{software interrupt priority level;} \\ 16 \leq IPL \leq 23, & \text{device interrupt priority level;} \\ 24, & \text{if clock interrupt priority level;} \\ 25 \leq IPL \leq 31, & \text{urgent condition interrupt priority level.} \end{cases}$$

Program data representation in VAX-11/780 is more sophisticated [Levy and Eckhouse (1980)]. Hence, Vax 11/780 PCB is represented by the following C structure:

```c
struct Vax11PCB
    {
    int PC R15;
    int SP R14;
    int FP R13;
    int AP R12;
    int GeneralRegister[12];
    struct ProcessSW ProcSW;
    struct ProgramSW ProgSW;
    };


struct ProcessSW
    {
```

```
        unsigned IPL: 5;
        unsigned PM: 2;
        unsigned CM: 2;
        unsigned IS: 1;
      }


struct ProgramSW
      {
        unsigned Carry:1;
        unsigned Overflow: 1;
        unsigned Zero: 1;
        unsigned Negative: 1;
        unsigned TraceTrap: 1;
        unsigned IOTE: 1;
        unsigned FLUTE: 1;
        unsigned DOTE: 1;
      };


struct VaxProcess
      {
        struct VaxProcess *Plink;
        struct Vax11PCB *Process;
        strucr VaxProcess *Nlink;
      };
```

IBM 360/370 and VAX 11/780 are the two most influential computer architectures. To better understand their influence here we provide the main differences between them:

(1) VAX 11/780 is a stack machine; it performs a model of computation in which the computer's memory takes the form of one or more stacks.
(2) IBM 360/370 is not a stack machine; it performs a model of computation in which computer memory is a linear array of memory locations.
(3) VAX 11/780 provides explicit hardware support for OS structuring on layers; IBM support for OS structuring is provided by PSW;
(4) Interrupts and Exceptions in VAX 11/780 are identified by dedicated memory locations called interrupt vectors; IBM uses a fixed number of Interrupt agents clustered in classes and are identified by IBM PSW.

9.8   Processor Activity

The computing activity performed by the processor of a computer system consists of a continuous execution of processes populating the PDS. Each PCB in PDS characterizes the status of a process executed by the processor. To start a process execution the processor's registers must be loaded with the appropriate information from a PCB in PDS. To interrupt a process execution, processor's registers must be saved into the appropriate PCB in PDS. Figure 9.6 illustrates this activity for the Mix Machine. Here PDS is a linked list of MixPCB-s.

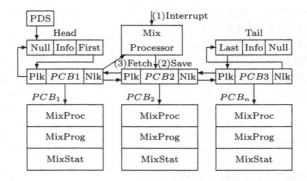

Fig. 9.6   Process Data Structure

The actions which start processing an interrupt are performed in two steps:

(1) Fetch (for start) or save (for interrupt) minimal information using one machine instruction;
(2) Fetch (for start) or save (for interrupt) the remaining information using an appropriate program (function).

The amount of information fetched or saved in step 1 depends on both the process and the event that determines process transition. The PSW in the IBM-360/370 and the PSL in the VAX-11/780 contain the minimal information that characterizes the processor activity. These registers are automatically saved in an appropriate data structure when the process is interrupted and need to be fetched by machine instructions when a process is started.

The contents of the processor registers while executing the current process is called the *processor context*. Switch context is the most frequent function executed by the PMS and consists of the sequence of operations:

(1) Save the processor registers into the *PCB* in the PDS of the current process;
(2) Select another process from the *PDS* to be executed by the processor;
(3) Load processor registers with the content of the new *PCB*.

Fact: switch context is the main operation performed by a PMS. The simulation of switch context allows us to really understand the events that may occur during a process execution and how to treat them. Context switching can be executed by a machine instruction, as is the case with the VAX-11/780 machine, or it can be executed by a sequence of machine instructions that can be packaged into a function. A generic function that simulates this action is:

```
SwitchContext (struct PCB *ActiveProc)
  {
    struct PCB *TempPCB = Fetch(ActiveProc);
    TempPCB->Pid = FindIdentity (ActiveProc,PDS);
    TempPCB->Priority = ChangePriority (TempPCB);
    Save(TempPCB,PDS);
    TempPCB = HighestPriority (PDS);
    Dispatch (TempPCB,ActiveProc);
  }
```

Here `ActiveProc` denotes the processor context. In simulation it is a datastructure simulating the processor. In a real case it may be the PSW. Other notation used in `SwitchContext()` are:

`FindIdentity()` is a function which determines the process Id of the current process in the PDS; if PDS is an array this is an indexed operation, otherwise it implies a traversal of PDS.

`ChangePriority ()` is a function used in simulation to modify the priority of currently executing process such that it will not be scheduled immediately;

`Save()` is the action that saves the processor registers into the PCB of the current process;

`HighestPriority ()` determines the process in the PDS to be scheduled next;

`Dispatch ()` fetches the processor's registers from the PCB.

Chapter 10

Memory Management System

. Various programs existent in memory at a given time require memory to be partitioned among computer users. The two main memory partitions are system memory area, occupied by programs in system software and user memory area, which is the memory available for user programs. While system memory area remains occupied by the same programs over long periods, the user memory area changes continuously.

Facts:

(1) System memory area is always occupied by system programs (such as RTE components) that provide services for user program development and execution.

(2) User memory area is however recycled between various user programs that require memory, use memory, and release memory.

(3) When no user program is in memory the user area is a contiguous block. In time it becomes distributed among the executing user programs, as seen in Figure 10.1.

System area	Program 1 area	Program 2 area	Program 3 area	Free area

0   1000 1001   2000 2001   5000 5001   8000 8001   10000

Fig. 10.1   Memory partitioning

Now, suppose that Program 2 in Figure 10.1 finishes; the memory configuration is shown in Figure 10.2. Program 4 requires 5000 locations to execute. Though there is enough free memory space for Program 4 it cannot be granted as a single block in this configuration.

133

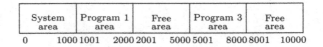

System area	Program 1 area	Free area	Program 3 area	Free area
0 1000	1001 2000	2001 5000	5001 8000	8001 10000

Fig. 10.2   Memory partitioning when Program 2 terminates

10.1   Memory Management System

The dynamic behavior of program execution divides the user memory area into a collection of disjoint blocks of variable size. To allocate such memory blocks, the system software needs information about their size, address, and state (busy or free). To optimize memory usage, Memory Management System (MMS) needs to represent the memory as a data and coalesce memory blocks thus reducing memory fragmentation. Rationale for MMS are:

- Programs need to be loaded into memory for execution;
- A program may require memory dynamically, during execution;
- A program may free memory dynamically, during execution.

Hence, software tools are needed to manage the inventory of memory.

Memory requirements of programs are processed by system software programs. Thus memory requirements need to be represented as data and operations. The generic representation of such requirements is expressed by functions such as `getMemory(Size)` and `freeMemory(Location, Size)`. `getMemory(Size)` finds a free block of memory of size *Size*, change its status to *busy*, and returns it to the requesting program. `freeMemory(Location, Size)` changes the status of the memory block at location *Location* of size *Size* to *free* and thus makes it available to other programs.

To perform memory management, a MMS makes assumptions about computer memory. A user program sees the memory as a large storage space destined to satisfy its memory requirements. The system sees the memory as a collection of storage blocks that change dynamically. To manage the dynamic of memory, the free memory blocks are maintained by the system into a list called Free List (FL) which initially consists of entire user memory. The two major objectives of memory management are:

(1) Ensure system efficiency by keeping memory blocks busy as long as possible;

(2) Ensure program convenience by providing memory space as soon as this is required and in the amount requested.

However, the objectives of memory management are conflicting: keeping memory blocks busy as long as possible may prevent programs from running. The compromise required can be achieved by minimizing the number of blocks on FL. Memory fragmentation is then measured by the number and the size of memory blocks on the FL. MMS maintains free memory blocks using FL, that is, $MMS = \langle FL, getMemory(), freeMemory(), maitainMemory() \rangle$ where:

- getMemory(Block) searches FL for a memory bloc using an optimization strategy such as *best-fit, worst-fit, first-fit*;
- freeMemory(Block) returns the Block to FL and minimize fragmentation by coalescing. This implies searching FL for the neighbors of the Block;
- maintainMemory() is a collection of functions that optimize memory usage by coalescing memory blocks on FL and by compacting memory contents, if necessary.

10.2 Optimization Strategies

The three strategies used for memory optimization while manipulating memory blocks on a FL are *Best-fit, Worst-fit, First-fit*.

Best-fit: allocate the smallest block on FL that fits a memory request. This minimizes the number of blocks on FL keeping their size as large as possible. Hence, it increases the probability that a free suitable block on FL is always available.

Worst-fit: allocate the largest block on FL that fits a memory request. The rationale is that the remaining block is large enough for the next request.

First-fit: allocate the first block on FL that fits the request. This allows fast block coalescing thus avoiding memory fragmentation.

In addition, one can use the hardware property of memory structuring that requires memory construction from memory blocks of size a power of 2 locations. Thus, if block size is a power of 2 then the equality $2 * 2^k = 2^{k+1}$ ensures free blocks fast coalescing.

10.3   Memory Compaction

Coalescing free memory blocks minimizes memory fragmentation, it doesn't prevent it. Memory fragmentation can reach a status where free memory become unusable because it is split into many small unusable blocks. By compaction, memory contents is moved to one end of the memory, generating one large block, thus increasing its usability.

Memory compaction means compacting all free blocks of FL into one large memory bloc. The problem with this optimization strategy is that compaction requires the system interruption and program reloading/linking.

10.4   MMS Design Assumptions

(1) Several programs reside in memory at the same time.
(2) Different programs have different memory requirements.
(3) The size of the memory block requested is not known in advance.
(4) Blocks of memory are acquired and freed in an unpredictable order.

10.5   Memory Blocks

A memory block is a data representation of a fragment of physical memory. A memory block contains two types of data: status information and user information. Both software programs and user programs operate on memory blocks. But, software programs operate on the status information, while user programs operate on the information contained in the block. Hence, memory blocks on FL are described by *memory block descriptors*. There are two approaches to defining memory block descriptors: variable size descriptors, where a descriptor contains both status and user information, and fixed size descriptors, where a descriptor contain only status information, the user information is pointed to from the memory block.

Status information in a memory block consists of the state of the block (busy or free), the number of contiguous locations that belong to the block (block's size), and the link of the block in the FL. When the block is busy, the user information is simply stored in the array of contiguous locations comprising the body of the memory block. The C expression of a variable size descriptor is:

```
struct VariableDescriptor
    {
    char State;
    int Size, Type;
    struct VariableDescriptor *Link;
    location Information[MaxSize];
    };
```

The C expression of a fixed size descriptor is:

```
struct FixedDescriptor
    {
    int Size, Type;
    struct FixedDescriptor *Link;
    location *FirstLocation;
    };
```

10.6   Free List

We examine here the design and implementation of a MMS using a FL where blocks are all either specified by variable-size or fixed-size descriptors.

10.6.1   *FL with variable size descriptors*

FL with variable size descriptors maintains the status information in the block itself. FL is a linked list of variable size blocks within the user memory area. The amount of status information in the block depends upon the goal and performance of the operations on the free list. The structure of a memory block that allows coalescing of free adjacent blocks in constant time is in Figure 10.3.

Plink	Tag	Size	Nlink
User information			
...			
User information			
UpLink	Tag	Null	Null

Fig. 10.3   Block structure of the FL

For constant time coalescing of adjacent free blocks the status information surrounds the user information. To implement the FL as a double-linked list the `Plink` and the `Nlink` chain the memory blocks on FL. The meaning of Tag field is defined by:

$$Tag = \begin{cases} 0, & \text{if the block is free;} \\ 1, & \text{if the block is busy.} \end{cases}$$

The `UpLink` field shows the address of this block in the user memory array. The `Size` field contains the number of locations in this block. The `Null` field record is chosen for uniformity reasons.

When a block of address A is freed, the status of its down and up-neighbors in the physical memory are discovered by one test: `if(A - 1).Tag == 0)` the downward-block in physical memory is free and it can be coalesced with the freed block; `if((A + A.Size + 1).Tag == 0)` then the upward-block in the physical memory is free and it can be coalesced with the freed block. The UpLink allows for easy and efficient examination of the other neighbors of a block.

The C definition of a memory block of this sort is:

```
struct MemBlock
    {
        struct MemBlock *Plink;
        boolean Tag1;
        int    Size;
        struct  MemBlock *Nlink;
        char  Block[Size];
        struct MemBlock *UpLink;
        boolean Tag2;
    };
```

At the initializations time the FL is one large block as shown in Figure 10.4.

Observation: The memory block used in the LMS has factored out the status information. If we decide to embed the value of the lexical element in the same block we obtain a variable size block. However, `NFB` may be used to record the number of free blocks on FL, and `NBB` may be used to record the number of busy blocks in memory at a given time. Further, FL.Head.NFB and FL.Tail.NBB are then used to describe the goodness of MMS. This can be done by simulation, before a MMS is deployed.

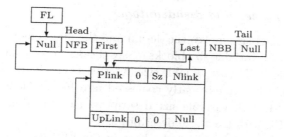

Fig. 10.4   FL: All user memory is available

10.6.2   *FL with fixed size descriptors*

FL with fixed size descriptors keep only status information in the block, Figure 10.5. Each descriptor contains only what is required by the software programs to maintain the free list. The memory area occupied by the free list can be granted to the software programs maintaining it upon request, from the system memory area or from the user memory area.

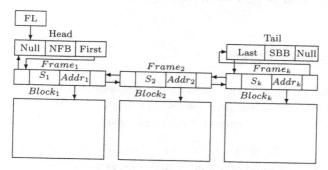

Fig. 10.5   Free list with fixed size frame blocks

Facts:

(1) To maintain the free list, MMS gets memory for descriptors like any user program gets memory for its data.

(2) Hardware support for MMS may be used to standardize memory blocks at the size of IO exchange record. This allows virtual memory (on level memory) implementation.

(3) The approach discussed here would implement Program Page Table in a VM environment.

10.6.3 *Advantages and disadvantages*

Descriptors of fixed size makes the design and the maintenance of FL simpler. Descriptors of variable size blocks makes the design and maintenance of FL more complex. FL with variable size descriptors can be easily traversed and adjacent blocks are efficiently coalesced into bigger blocks. However, operations on FL with variable size descriptors lack the simplicity of the operations on FL with fixed size descriptors.

The information suggested to be kept in the FL.Head and FL.Tail in Figure 10.5 are:

- The field **FL.Head.NFB** may be used for the number of free blocks, as in the case of variable-size descriptors;
- The field **FL.Tail.SBB** in the tail of the FL may be used for the size of the biggest block;
- The S_1, S_2, ..., S_k in the descriptors are the sizes of the blocks they describe.

This information is used to develop tools that measure the goodness of MMS.

10.7 Simulating MMS

A valuable challenge project may be the implementation of a MMS using fixed-size memory block descriptors. The implementation of this project may be facilitated by a correct implementation of the LMS because:

(1) The memory block descriptors have been already implemented;
(2) The operations needed to manipulate the memory blocks have also been implemented;
(3) What remains is the part of the project that handle value field required by malloc(), maintains the status informations, and perform allocation according to given criteria.

The C expression of a free list with fixed size blocks is:

```
struct FixedDescriptor
      {
        struct FixedDescriptor *Plink, *Nlink;
        int Size;
        char *Location;
```

```
        };
struct FLHeadTail
        {
        struct FixedDescriptor *Plink, *Nlink;
        int     Nfb, Sbb;
        }*FreeList, Head, Tail;
```

Services offered by MMS to other programs (user and software) are defined as operations on the FL.

- getMemory(Size) searches the FL for a memory block of size Size and returns a pointer to it, if found, otherwise it returns a null pointer;
- freeMemory(Address, Size) frees the memory block at the address Address of size Size and returns it to the free list. This implies the block coalescing with its neighbors.

The MMS simulates the physical memory using an abstraction of memory-block (a data type) and is specified by the tuple: $MMS = \langle FreeList; getMemory, freeMemory \rangle$.

10.7.1 Buddy algorithm

A particularly attractive simulation of a MMS that minimize the memory fragmentation by an efficient operation of coalescing free memory blocks is obtained by using the *buddy algorithm*. This algorithm uses the following observation: *for technological reasons the number of location units (bytes) which compose the real memory of a computer is a power of 2.* That is, the size of the Real Address Space (RAS) is 2^n for a given n. For examples: a Kilobyte memory (KB) contains 10^3 bytes has the size 2^{10}, a Megabyte memory (MB) contains 10^6 bytes has the size 2^{20}, a Gigabyte memory (GB) contains 10^9 bytes has the size 2^{30}, a Terabyte memory (TB) contains 10^{12} bytes has the size 2^{40}, a Petabyte memory (PB) contains 10^{15} bytes has the size 2^{50}, an Exabyte memory (EB) contains 10^{18} bytes has the size 2^{60}, a Zetabyte memory (ZB) contains 10^{21} bytes has the size 2^{70}, a Yotabyte memory (YB) contains 10^{24} bytes has the size 2^{80}.

10.7.2 Buddy property

The essential property of a block of memory of size 2^n, called the *buddy property*, is that it contains exactly two sub-blocks of memory of size 2^{n-1} called buddies for n. For example, consider a block of memory of size

$16 = 2^4$. If the address of this block is B then the two buddies for 4 are of addresses B and B + 8 and their size is $8 = 2^{4-1}$.

Let us denote by B_{n_0} and B_{n_1} the two buddies for n. Since they have size 2^{n-1}, B_{n_0} and B_{n_1} have the buddy property as well. Thus, we obtain four blocks of memory of size 2^{n-2}. With these four blocks we can construct 6 pairs of memory blocks of size 2^{n-2}. However, only two of these pairs are buddies for $(n-1)$. In general, for given n and k we can construct 2^k blocks of memory of size 2^{n-k} which can be paired in $(2^k - 1) \times 2^{k-1}$ distinct pairs. But only 2^{k-1} of these pairs are buddies for $n - (k - 1)$. Moreover, for a memory space of size 2^n, for any $k < n$ and any memory block B1 of size 2^{k-1} there exists precisely one memory block B2 of size 2^{k-1} such that B1 and B2 are buddies for k.

Buddy Compactness Property: Two blocks of memory B_1 and B_2 of size 2^k and addresses A_1 and A_2 are buddies for $k + 1$ in a memory space of size 2^n, $n \geq k$, iff their addresses are related by the relation:

$$A_i = \begin{cases} A_j + 2^k, & \text{if } remainder(A_j/2^{k+1}) = 0; \\ A_j - 2^k, & \text{if } remainder(A_j/2^{k+1}) \neq 0. \end{cases}$$

where $i, j = 1, 2$ and $i \neq j$. Figure 10.6 illustrates the buddy compactness property. Note that if $p = 2m$ then $A_j = (2m+1)2^k$, $A_j \bmod 2^{k+1} \neq 0$ and

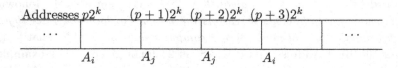

Fig. 10.6   Buddy compactness property

$A_i = A_j - 2^k$; if $p = 2m + 1$ then $A_j = (m+1)2^{k+1}$, $A_j \bmod 2^{k+1} = 0$ and $A_i = A_j + 2^k$.

Formal Proof: Assume that the relation is satisfied. Since B_1 and B_2 have the same size, 2^k, and since their addresses differ by 2^k they are contiguous. Putting them together we obtain a new block of memory of size $2 \times 2^k = 2^{k+1}$, i.e., B_1 and B_2 are buddies. Now, let B_1, B_2 be buddies for $k+1$ of addresses A_1, A_2 respectively. I.e., there exists a contiguous memory block B of address A such that $A \bmod 2^{k+1} = 0$ and size of A is 2^{k+1}, such that $A = A_1$ or $A = A_2$. If $A = A_1$ then since A is a multiple of 2^{k+1} and $A_2 = A_1 + 2^k$, A_2 is not multiple of 2^{k+1}, i.e., $remainder(A_1/2^{k+1}) \neq 0$ and $A_1 = A_2 - 2^k$. If $A = A_2$, then because A is a multiple of 2^{k+1}, A_2 is a multiple of 2^{k+1} and thus $remainder(A_2/2^{k+1}) = 0$ and $A_1 = A_2 + 2^k$, obviously.

Examples:

(1) Consider a memory of size 2^4 and addresses 0 to 15. Let k+1 = 2 and two blocks of memory of size $2^{2-1} = 2$ and addresses 14 and 10. Applying the above relation we have $10 = 2 \times 4 + 2$, and $remainder(10/4) \neq 0$; $14 = 3 \times 4 + 2$, and $remainder(14/4) \neq 0$ thus, the blocks of size 2 and addresses 14 and 10 are not buddies for 2.

(2) Consider now the same memory of size 2^4 and addresses 0 to 15. Let k+1 = 2 and the two blocks of memory of size 2 and addresses 14 and 12. Since $12 = 3 \times 4$, $remainder(12/4) = 0$; moreover, $14 = 12 + 2$ and they are buddies for 2.

10.7.3 *Using buddy property*

Assume that MMS policy consists of maintaining the free memory blocks of size 2^k for some $k < n$. Then MMS can implement the getMemory(S), freeMemory(A,S) for each request by the following strategy:

(1) Determine the smallest k such that the size S satisfies the relation $2^{k-1} < S \leq 2^k$. The following formula can be used:

$$k = \begin{cases} log_2(S), & \text{if } log_2(S) \text{ is an integer}; \\ log_2(S) + 1, & \text{otherwise.} \end{cases}$$

(2) getMemory(S) returns a block of memory of size 2^k.
(3) freeMemory(A, k) returns the block of memory of address A and size 2^k to the FL. If the buddy of this block is free, compact then into a larger buddy of address B and size 2^{k+1} and repeat the freeMemory(B, k+1).

Design decisions:

(1) Determine the minimum size of the allocable buddy, say k, and maintain the free buddies on an array of $n - k$ free lists, Figure 10.7.
(2) Free lists are double-linked lists defined by a header and a tail;

(3) Information in header and tail is used by OS people to compute the goodness of the system they implement;

(4) The field *address* of a header is the number of the buddies in the list;

(5) The field *address* of a tail collects statistics about free list usage.

The buddy size is computed by the formula $size = 2^{k+i}$, where k is fixed such that 2^k is the size of the smallest block maintained on the free list.

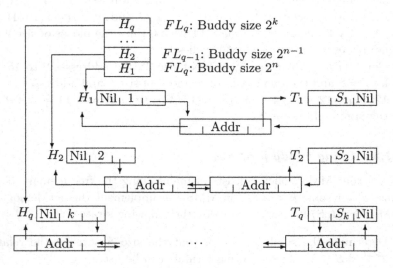

Fig. 10.7   A buddy-system free lists

10.7.4   *Implementation*

The C data structures required for the specification of the free lists $FL[1..q], q = n - k$ is an array of pointers to the free list elements and may be defined by the C structure called *element* where the field *address* is a buddy address.

```
struct   element
     {struct element *PLink;
      int      address;
      struct element *NLink;
     };
```

Simulation definitions:

```
#define n 24 /* The memory size is $2^{24}$ */
#define k  8  /* The size of the smallest block is $2^8$*/
#define q n-k  /* There are 24-8 = 16 free lists */
#define FFA  'the first free address'
#define boolean int
typedef struct element *elemptr;
elemptr FL[q];
struct element head[q], tail[q];
```

Supporting functions: here we provide C pseudo-code to express functions composing the buddy system.

```
/* exp2(k): computes the expression 2^k */
int exp2(int k)
    {int j := 1; /* That is, j := 2^0 */
     j := j << k; /* That is, j := 2^0 * 2^k */
     return (j); /* That is, return 2^k */
     }


/* log2(size): computes the index of FL maintaining buddies of
size size */
int log2(int size)
    {int k := 0;  size := size - 1;
     while (size > 0)
         {
           size := size >> 1; k := k + 1;
         }
     if (k > m)
        return (k-m);
     else
        return (0);
    }


/* makeFL(): set the initial configuration of FL[1..q]*/
makeFL ()
      {int i;
       for (i = 0; i < q+1; i++)
           {
             FL[i] = List(head[i], tail[i]);
```

```
            head[i].address := 0;
            tail[i].address := 0;
          }
      i = Exp2(m+q);
      head[q].address = 1; tail[q].address := i;
      PrePend (FFA, i);
    }
```

```
/* searchBuddy(A,S): searches FL for the buddy of A of size */
    elemptr SearchBuddy(buddy, size)
    int  buddy, size;
    {elemptr tempptr;
     boolean searched := false;
     int k := log2(size); tempptr := FL[k]->NLink;
     while (tempptr->NLink != null)
          {if (tempptr->address = buddy)
             {searched = true;
              break;
             }
           else
             tempptr = tempptr->NLink;
          }
       if (searched)
         return(tempptr);
       else  return(null);
    }
```

```
/* deleteBuddy(buddyptr): deletes (buddyptr) from FL */
    deleteBuddy(buddyptr)
    elemptr buddyptr;
    {buddyptr->PLink->NLink = buddyptr->NLink;
     buddyptr->NLink->PLink = buddyptr->PLink;
    }
```

```
/* prePendBuddy(A, S): prepends buddy address A on its FL */
    prePendBuddy(buddy, size)
    int buddy, size;
        {int k = Log2(size);
         elemptr temp;
```

```
        temp = (elemptr) malloc(sizeof(struct element));
        temp->address = buddy;
        temp->PLink = FL[k];
        temp->NLink = FL[k]->NLink;
        FL[k]->NLink->PLink = temp;
        FL[k]->NLink = temp;
        }

/* splitBuddy(A, S): splits the buddy A */
/* prepend second buddy on its FL[k] */
/* returns first buddy to satisfy memory request */
int splitBuddy(buddy, size)
    int buddy, size;
        {int buddy1, k;
         k = size >> 1;
         buddy1 = buddy + k;
         prePendBuddy(buddy1, k);
         return(buddy);
        }


/* composeBuddy(A1, A2): composes two buddies for a k of
addresses A1 and A2 */
/* into a new buddy for k + 1 and returns its address */
int   composeBuddy(buddy1, buddy2)
    int buddy1, buddy2;
        {if (buddy1 < buddy2)
            return (buddy1);
         else
            return (buddy2);
        }


/* getBuddy(): get memory service */
int   getBuddy (int size)
    {elemptr tempptr;
     int i, j, k, s, buddy1, buddy2, splitBuddy();
     k = log2(size); i = k;
```

```
    while (i <= p)
        {tempptr = FL[i]->NLink->NLink;
         if (tempptr != null)
           break;
         else i = i + 1;
        }
    if (i > p)
      buddy1 = -1;
    else
      {buddy1 = FL[i]->NLink->address;
       deleteBuddy(FL[i]->NLink);
       for (j = i; j > k; j--)
         {s = exp2 (m + j);
          buddy2 = splitBuddy(buddy1, s);
          buddy1 = buddy2;
         }
      }
    return(buddy1);
    }

/* freeBuddy(): frees memory service */
freeBuddy(int address, int size)
  {elemptr tempptr, SearchBuddy();
   int rest, divider, sz, buddy1, buddy2, ComposeBuddy();
   buddy1 = address; sz = size;
   divider = size << 1; rest = (address % divider);
   if (rest = 0)
     buddy2 = address + size;
   else
     buddy2 = address - size;
   tempptr = SearchBuddy(buddy2, size);
   while (tempptr != null)
       {deleteBuddy(tempptr);
        buddy1 = composeBuddy(buddy1, buddy2);
        sz = divider;
        divider = divider << 1;
        rest = (buddy1 % divider);
        if (rest = 0)
          buddy2 = buddy1 + sz;
```

```
        else
          buddy2 = buddy1 - sz;
        tempptr = searchBuddy(buddy2, sz);
        }
  prePendBuddy(buddy1, sz);
  }
```

Contrast: memory control unit (in hardware) defines a generic data type on the physical memory specified by:

$$Memory = \langle Array\ of\ Location, StoreFetch, Fetch, Store \rangle$$

Memory management system defines a generic data type on memory abstraction specified by:

$$Memory = \langle FreeLists, getMemory(), freeMemory() \rangle$$

Chapter 11

I/O Device Management System

As in the case of processor and memory, to manipulate I/O devices by program they need to be represented as data. To develop a device data representation we first look at the device functional characterization.

An I/O devise is characterized by:

(1) The information carrier, i.e., the physical medium on which information is recorded;

(2) The Record of Information on the Carrier (RIC), i.e., the unit of information recorded on the carrier;

(3) The structure of the records on the carrier, also called the FILE type organized on the carrier. This structure has a double existence, as seen be the computer user on the information carrier, called here Device External File, and as seen be the processor in computer memory, called here Device Internal File.

(4) Operations performed by the device.

The information carrier allows us to classify the I/O devices of a hardware system in classes. All I/O devices with the same information carrier constitutes a class of I/O devices. For example, all magnetic tape units constitute the class of magnetic tapes and all disk drive units constitute the class of disk drives. The individual devices within a class perform I/O operations. The goal of looking at device classes rather that individual devices is to simplify the design of Input/Output Management System (IOMS). Hence the I/O devices are represented as data using a two-level linked list: a linked list of *Device Class Descriptors* (DCD) and a linked list of *Device Descriptors* (DC). The DCD is a data structure which records the characteristics of a class of devices. The DD is a data structure which records the characteristics of a single device in a class of devices. That is, each I/O device in a class is maintained in a DD on the linked list that has as header the DCD of the class to which the I/O device belongs.

11.1   Protocol for Device Usage

I/O devices perform destructive operations. That is, during the information exchange, the information held in a memory area is destroyed by an input operation whose target is that memory area, and the information on the device carrier record is destroyed by an output operation whose target is that device carrier record. Therefore I/O operations need to be performed under the control of the OS using the following protocol of I/O device use:

(1) Acquire the device;
(2) Use the device once acquired;
(3) Release the device when no longer in use.

Facts:

(1) The protocol of I/O device use must be strictly observed by each program that needs to use I/O devices.
(2) Programming languages implement the protocol of I/O device use providing appropriate libraries of I/O operations, such as <stdio.h> in C.
(3) The protocol is usually implemented in the I/O library by a sequence of three operations performed by the functions called **open, use** i.e., doIO, and close.

I/O device use, i.e., doIO, is diversified by the kind of information exchange the device can be involved in. For examples, under Unix we have characters, formatted data types, lines, files.

11.2   Efiles and Ifiles

A program uses I/O devices to transfer information from the environment to the system and vice versa. The program specifies the devices involved in its I/O operations as computing abstractions which are usually referred to as files. We refer to these abstractions by their names called *file names.* The file names that appear in the user programs denote computing abstractions which live in the programs not in the hardware system. Therefore we call them here *external files*, or Efile-s. An information carrier that is the actual target of an I/O operation lives in the hardware system and is called an *internal file*, Ifile or device file.

An Efile is a (potentially infinite) ordered collection of abstract data records. The abstract data records that are the elements of an Efile are similar to the record of the information carrier (RIC) of a given class of I/O devices. For example, a string of characters that ends with CR (LF) is the record of information characterizing the keyboard. An Efile is defined by a File Descriptor (FD) which specifies: the class of I/O devices that accommodate such information carrier, information record type, order relation among the records on a file of that type, access methods to the records. Various systems can standardize File Descriptors. For example, in Unix a FD is standardized by the keyword FILE and we refer to it as the FILE data type.

An Ifile is an ordered collection of physical records on the information carrier of an I/O device. For example, a collection of disk sectors on a disk is such an Ifile. The I/O records of an Ifile are the objects of the actual input/output operations. The information records in an Ifile are device-dependent and are specified by descriptors, such as device class descriptors or device descriptors.

Facts:

- Programmers operate on Efile-s while the actual information represented in an Efile resides in a device file of the system.
- A program can execute I/O operations only if its Efile-s are bound to devices on which similar Ifile-s are maintained.
- The binding of an Efile to a similar Ifile is called *opening an Efile* (defined by the user program) on an Ifile (defined by the system).

11.3 Information

The information processed by a computer system can be transient or persistent. Transient information is the information that lives in the system *only* during the life of the process that processes it. For example, data stored in memory during program execution disappear when process performing the program terminates. Persistent information is the information that survives the process that processes it. For examples, program performed by a process may be persistent, that it, it may have a disk copy which allows the system to perform it repeatedly. In addition, the results of a computation performed by a process may be persistent, i.e., they must survive the process termination.

Persistent information is maintained in the system on Ifiles (device files). In order to be processed Ifiles must be created on devices and their Efile names must be known. To access information in an Ifile the program (programmer) must know its Efile name and must have access rights to it. Examples persistent information in Unix system are:

(1) The Ifile processed by a LMS is known to the processing program as an Efile (the Efile name is in the program home directory) and it must be readable.
(2) The Ifile that contains the program performed by the LMS is known to the system and the shell can use its Efile name (such as a.out) to create the appropriate process.
(3) The Ifiles that contain the information in the lists created by the LMS must be created by the program and their Efile names must be written in the appropriate directories.

11.4   File Abstraction

To manipulate files (Efile in the program and Ifile in the system) the operating system represents them as abstractions defined by the tuple:

$$File = \langle FileName, FileType, Operations \rangle$$

where:

(1) FileName is a name that uniquely identifies the file;
(2) FileType is a file descriptor (FD) that specifies the structure of the information in the file;
(3) Operations are the operations that can be performed on the file, such as read, write, execute, etc.

Efile are declared by programmer in her source program using PL conventions. Ifiles are created by system calls issued by software tools (such as editors) or by user programs. The structure of an Ifile creation system call should be: `makeFile(Name, Carrier, accessRights, acceessMethod)`. Different operating systems may use different system calls for file creation.

11.4.1 *File creation in Unix*

The Unix system calls that create Ifiles are: `create (pathName, mode)` and `open (pathName, Flags, mode)` where:

(1) `pathName` is the Efile name used to access the information it contains;
(2) `mode` defines the operations to be performed on the file (read, write, read/write);
(3) `Flags` describe right-restrictions (read-only, write-only, etc.) to the information in the file.

All files in Unix are created on disk, hence no need to specify it [Googheart and Cox (1994)]. A program or interactively a computer user creates an Ifile using an `open()` whose syntax synopsis is `open(FileName, FileType, ModeOfOperation)`. In general, when this calls is encountered in a program it is processed by a system function which performs the following actions:

(1) Search for the device class specified by the FD of the *EfileType*; if not found suspend the program. Since Unix Ifiles are either standard input (the keyboard of the terminal), the standard output (the terminal screen), or the disk, this action is a case-statement in Unix.
(2) Search device class found in (1) for a free device; if not found enqueue the calling program at the device class.
(3) Associate the device discovered in (2) with the `FileName` contained in the call. This is done by linking a copy of the FD of the `EfileType` with the DD discovered in (2) using appropriate pointers.

Example open() in Unix are:

```
#include <fcntl.h>
int fd; /* FD in C is an integer (index in the file table) */
int open(char *name, int flags, int perms);
fd = open(name, flags, perms);
```

and

```
FILE *fp, *fopen(char *name, char *mode);
fp = fopen (name, mode);
```

Note that `open()` is a system call used by `fopen()` and is well documented in the C language standard [Kernighan and Ritchie (1988)].

11.4.2 *Using I/O devices*

Efile-s can be subject to I/O operations only after they are opened. The I/O operations are expressed (in the program) on Efiles but they are carried out on the associated Ifile. I/O operations are initiated by machine instructions in the user program. The generic form of the machine language instruction performing an I/O request is doIO (FileName, Amount, Destination, Semaphore). This instruction specifies an I/O request to the device bound by to the FileName by a previous open() operation. Note that during an IO operation the information carrier of the device may be shared in mutual-exclusion (by locking and unlocking it). The parameters FileName, Amount, Destination are as usual. The Semaphore is used for the synchronization with the control processor executing the operation. Hence, the execution of doIO() requires the following services from software:

(1) Organize the parameters in the doIO() operation as a structure called the Input-Output Record Block (IORB);
(2) Send the IORB thus constructed to the device as a record in the queue of requests waiting to be serviced by the device.

Fact: The device itself is controlled by a program called the *device driver* which operates on the device descriptor. The generic form of a device driver in the language of actions is:

```
DeviceDriver::
local DD: Pointer to DeviceDescriptor,
   Queue: queue of IORB, Temp: IORB;
   l_0: repeat
      l_1: await (DD->Queue not empty):^l_1;
           l_2: Temp = Next(DD->Queue); StartIO(Temp):^l_2;
                l_3: await (IO Completion); TerminateIO:^l_3;
      :^l_0 forever
```

However, this arrangement of a device driver leads to inefficient use of the I/O processor which starts the I/O operation and waits for its termination. The functions composing the device driver are Next(), StartIO(), and TerminateIO. The Next(DD− >Queue) moves the next IORB from the devise waiting queue Queue into a temporary IORB called Temp. The StartIO(Temp) starts the I/O operation specified in the IORB Temp. At this point the requesting process can be suspended until the event "IO Completion" occurs. The TerminateIO moves data from the device buffer into memory when the event "IO Completion" occurs. Other house-cleaning actions are also possible at this time.

Devices should be made available to other programs after the completion of the current information exchange operation. This is done by close() function which removes the link between the Efile and the Ifile established by the open(). The syntax of the close() call in Unix is close(FileName). The function close(FileName) searches for the DD associated with FD by *open(FileName)*, removes the association $DD \leftrightarrow FD$ set by open(FileName), and switches the device status to free.

11.5   Device Data Structure

As mentioned above, the device data representation is the Device Data Structure (DDS), a two-level linked list that consists of a linked list of DCD-s where each DCD has as records a linked lists of DD-s within a device class. Each Device Descriptor (DD) contains:

(1) A pointer to the queue of input-output request blocks (IORB) waiting to be serviced by the device;
(2) A pointer to the DeviceDriver action performing the I/O operations requested to the device;
(3) A pointer to the file descriptor (FD) of the Ifile on which the device operates..

The C language expression of a DD is:

```
typedef  void * (*Driver)(void *)
struct DeviceDescriptor
       {
         char    State;
         struct FD *ToFD;
         struct IORB *ToIORB;
         Driver DeviceDriver (void *);
         struct DeviceDescriptor *ToNEXT;
       };
```

The C language expression of a DCD is:

```
typedef  void * (*AccessMethod)(void *)
struct DeviceClassDescriptor
       {
```

```
    struct DeviceClassDescriptor *Nlink, *Plink;
    char  *ClassName;
    char  *ClassStatus;
    struct DeviceDescriptor *ToFirstDV;
    struct InfoRecord *ToInfoRecord;
    AccessMethod accessMethod (void *);
    struct Operations  *ToOperations;
};
```

The C expression, of the DDS is:

```
struct DDSHeadTail
{
 struct DeviceClassDescriptor *Plink;
 int Value;
 struct DeviceClassDescriptor *Nlink;
};
```

Note that `Value` field of the `DDSHead` may contain the maximum number of device classes supported by the system and `Value` field of the `DDSTail` may contain the number of device classes currently attached to the system. Figure 11.1 shows a graphic representation of the device data structure.

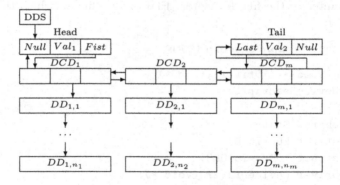

Fig. 11.1   Device Data Structure, DDS

The implementations of a DDS is sketched here by the action `CreateDDS`:

```
CreateDDS::
 in m: integer where m = |Device Classes|,
```

```
DVC: array[1..m] of integer where DVC[i] = |DeviceClass[i]|;
local DDS: pointer to DDSHeadTail,
  DDSHead, DDSTail: DDSHeadTail,
  DCD: array[1..m] of DeviceClassDescriptor,
  DD: DeviceDescriptor, ToDD: pointer to DeviceDescriptor,
  i,j,k: integer where i = 1, j = 1, k = 1;
  DDS = MakeList (DDSHead, DDSTail);
  1_0: while (i <= m) append (DDS, DCD[i]); i := i + 1:^1_0
  1_1: while (j <= m) do
    1_2: while (k <= DVC[j]) do
    ToDD:=GetMemory(sizeof(DD));Attach(DDS,j,ToDD);k:=k+1;
    :^1_2
    k := 1; j := j + 1
  :^1_1
```

The action **CreateDDS** uses the list management system to create a DDS at system initiation time.

11.6   Performing I/O Operations

The protocol of I/O operation use in a program consists of:

Define the external file **FileName** of type **EfileType** where **EfileType** is given in the programming language used to express the computation. For example, EfileType in Unix is defined by the declaration **FILE *f;**.

Open the external file **FileName** which is an abstraction that contains the information to be exchanged with the system. For example, in Unix this is done by the assignment **f = fopen("FileName", "mode");**.

Issue I/O requests through appropriate **doIO()** operations. For example, using the keyboard and the screen in Unix:

```
printf("\nInput a file name: "); /* output to the screen */
scanf("%s", fileName); /* input a typed string in fileName */
```

doIO() is usually translated by the compiler which generates two things:

(1) An **IOprogram** to be performed by the device. Let **IOprogAddr** be the address of this program.

(2) A machine instruction in the program where **doIO()** is located that has the goal to initiate the execution of the **IOprogram**. This instruction is usually a pattern of the form **startIO,DvAddr IOprogAddr**.

The `IOprogram`, whose address is `IOprogAddr`, is standard and is constructed by the compiler. It usually contains: the code of the I/O operation to be executed by the device, the quantity of information the device is asked to exchange by the respective I/O operation, if any, and the address of the memory location where the information is stored, or from where information is fetched. The `DvAddr` is the device address which is one of: a number, an address containing a number, or a dedicated memory location identifying a specific device in the system. The device activation is performed by control processor during its operation cycle that interprets the instruction `StartIO,DvAddr IOprogAddr`. The instruction representing an I/O operation is fetched by the control processor (as usual). The control processor selects the I/O processor encoded in `DvAddr` to execute the I/O operation and transmits the `IOprogram` at the address `IOprogAddr` to that processor. The I/O processor activates the I/O device addressed by `DvAddr` to perform the `IOprogram` at the address `IOprogAddr`.

There are three approaches to addressing a device: direct addressing, channel addressing, and memory addressing. Direct addressing is used when the device is controlled by the CPU. In this case the `DvAddr` is a binary number encoded in the instruction. Channel addressing is used when device operates under the control of an I/O processor called the Channel. Usually in this case the device is identified by a tuple ⟨*ChannelNumber, DeviceNumber*⟩ which is encoded as the contents of the memory address `DvAddr` provided in the instruction. Memory addressing is used when devices are memory mapped. In this case `DvAddr` is the address of a *dedicated memory location* (or a control register). In this case the operations of device initiation, I/O execution, and I/O completion are usual operations on that memory location.

11.7   Examples of I/O Programming

We examine I/O devices with direct addressing, I/O channel, and memory mapped [Rus and Rus (1993)].

11.7.1   *I/O with direct addressing*

I/O operations are executed by the CPU as any other ordinary operations. Mix machine is a good illustration of this. The binary pattern representing a Mix machine I/O operation is shown in Figure 11.2. When the device

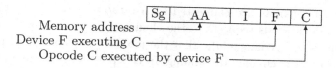

Fig. 11.2   Mix I/O instruction-word

completes its operation it raises a flag. The termination of the I/O operation is tested either within the same operation cycle or by a special Test DeVice status operation, TDV. Mix processor tests the termination of I/O operations by an explicit test device status operation which checks the device's flag. The communication between control processor and I/O device is performed by the following instructions:

- **Start device:** Mix machine has two such operations, IN, for reading information, and OUT, for writing information.
- **Test device:** Mix machine uses JBUS (*jump if device is busy*) and JRED (*jump if device is ready*).
- **Control operations:** Mix machine uses IOC. For example, to move a read-head to a given track on a disk, one writes: IOC, DiskNr, TrackNr.

The amount of information involved in an I/O operation in not specified since it is equal to the size of the record of the information carrier (RIC). For example, an 80 column card reader will always read 80 characters, a 120 characters line printer will always print 120 characters; the head of a 100 words sector disk will read/write 100 memory words. MIXAL [Peterson (1978)] is the assembly language of MIX machine. MIX machine I/O devices are identified by binary numbers that are codified on the F field of the MIX instruction. MIXAL I/O operations are:

```
[Label]  IN   Address (Device);
[Label]  OUT  Address (Device);
[Label]  IOC  Address (Device);
[Label]  JBUS Address (Device);
[Label]  JRED Address (Device);
```

11.7.2   *I/O with channel addressing*

The I/O processor called the channel has been invented to release the control processor from the burden of controlling I/O operations. Control processor and the channel are connected by a *master*⟷*slave* relation. The control processor sends requests to the channel. The channel executes the requests and sends signals telling that the job has been done. Control processor activates the channel by sending an I/O program. Channel initiates the I/O device to execute the I/O program and controls its execution. Upon completion of the I/O program, channel sends an interrupt signal to the control processor. A graphic image of this relationship is in Figure 11.3.

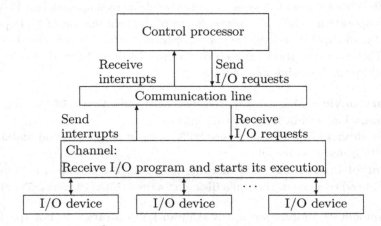

Fig. 11.3   Channel communication protocol

To free the control processor of the burden of moving information among device buffers and memory, the channel is provided with Direct Memory Access (DMA). To control the I/O operation, the channel has two main registers: an *I/O program counter* and an *I/O state register*. The channel I/O processor is illustrated by the architecture of the IBM 360/370.

The IBM-360/370 I/O State Register is called the Channel Status Word, CSW. CSW, Figure 11.4, is similar to PSW of IBM 360/370 and is assigned to the dedicated memory address 0064. The I/O Program Counter in IBM-360/370 is called the Channel Address Word, CAW, and is assigned at dedicated memory address 0072, Figure 11.5. Each I/O operation is structured as a Channel Command Word, CCW, Figure 11.6. An IO program (called channel program) is a sequence of CCWs. A CCW is always allocated at a double-word of address $8k$ for some integer k. The bytes $8k$, $8k+1$, $8k+2$, $8k+3$, $8k+4$, $8k+5$, $8k+6$, $8k+7$ are the bytes of the double word representing this CCW. The Opcode is the code of the I/O operation codified

PK	0000	Address of CCW executed		
64	65	66		67
Status info		Byte counter		
68	69	70		71

Fig. 11.4   Channel Status Word, CSW

PK	0000	Next CCW to be executed	
72	73	74	75

Fig. 11.5   Channel Address Word, CAW

Opcode	Memory data address		
$8k$	$8k+1$	$8k+2$	$8k+3$
Flags NU	Byte counter		
$8k+4$	$8k+5$	$8k+6$	$8k+7$

Fig. 11.6   Channel Command Word

by the CCW. The memory data address is a physical address in memory where (or from where) data is directed by the operation represented by the Opcode. The byte counter shows the number of bytes involved in the operation. NU stands for "Not Used", that is, the bits 37, 38, 39, 40 of the CCW are not used. The bits 32, 33, 34, 35, 36 of CCW are directives to the channel, called *flags*:

Bit 32 *called chain data*, tells Channel to interpret next CCW of IO program as the data extension of current CCW;

Bit 33, *called chain command*, tells Channel to interpret the next CCW of IO program as a new I/O operation, i.e., upon completion of current operation, channel performs 0072 := (0072) + 0008;

Bit 34, *called suppress length*, asks the channel to suppress the signaling of an incorrect length. This is done in conjunction with CSW;

Bit 35, *called skip flag*, asks the channel to skip to the CCW with the address contained in the current CCW, i.e., to perform 0072 := (CCW).Bits[8..31];

Bit 36, *called programmed interrupt*, asks the channel to generate an interrupt.

Channel executes I/O program in sequence if the CCW.Bit[33] is set and performs a branch to a given CCW if CCW.Bit[35] is set. The control processor activates a channel by storing the address of the channel program in the location 0072 and by sending an I/O request. The I/O requests are machine language instructions with the opcodes SIO,HIO,TIO,TDV where:

- Start I/O, SIO, tells the channel to start the execution of the I/O operation whose CCW address is the location 0072.
- Halt I/O, HIO, tells the channel to halt the execution of the current I/O operation.
- Test I/O, TIO, tests the state of the channel. The result is stored in CC and can be used in test and branch operations.
- Test I/O device, TDV, tests the state of a device. The result is stored in CC and can be used in test and branch operations.

Graphic, an IBM instruction of an I/O request is shown in Figure 11.7. The

Opcode	Unused	Base	Displacement
$k+1$	$k+2$	$k+3$	$k+4$

Fig. 11.7   I/O request format

instruction opcode is one of SIO, HIO, TIO, TDV. Base and Displacement specifies the address of a memory location where the address of device is stored. Let B and D be the base register and the displacement encoded in the I/O instruction. Then the device address is computed as shown in Figure 11.8 Note that at most 256 channels and at most 256 devices on

$C(B) + D$	Unused	Channel	Device
k	$k+1$	$k+2$	$k+3$

Fig. 11.8   I/O Device address

every channel can be used with the IBM 360/370 architecture. Channel's instruction cycle performs as follows:

(1) Executes I/O operation codified in the CCW;

(2) Upon completion, based on the flags in current CCW do:

- If CCW.Bit[32]=1 continue operation execution taking the new count from CCW + 8.
- If CCW.Bit[33]=1 perform $CAW := (CAW) + 8$.
- If CCW.Bit[35]=1 perform $CAW := CCW.Bits[8..32]$.
- Otherwise initiates an interrupt telling that operation is complete.

Channel programming requires the programmer to performs the following actions:

(1) Design a channel program as a sequence of CCW-s;

(2) Construct device address as seen in Figure 11.8;

(3) Load the address of the first CCW into the CAW (0072);

(4) Issue a SIO on the device address.

The assembly language provides support for IO programming. We illustrate channel programming with the following examples:

Example 1: write a channel program to flush the cards in a card reader until the end of file. The channel program which executes this operation is:

```
CCW1  READ, BUF1; ChainData, 72;
CCW2  NOP, BUF2;  ChainCCW, 8;
CCW3  NOP, CCW1;  JUMP, 0;
BUF1  DS C 72;    BUF2  DS C 8;
```

Assuming that the card reader is the second device on the first channel, its address is defined by the assembly language declaration CardReader DC X'00000102';. To prepare the channel to execute the above program, the programmer writes in her program the sequence: LA R1, CCW1; ST R1, CAW;. Then the programmer write the code: SIO CardReader that when executed by the processor will start the I/O program.

Example 2: write a channel program to print a message on the current page, ejects page, and then print a header on top of the next page. The channel program is:

```
CCW1  PRINT, MESSAGE; ChainCCW,  =F'11';
CCW2  PRINTH, HEADER; NOP, =F'15';
MESSAGE  DS C'END OF PAGE'; HEADER  DS C'TOP OF NEW PAGE';
```

assuming that printer is the 4th device on channel 1 and can execute PRINT and PRINTH: the programmer defines the printer by the declaration

PRINTER DC X'00000104'; To prepare the channel to execute the above I/O program the programmer writes in her program the sequence: LA R1, CCW1; ST R1, CAW;. Then she issues the I/O request: SIO PRINTER. Note that the mnemonics DS and DC stand for define storage and define constant.

11.7.3 *Memory mapped devices*

The PDP-11 identifies every device in the system through a pair of two-byte memory locations called the Device Status, DS, and Device Buffer, DB. For a given device, DS and DB are dedicated memory locations in the architecture, as were CSW and CAW in IBM 360/370 architecture. The device operations are defined as follows: Read:DataCarrier $\Longrightarrow$ DB; Write:DB $\Longrightarrow$ DataCarrier. Operations on DS and DB are interpreted as operations on the device they represent. For example, if DS and DB are two bytes locations denoted by DS1, DS2 and DB1, DB2, respectively then we have:

$$DS1 = \begin{cases} 00000000, & \text{if the device is ready;} \\ 00000001, & \text{if I/O request is initiated;} \\ 10000001, & \text{if device is ready for next operation.} \end{cases}$$

The operation completion status is represented by DS2 and is defined as follows:

$$DS2 = \begin{cases} 00000000, & \text{if the operation completed correctly;} \\ 10000000, & \text{if an error occurred during operation.} \end{cases}$$

During the operation cycle hardware interprets DS1 and DS2 as follows:

```
if DS1 =  0 the device is idle;
if DS1 =  1 initiate device operation;
if DS1 >= 0 the device is busy operating;
if DS1 < 0 the device is ready for the next operation;
if DS2 < 0 erroneous operation;
if DS2 >= 0 no error in operation
```

Note that only bit 0 in DS1, bit 7 in DS1, and bit 7 in DS2 are significant; they are called INIT, READY, and ERROR respectively. Hence, device status is characterized by the tuple DS = ⟨ERROR, READY, INIT⟩ This provides easy programming of the operations it can perform.

Read Operation: the start condition is $DS = \langle 0,0,0 \rangle$.

```
DS = <0, 0, 0> the device is idle;
DS = <0, 0, 1> initiate device operation;
DS = <0, 1, 0> the operation has completed without error;
DS = <1, 1, 0> the operation has completed with error.
```

Hardware performs automatically:

When INIT:=1 the device starts reading the information from its info carrier.

Upon completion, device sets READY:=1; if successful ERROR:=0, otherwise ERROR:=1.

When a fetch from DB is performed hardware sets READY:=0, signaling that the next character can be read.

Graphic this is shown by the Figure 11.9. Consequently system program-

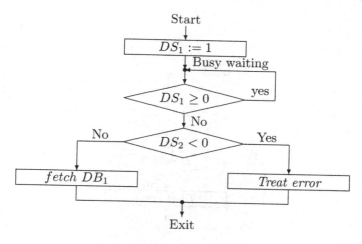

Fig. 11.9   Flow diagram of read operation

mers can treat the variables DS and DB in their programs as global variables. The system generator binds the variables DS and DB to device physical addresses.

Write Interpretation: for the write operation the tuple $DS = \langle ERROR, READY, INIT \rangle$ is interpreted as follows:

```
DS = <0, 0, 0> the device is not ready for operation;
DS = <0, 1, 0> the device is ready to write;
DS = <0, 0, 1> the  device is writing;
DS = <0, 1, 0> the operation has completed without error;
DS = <1, 1, 0> the operation has completed with error.
```

Hardware perform automatically:

If $DS = \langle 0, 1, 0 \rangle$ and data is stored in DB1, the device starts sending it to its information carrier and sets READY to 0. Hence, during device operation DS1 $\geq$ 0.

When operation has completed, the hardware sets READY to 1 and thus DS1 < 0.

If the operation is erroneous then ERROR is set 1, otherwise ERROR is set to 0. Hence, DS2 $\geq$ 0 means no error occurred and DS2 < 0 means an error occurred during data transfer.

Graphic this is shown by Figure 11.10 To free the control processor of

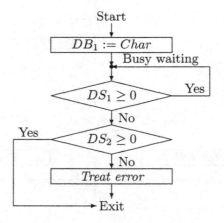

Fig. 11.10 Flow diagram of write operation

the burden of waiting for an operation completion, an I/O processor can also be provided in this type of architecture. I/O processor (when present) executes I/O programs while the control processor performs other activities in parallel. Such an I/O processor is similar to a channel and is usually implemented by a microprocessor.

Chapter 12

Computation Activity and Its Management Tools

Unlike other computer resources, which are tangible entities and require management tools, computation performed by a computer platform is not tangible. It is a dynamic abstraction observable through the effect the events that occur during a computation task have on the other resources of the system. For example, an interrupt event may result in a switch-context operation (see section 9.8), an exception may result in the increase or decrease of the resources allocated to the currently running program, a message may result in complete change of computation configuration. Therefore, software tools that manage computation activity actually manipulate the events that may occur during computation and have the goal to preserve computation consistency and to maintain the computer busy as long as possible.

12.1 Events

The events which a computing system is designed to be sensitive at belong to the computer architecture and are called interrupts and exceptions. Interrupts are generated outside the computing task performed by the processor i.e., outside of the Run action, see Chapter 8, and thus occur asynchronous with this task. Exceptions are generated by the computing task, i.e., by the Run action, performed by the processor and thus occur synchronous with this task. The occurrence of an event may have as the side effect the interruption of the task performed by the processor in order to treat the event. The events are treated by the interrupt system, which consists of a collection of functions in the system software designed to handle the effect events may have on the computation performed by the processor. Therefore, the major behavior of the interrupt system is defined in terms of the *computing activity* performed by the computer system and of the events that may interrupt this activity.

The events that can occur during process execution are defined by the interaction between the processor and its environment. The mechanism of this interaction is part of the processor physical structure. That is, the hardware system is designed so that the processor is sensitive to a given collection of interrupt agents that can signal the processor during its activity. Interrupting events are recorded (synchronous or asynchronous with instruction cycle) using appropriate registers, usually components of the PSW. Instruction cycle is designed such that the processor, through the function Next() (see Chapter 8) checks certain registers before starting a new instruction cycle. These registers are signaled by external agents (that belong to the processor environment) synchronously or asynchronously with the current processor activity. Upon the receipt of such a signal, the processor *may* interrupt its current activity, and, depending upon the priority of the signal, it *may* start treating the respective signal.

12.1.1   *Interrupt event characterization*

An interrupt event is characterized by three elements: the agent which issued the event, the effect of the event on the current process, and the effect of the event on the PDS.

The interrupting agent is identified by an Interrupt Identification Code (IIC), usually a number, stored into a dedicated register that usually belongs to the PSW. A hardware mechanism associated with IIC (for example a code stored into a dedicated register) allows the system to recognize it. When IIC is preserved in PSW, the simplest method to treat such an agent consists of two dedicated memory locations: OldPSW, where PSW of current process is saved, and NewPSW, where the PSW of the process treating the interrupt event is stored. Since IIC is usually part of PSW, it can be discovered in OldPSW.

When an interrupt signal is received and accepted, OldPSW allows the processor to automatically save the state of the currently executing process. Since the IIC belongs to the state, it is saved in the OldPSW. The NewPSW allows the processor to automatically fetch the PSW of a predefined process designed to recognize the interrupting agent and start treating the interrupt signals issued by the agent. Since OldPSW is predefined, it is available to the process initiated by NewPSW, hence this process can treat the interrupt identified by IIC. The effect of an interrupt event on the processor could be one of:

(1) Processor interrupts its current activity performing automatically:

```
OldPSW := PSW;
PSW := NewPSW
```

(2) Processor leaves the interrupt event pending and continues;
(3) Processor ignores the interrupt event.

The effect of an interrupt event on the PDS could be one of:

(1) Change the state of one or more processes in the PDS. For example, if the completion of an I/O requested by process P1 interrupts, the PCB(P1) in PDS may undergo a transition from **Suspended** to **Ready**.
(2) Leave process state in PDS unchanged. For example,if power-off happens, current state off all processes in PDS should be preserved.

There are two classes of processes in the PDS: user processes and system processes. User processes are those that perform computations requested by system users; system processes are those that provide services to user or system processes. The effect of interrupt events on the two classes of processes is different. However it is accomplished by the same hardware and software mechanisms. Hence, the two classes of processes in PDS must be carefully differentiated. PMS can differentiate between the two classes of processes by assigning them different Process Identification Numbers (PID)-s.

12.1.2   *Examples interrupt agents*

We identified two classes of interrupt agents: asynchronous with processor instruction cycle (called interrupts) and synchronous with processor instruction cycle called exceptions. Since the two classes of interrupt agents are different, they need to be treated differently, though the mechanism of treatment is the same.

Common interrupt agents are: computer user, power off, other interrupt agents.PDS must contain low priority processes whose state could be changed to blocked by any interrupt event. Examples such processes are:

• a process which does nothing specified by the action

```
DoNothingLoop::
   l_: repeat
```

```
    skip; /* waiting for something to happen */ \\
  1_0 forever
```

- a process which computes the next decimal digit of π,
- a process playing a new chess game with somebody,
- a process working on a new musical composition;
- a process writing a new poems, etc.

When an interrupt event occurs, the process currently being executed may undergo a state transition. The processor identifies the interrupting agent in two steps:

- during instruction cycle processor checks special registers for synchronous or asynchronous signals;
- the identification code of the interrupting agent is stored into another special register (usually in PSW); if it belongs to the state, it can be discovered later.

When the interrupting agent has a higher priority than that of the current process the current process is interrupted, i.e., a switch context is performed, and a new process that treats the interrupt event is initiated. Remember, software system differentiates between two kinds of interrupts: external interrupts or simply interrupts, which are initiated outside of the current process and internal interrupts or exceptions, which are initiated by the current process.

While the interrupts are usually treated by system processes with increased rights to the computer resources, exceptions are treated by processes (system or user) with the same rights as the interrupted process. According to the stage reached by the instruction cycle when an exception arrives, exceptions are usually classified as follows:

- **System calls:** are service requests issued by the running process. System calls are identified by a special machine operation which generates the interruption action, (originally called supervisory call, SVC) whose parameters determine the service requested. The service is performed by a predefined procedure in the software.
- **Traps:** operations that violates their algorithms. Examples are overflows and underflows. However, any machine operation which is hardware defined, but whose execution violates its definition, is a trap.

- **Faults:** operations that cannot be terminated, The operands of the operation may not be available. Example is page fault in systems with virtual memory.
- **Aborts:** operations that are undefined either in the hardware or in the software, hence such an operation is illegal and process must be aborted. Example of abort is memory violation.

12.2 Computing Activity

Computing activity of a computer system is accomplished by the processor of a computer platform from its initiation and consists of a continuous sequence of computing tasks performed between switch context operations. Recall that switch context operations (see section 9.8) are performed on process data structure, PDS. PDS is composed of PCB-s of the processes competing for execution. Each $PCB_i \in PDS$ represents a process $P_i = \langle Processor, Program_i, State_i \rangle$ where $Processor$ is the control processor that executes computations encoded in the $Program_i$, and $State_i$ is the status of its execution, $i = 1, 2, \ldots, k$.

The main process states of a process during computing activity are:

- **Running:** processor registers contain the PCB.
- **Ready:** process has all the necessary resources allocated except the processor, so the process is ready to run but it is not yet running. The process state could be $ReadyIn$, that is the process waits for execution in main memory, or the process state could be $ReadyOut$, that is, the process waits for execution in the external memory, with its PCB residing in main memory.
- **Blocked:** the process execution is suspended. Again, the process state could be $BlockedIn$, that is, the process is suspended in the main memory, or it could be $BlockedOut$, that is, the process is suspended in the external memory with its PCB residing in the main memory.

A computer process is characterized by its state transitions determined by the events that may occur during its life in the system. Considering the set $States = \{Running, ReadyIn, ReadyOut, BlockedIn, BlockedOut\}$ as the process states and the set $Events = \{Interrupt, Exception\}$ as events that can happen during process life in the system, process state transitions can be seen as mappings $Transition : S \times E \rightarrow S, S \in States, E \in Events$, and are shown in the diagram in Figure 12.1. In a real system both $States$ and $Events$ are refined and the process state transition diagram becomes much

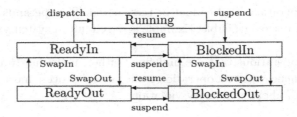

Fig. 12.1   Process state transition diagram

more complex. The process state transition is implemented by the execution of some operation of process data type on the PCB representing the respective process, see Figure 12.1. These operations have been introduced in Chapter 9, and are reviewed here as follows:

- **dispatch(PCB)**: state of the process represented by PCB becomes **running** and ControlProcessor:= PCB.
- **suspend(PCB)**: state of the process represented by PCB becomes **blocked** and SwitchContext(PCB,PDS) is performed.
- **resume(PCB)**: state of the process represented by PCB becomes **ready**.
- **SwapOut(PCB)**, **SwapIn(PCB)**: process represented by PCB is swapped-out (swapped-in) while preserving its state.

Process states are usually implemented by queues of processes waiting for some event to happen in order to change state as appropriately. Examples such queues are:

- Processes waiting for an I/O device to become free;
- Processes waiting for a block of memory to become available;
- Processes waiting for the processor to become available.

12.2.1   *Process cycle*

The process cycle of a process P is measured by the time interval between **dispatch(PCB(P))** and **suspend(PCB(P))** (see Figure 12.1).

Tools handling computing activity of a computer system are independent of the actual computing tasks performed by the processor when an interrupting event occurs. Therefore we discuss these tools in terms of process cycles rather than computing tasks performed by the processor. To better understand the goal of these tools we need to contrast the two terms, *instruction cycle* and *process cycle*:

Instruction cycle (or processor cycle) is measured by the time interval processor takes to execute an instruction.

Process cycle is measured by the number of instructions cycles performed by the processor for a given process before a switch-context occurs.

For a given hardware architecture, instruction cycle is usually a constant (with small variations determined by instruction complexity) while the size of process cycle depends upon the process executed by the processor.

In other words, process cycle is measured by the number of instructions performed by the processor before an interrupting event occurs. Notice that a process can suspend itself asking for a service by issuing a `system call` (i.e.,an exception). The size of the process cycle determines the process granularity. The larger the process cycle of a process is the more coarse the process is considered and thus, the longer it may hold the processor during its execution.

Computing activity of a computing system consists of the continuous execution of process cycles where processes are selected for execution from the process data structure. The transitions among the states of various processes depend upon process granularity and the events that can occur during process execution. The states of processes in PDS change according to the dynamical events that generate process transitions and process cycles. The state transition happens when one of the following events occur:

(1) process relinquish the processor by suspending itself waiting for a service;

(2) process execution is interrupted by some internal event (synchronous) with process execution;

(3) process execution is interrupted by some external event (asynchronous) with process execution.

12.2.2   *Computation representation*

The computation performed by a computing system is thus represented by three components:

- The processor, viewed as a dynamic object executing processes.
- The process data structure, PDS, which is a queue of processes competing for the processor.

- A collection of interrupt agents which can attempt to interrupt the computation activity of the processor and thus may determine a state change of some processes in PDS.

The interaction between the three components of a computing system is shown in Figure 12.2.

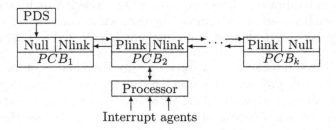

Fig. 12.2   Computing task of the processor

Computing activity of a computer system can thus be formalized by the following action called ComputingActivity:

```
ComputingActivity::
  in PDS : list of processes in any state;
  local PCB : Process Control Block;
  local PSW : register to receive interrupts;
  1_0: PCB:= NextProcess(PDS); ProcRegisters := PCB:1^0
   1_1: repeat
    1_2: ProcessCycle(PCB) || EventOccurrence(PSW) :1_2^
     /* Events in two sides of "||" may occur concurrently */
    1_3: if (Interrupt) Treat Interrupt(PSW);
         else if (Exception) Treat Exception (PSW);
         else SystemError; 1_3^
    1_:4 SwitchContext(PDS); 1_4^
   forever  :1_1^
```

Since PDS is never empty, user service requests are treated as interrupts and program termination is treated as an exception. We use the following notations in the action ComputingActivity:

- NextProcess(PDS) is a function that finds the PCB of a process from PDS satisfying some execution criteria (for example highest priority) and returns it.

- At label 1_3 the processor checks registers to find if it needs to handle an interrupt or the running process voluntarily suspends itself.
- Among the events that suspend a process execution is also the process completion. Therefore the computing activity performed by a processor continues as long as processor is plugged in and power is on.
- SystemError is an action that requires system maintenance.

This model of computation activity works for both uniprocessor and multiprocessor systems. However, when used for multiprocessor systems all processors operating on the same PDS must be similar. The model works for heterogeneous systems as well but a separate PDS is required for each class of similar processors.

12.2.3 *Priority levels*

Computer user is an agent that should be allowed to interrupt the computation activity performed by the processor. Since any user may have any number of processes in the system there is a potentially infinite number of processes competing for execution by processor. However, any computer architecture can support only a finite number of interrupting agents. Consequence is that the collection of processes competing for execution are split by their priorities into equivalence classes. A class of priority equivalent processes is characterized by a number called Interrupt Priority Level (IPL). If a priority level is associated with any process, the processes become interrupt agents. Therefore process execution can be treated as the processing of an interrupt signal sent by a process agent. Thus, computer users too become interrupt agents who send interrupt signals asking the processor to execute their programs. Since an interrupt handler is a process that may be interrupted, it has an IPL, which is a software component of the process performing a computation. On the other hand, a physical agent may have a priority which the agent can store in a dedicated register called Interrupt Priority Register (IPR) which is a hardware component of the processor. When the agent wants to send a message to the processor, it stores its priority number into this register. So, while IPL is a software component associated with the running process, the IPR is a hardware component associated with the agent. The relationship between IPL and IPR allows the interrupt system to manage a computation according to the agent and process priority. When $IPR > IPL$ the running process can be interrupted. The process executing an interrupt handler is not different from other processes. Therefore, IPL is associated with process execution. Hence, IPL organizes processes in the system on a hierarchy of priority levels, therefore the place of IPL is in the PSW.

12.3 Interrupt System

Interrupt system is discussed further using the systematic approach for ad hoc system construction described in Section 3.1. For reader convenience we review this approach here. It consists of iterating the steps:

(1) Define system's major behavior;
(2) Identify system's components;
(3) Specify each component's functional behavior;
(4) Provide an algorithmic expression of the system in terms of its components;

until system is well defined.

12.3.1 *Major behavior of interrupt system*

The major behavior of an interrupt system is to receive interrupt signals sent to the processor by various predefined agents, change processor state according to the interrupt signal received, initiate a system process called *interrupt handler* to handle the interrupt signal, update the PDS accordingly, and resume computation.

12.3.2 *Components of interrupt system*

The major behavior of the interrupt system is accomplished by hardware and software elements called here *interrupt system components*.

12.3.2.1 *Hardware Components*

A complete set of hardware components of an interrupt system are:

- An Interrupt Signal Register, ISR;
- An Interrupt Identification Register, IIR;
- A Save State Register, SSR;
- A New State Register, NSR;
- An Interrupt Control Register, ICR;
- An Interrupt Priority Register, IPR.

Interrupt Signal Register: IRS is a communications register which allows agent to send interrupt signals to the processor. ISR facilitates the receipt of an interrupt signal by the processor without affecting its current computing task. That is, the interrupt agent can set ISR at its own convenience while the processor checks it at the end of every instruction cycle.

Interrupt Identification Register: IIR accommodates the code that identifies the interrupt agent in a class of similar agents. When the class of similar agents recognized by IIR contains just one agent, the ISR may be used as IIR as well.

Note that ISR may be associated with a class of agents while IIR identifies an agent in this class. For example, there may be one ISR for all I/O devices while each device is identified by a particular code stored in the IIR.

Save State Register: The purpose of the SSR is to save the (partial) state of the process executing on the processor when the interrupt signal arrives and it is accepted. Recall that in the mechanism we suggested to perform a computation interruption the SSR was called the `OldPSW`. SSR must have room for IIR and PC, at least.

New State Register: The purpose of the NSR is to provide a gate to enter the interrupt system. Hence, the NSR is the PSW of the program that is initiated to treat the interrupts. Again, recall that in the mechanism we suggested to perform a computation interruption the NSR was called the `NewPSW`.

Interrupt Control Register: ICR provides a mechanism to control the interrupt signals. Functionally ICR can be defined by the equation:

$$ICR = \begin{cases} set, & \text{if interrupt identified by ISR and IIR is enabled;} \\ off, & \text{if interrupt identified by ISR and IIR is disabled.} \end{cases}$$

This means that by hardware an agent can send an interrupt signal setting its ISR. However, by software the signal sent by the agent can be disabled by appropriate setting of its ICR. That is, ICR is usually accessible to the program. This allows the interrupt system to enable/disable interrupt signals as required by the computation task performed by the processor.

Observations:

- A signaling agent associated with ICR has its signal stored in its ISR when the interrupt is enabled.

- If an interrupt is disabled then the interrupt signals sent by the agent associated with this ICR are not to be stored in its ISR.
- According to the interrupt system's philosophy, this signal could remain pending or it could be completely ignored.

Interrupt Priority Register: IPR provides a mechanism that allows an interrupt signal to interrupt an interrupt handler. That is, if IPR(CurrentProcess) $\geq$ IPR(InterruptingAgent) then the interrupt should not be allowed. On the other hand, if IPR(CurrentProcess) < IPR(InterruptingAgent) the interrupt signal has higher priority and interrupt should be allowed.

Fact is that due to optimization reasons, any particular computer platform may use only part of the equipment provided in this general model.

Hardware components of an interrupt mechanism are integrated by the instruction cycle. Instruction cycle is the generic procedure wired in hardware which recognizes and initiates treatment of interrupt signals as shown in Figure 12.3.

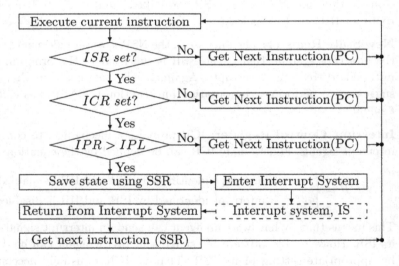

Fig. 12.3   Hardware components of interrupt system

The cost/efficiency trade-off determines the amount and the quality of hardware dedicated to interrupt systems. Since ISR and ICR registers are either set or off they can be one-bit registers. Thus, all ISR-s and ICR-s can be arranged as two fixed size registers called here the Register Recording Interrupt Signals (RRIS), and the Register Recording

Control Signals (RRCS), respectively. Thus, if $sizeof(RRIS) = n+1$, then $\forall i, 0 \le i \le n$

$$RRIS[i] = \begin{cases} 1, & \text{if interrupt agent } i \text{ has sent an interrupt signal;} \\ 0, & \text{if interrupt agent } i \text{ has not sent an interrupt signal.} \end{cases}$$

Similarly,

$$RRCS[i] = \begin{cases} 1, & \text{if interrupt signals from agent } i \text{ are enabled;} \\ 0, & \text{if interrupt signals from agent } i \text{ are disabled.} \end{cases}$$

Further, if agent priority is implemented by the position of its ISR, ICR in RRIS, RRCS, then no IPR is needed. The structure of the RRIS and RRCS is in Figures 12.4.

Agent n	Agent n-1	$\cdots$	Agent 1	Agent 0

Fig. 12.4 Structure of RRIS and RRCS registers

Thus, the bits of the RRIS are set by the hardware. The bits of the RRCS are set by the software. In hardware, the ability to interrupt is provided to a given agent; in software, this ability can be suspended. A bit is loaded by hardware into the correct location of the RRIS only if the corresponding bit of the RRCS is set by the software. If agent i is enabled and it sends an interrupt signal while agent j is running, i will interrupt j only if $i > j$ in the above ordering. In conclusions, only RRIS, RRCS, IIR, SSR, and NSR are needed in order to implement the interrupt system. IIR is in PSW, SSR and NSR are dedicated memory locations.

12.3.2.2 *Software Components*

The software components of an interrupt system are: the Array of Expected Events (AEE), the Kernel of the Interrupt System (KIS), the Interrupt Handlers (IH)-s, and Return from the Interrupt System (RIS).

Array of Expected Events: AEE records the events expected to interrupt the current process. Each component of AEE characterizes an interrupt event in terms of the following three elements:

- Interrupt Identification Code (IIC) to be matched with IIR to determine the identity of the interrupt agent in a class;
- Interrupt Handler Address (IHA), the address of the interrupt handler designed to treat this event;

- Process Waiting Queue (PWQ), the queue of processes waiting for the event identified by the *IIC* to occur.

Components IIC, IHA, PWQ are pointed to from the entry $AEE[i]$ where i is the order number of the interrupt agent. The interrupt identification code $AEE[i] \rightarrow IIC$, $i = 1, 2, \ldots, Size$, where $|AEE| = Size$, is used to identify the interrupt signal stored in IIR. $AEE[i] \rightarrow IHA$ is the address of the Interrupt Handler designed to treat the interrupts sent by agent IIC. $AEE[i] \rightarrow PWQ$ is a pointer to the queue of processes waiting for an interrupt sent by this agent to occur. Thus, C expression of the AEE is:

```
typedef int (* InterruptHandler)();
struct AEEEntry
      {
        int IIC;
        InterruptHandler    IHA;
        struct WaitingQueue *PWQ;
      }AEE[Size];
```

where $Size$ is the number of interrupt agents (classes) recognized by the system.

Kernel of Interrupt System: KIS is a general procedure which determines the interrupt handler designed to treat a particular interrupt. The algorithm for KIS is called a *skip-chain* and operates on AEE as shown in Figure 12.5.

The action expressing KIS behavior is:

```
KIS::
    in AEE: array[0..n] of AEEEntry,
       IIR, AEESize: integer where AEESize = n,
       alpha: channel of strings;
    local i: integer where i = 0,
          Flag: boolean where Flag = False;
    1_0: while ((i < AEESize) and (Flag = False)) do
                if (IIR <> AEE[i]->IIC) then i := i+1
                else Flag = True:^1_0
    1_1: if Flag = False then
             Send(alpha,''Unrecognized interrupt'');
         else
             Initiate interrupt handler AEE[i]->IHA :^1_1
    1_2: RIS():^1_2
```

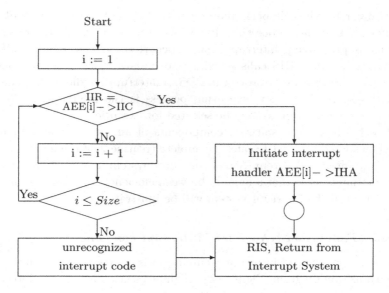

Fig. 12.5 Kernel of interrupt system

Note that this action transfers the control to the appropriate component of the system.

Interrupt Handlers: Each interrupt recognized by KIS is provided with a procedure called `interrupt handler` to be executed when the respective interrupt occurs. Interrupt handlers execute two kinds of activities: manipulate the associated interrupt signals, and treat the related events. For example, an I/O interrupt handler terminates the I/O operation and sends information about its status to the device driver, thus enabling it to reactivate the device if necessary. A timer interrupt may suspend the current process and dispatch another process to execute. A real-time interrupt may perform specific computations determined by the real-time event: open valves, close valves, pull levers, etc. Processes waiting for an event to arrive are maintained in the PWQ[ISR] pointed to from the AEE. For example, if interrupt signal i occurs, the interrupt handler for this signal may release one or more processes from the queue pointed to by $AEE[i] \rightarrow PWQ$. The number and the identity of processes released from $AEE[i] \rightarrow PQW$ depend upon the interrupt signal and a given queuing discipline.

Return from Interrupt System, RIS: An interrupt handler returns control to a procedure of the interrupt system called the *Return from Interrupt System* (RIS). An interrupt handler may also return an integer specifying the manner in which it performed its task. RIS restores the state of the processor for further processing. It initiates the KIS if while an interrupt handler is processing, interrupt signals occurred and are pending. If no pending interrupts, RIS calls scheduler to update PDS. Scheduler determines the highest priority process in PDS. If interrupt handler didn't change priorities in PDS the new executing process is the interrupted process, otherwise another process may be selected for execution.

The hardware and software components of an interrupt system have been considered in order to offer a complete treatment of the interrupt signals in an interrupt system. A real computer system, however, implements these mechanisms so that a balance between efficiency and cost is achieved. This aspect of the interrupt system will be illustrated further.

12.3.3   *Functional behavior of interrupt components*

Functional behavior of interrupt components is expressed by the interrupt state transition diagram, Figure 12.6. Significant attributes of an interrupt system are the times involved in the transition from current process to process execution after the treatment of the interrupt. These times are directly related to the amount of information to be saved, to be restored when the context is switched back again, and the number of interrupts pending during interrupt handling. A critical measure of performance is defined by the constant called the *Interrupt Response Time* (IRT), $IRT = t_0 + t_1 + t_2$. Note that IRT does not depend on the interrupt agent and the interrupted process. There are some variation in t_0, t_1. However, t_2 depends on the KIS and its complexity is $O(Size)$ or $O(log(Size))$. t_3 is

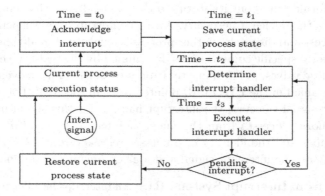

Fig. 12.6   Interrupt state transition diagram

defined according to the specific interrupt agent. To improve performance, the operations executed at times t_0, t_1, t_2 can be hardware wired.

Note that in a real-time system the sensors connected to the processor are the interrupt agents to be treated within the real-time constraints of the application. In this case the interrupt response time is critical.

12.3.4 *Algorithmic expression*

The algorithmic expression of the interrupt system is shown in Figure 12.7, and is given in terms of the three main components:

- A gate to enter the interrupt system, EIS;
- The kernel of interrupt system, KIS;
- A gate to exit the interrupt system, RIS.

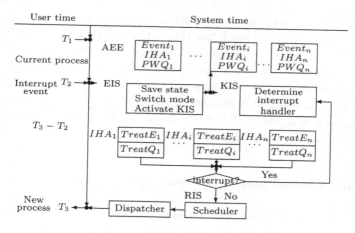

Fig. 12.7   Algorithmic expression of interrupt system

The entity $(T2 - T1)$ on this figure represents the time spent by the processor executing user processes. The entity $(T3 - T2)$ represents the time spent by the processor in the interrupt system. Scheduler and Dispatcher are factored out because they belong to the PMS.

Enter Interrupt System (EIS) contains both hardware-wired and software-implemented operations. To minimize IRT, EIS tends to be hardware implemented and consists of three operations executed automatically within the same instruction cycle.

- Save state of the current process;
- Switch mode of processing;

- Activate the Kernel of the Interrupt System.

When a valid interrupt signal is received, a summary of the state of the current process is automatically saved in SSR. Both the summary of the state and SSR are predefined for a given computer system. SSR and NSR registers may be arranged as the arrays OldState[] and NewState[] where Old-State[i] and NewState[i] are the SSR and NSR of the interrupt agent i (see interrupt system in IBM 360/370, Section 12.4.2). Then, to save the state of the current process when interrupt i occurs, `Store PSW OldState[i]` and `Load PSW NewState[i]` are automatically executed, within the same instruction cycle, while changing the processing mode, thus providing access to privileged instructions.

The processing rights concern the access to privileged instructions and access rights to memory. The access to privileged instructions is valid for both interrupts and exceptions. The increasing memory access rights is valid for interrupts only. Rationale for this is that exceptions comes from current process and therefore they should be treated in the current process own address space. On the other hand, an interrupt is an asynchronous event initiated outside the current process. Consequently it should **not** be treated in the computing environment of the current process. When the interrupt signal belongs to a cluster, its interrupt handler is determined and activated using a cluster dedicated KIS and AEE.

12.4   Actual Implementations of Interrupt Systems

Cost/efficiency trade-off make interrupt systems cluster agents into classes of interrupts. Consequently hardware and software are provided for classes of agents. Classes are arranged in the AEE in a hierarchy where lower level interrupts are ignored until the higher level interrupt handlers run to completion. There are four main approaches for clustering the interrupt agents into classes and designing the interrupt system accordingly: single priority single level, single priority multiple level, multiple priority single level, and multiple priority multiple level.

Single Priority Single Level: In this approach there is no IPR and only one cluster is allowed. Hardware components are $(ISR, ICR, SSR,$ $NSR, IIR)$, i.e., $|RRIS| = 1$, $|RRIC| = 1$. The ICR is either on or off, and interrupts are either totally enabled or disabled. Software components are AEE and one skip-chain that identifies the interrupting agent. The resulting system is characterized by relative slow interrupt resolution, i.e. the time interval t_2 is too large for some applications.

Single Priority Multi Level: In this approach there is no IPR and a given number $n \geq 1$ of clusters are allowed. Hardware components are $(ISR[n], ICR, SSR[n], NSR[n], IIR)$. All agents can send interrupt signals at once. $|ICR| = 1$ implies interrupts enabled or disabled. $|ISR| = n$ implies interrupts may be pending. If $ISR[i] = 1$ and the cluster i contains one agent then $AEE.IHA[i]$ is activated by the indirection `Jump Indirect NSR[i]`. If cluster i contains more agents then a skip-chain is necessary. The time interval t_2 is an indirection or what does it takes to determine the signaling agent in a cluster.

Multi Priority Single Level: In this approach there is an IPR register and one cluster is allowed. The IPR provided in hardware allows an agents to require an interrupt while the interrupt handler processing an interrupt of another agent is active. The IPL of the running process in conjunction with the IPR of the signaling agent determines the event. One pair (ISR,ICR) and one pair $\langle SSR, NSR \rangle$ are provided. Hence, only one interrupt agent can signal at once. However, an interrupt signal can interrupt an interrupt handler if ICR allows it and its IPR is higher than the IPL associated with the current process. A general skip-chain determines the interrupt handler associated with the interrupt agent. However, the interrupt agent can be a cluster of agents.

Multi Priority Multi Level: In this approach there is an IPR register and more clusters are allowed. A complete hardware equipment needs to be provided. A skip chain is provided for each cluster. Though there may be many agents in a cluster only one agent can signal at once. But interrupt agents of different clusters may interrupt each other. If only one interrupt agent composes a cluster the interrupt handler is initiated by an indirection, hence good resolution (small time t_2).

To decrease cost and improve performances actual architectures use combinations of these approaches. Further we sketch most influential interrupt systems of various computer architectures.

12.4.1 *Interrupt system in PDP-11*

PDP-11 is a series of 16-bit minicomputers manufactured by DEC (Digital Equipment Corp.) from 1970 to 1990-s and was taken as basis for PC-s. In this architecture interrupts agents are I/O devices. An I/O device is identified by two dedicated memory locations: device status, DS, and device buffer, DB. To facilitate the handling of interrupts New Status Word (NSW) and New Program Counter (NPC) are added, thus obtaining a *Device Identification Vector* (DIV) consisting of (DS, DB, NSW, NPC), shown in Figure 12.8

Device Identification Vector

	$Byte_2$	$Byte_1$
DB	$Byte_2$	$Byte_1$
DS	$Byte_2$	$Byte_1$
NPC	$Byte_2$	$Byte_1$
NSW	$Byte_2$	$Byte_1$

Fig. 12.8   DIV of PDP-11

Functionally, a device is identified by the tuple (`Error`,`Ready`,`Init`) of DS, as seen in Figure 12.9. The bits (`Error`, `Ready`, `Init`) define the

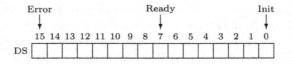

Fig. 12.9   DS of PDP-11

device state. Others bits of DS are available to be used for interrupts. Thus, the Bit_6 of DS is used as the interrupt control register:

$$Bit_6 = \begin{cases} 1, & \text{if interrupt generated by device is enabled;} \\ 0, & \text{if interrupt generated by device is disabled.} \end{cases}$$

Since DS is accessible to the program, this architecture allows easy disabling and enabling of interrupts by the interrupt handler. The Bit_7 of DS is used as the ISR. It is set by the hardware when the device sends an interrupt. For example, an I/O device sets $DS[7]$ when it is ready to execute the next I/O request. The device driver can be called from this interrupt to complete previous operation and to decide the further activity of the device. The IPR is specified by the three-bit field $NSW[5..7]$. Hence, there are 8 priority levels allowed by PDP-11 architecture. IPL of the current process is loaded in $PSW[5..7]$, i.e., processes execute with a given priority number called a priority level. The PSW of the interrupt handler is at the address NPC

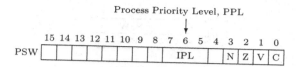

Fig. 12.10   Process priority level

and its IPL is in the bits $NSW[5..7]$. The PSW of the PDP-11 is shown in Figure 12.10. Hence, the PDP-11's skip-chains is:

```
Identify the interrupt agent using the  DIV;
The PSW of the interrupt handler is the DIV.NPC;
Agent priority is on the bits DIV.NSW[5..7];
Processor checks whether DIV.NSW[5..7] <= PSW[5..7]
 If true, continue with Next(PC);
 Otherwise
    Save PC, PSW in two temporary locations, T_1, T_2;
    Load PC and PSW from the DIV.PSW and DIV.NSW, repsectively;
    Push T_1 (i.e., the old PC), onto the stack.
    Push T_2 (i.e., the old PSW), onto the stack.
```

Note that since PC and PSW are those of the interrupt handler, the processor runs the interrupt handler. The interrupt handler completes its activity performing the statements:

```
PSW := Top(stack);
Pop(stack);
PC := Top(stack)
```

which resumes the interrupted process. The above code can be preceded by the initiation of a scheduler/dispatcher. The algorithm performed by PDP-11 in order to enter the interrupt system is shown graphically in Figure 12.11.

12.4.2   *Interrupt system in IBM 360/370*

In this architectures interrupt system is based on five clusters:

(1) **External interrupt:** interruption key on the control panel, the timer, another processor, special devices.

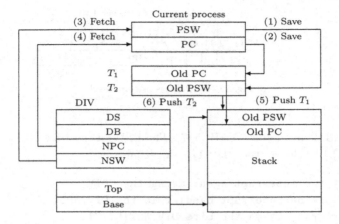

Fig. 12.11   Interrupt treatment in PDP-11

(2) **Supervisory call interrupt (Exceptions)**: allows a user program to request services provided by the OS and to switch processing mode to the supervisor.

(3) **Program interrupts (Exceptions)**: 15 exceptions, 8 overflows and 7 improper instructions.

(4) **Machine check interrupt**: caused by hardware malfunction. The interrupt handler is a diagnostic procedure.

(5) **I/O interrupts**: I/O operation completion; device identification code is in the PSW of current process, see Figures 9.3 and 11.4.

In this architecture exceptions that can be disabled are called program interrupts, and are: fixed point overflows, decimal overflow, exponent underflow, and lost significance. On the other hand the interrupts are called system interrupts, and eight of them can be disabled (masked) by the system. The hardware support for interrupt system provided in this architecture consists of an ISR and a pair $\langle SSR, NSR \rangle$ for each of the five classes of interrupts. There is no explicit ICR. However, some of the system interrupts can be disabled using bits 0..7 of the PSW and some of the program interrupts can be disabled using the bits 36..39 of the PSW. There is no explicit IIR. Bits 16..31 of the PSW serve as interrupt identification code. The skip chain determines the interrupt agent taking the IIC from SSR[16..31] of the cluster where the PSW of the current process is saved.

In this architecture SSR is called OldPSW and NSR is called New-PSW. Thus, the five pairs of $\langle SSR, NSR \rangle$, are organized in two arrays, of double words, OldPSW[0..4] assigned at the dedicated memory locations 0024..0056 and NewPSW[0..4] assigned at the dedicated memory locations 0088..0120, shown in Figure 12.12. Thus the PSW of the interrupted process is saved in OldPSW[i] when an interrupt in the cluster $0 \le i \le 4$ arrives, and the PSW of the skip chain that determines the interrupt agent in the cluster $0 \le i \le 4$ is fetched from NewPSW[i]. Hence, when an interrupt of

	OldPSW[0..4]
0024	OldPSW when external interrupt
0032	OldPSW when system call
0040	OldPSW when program interrupt
0048	OldPSW when machine check
0056	OldPSW when I/O interrupt
	NewPSW[0..4](PSW of KIS)
0088	External interrupts
0096	Supervisory call interrupts
0104	Program interrupts
0112	Machine check interrupts
0120	I/O interrupts

Fig. 12.12 NSR and SSR in IBM-360/370 architecture

cluster i, $0 \le i \le 4$, occurs the following section of code is performed:

```
0024 + 8*i := (PSW); /* Save the old PSW */
PSW := (0088 + 8*i); /* Fetch the new PSW */
```

Thus, a skip chain is provided for each interrupt cluster to determines the interrupt agent using the OldPSW[i] where the PSW of the interrupted process was saved. Since there is no ICR, interrupts are enabled and disabled by the following rules:

- The I/O interrupts remain pending, while four of the 15 program interrupts are ignored.
- The machine check interrupt, when masked (disabled), is ignored.
- The actual meaning of masking (disabling) an interrupt in this architecture is specified by the hardware and cannot be changed.

Since there is no IPR, interrupt handlers can be interrupted following the rules:

(1) Machine check has the highest priority.
(2) The next highest priority is associated with the program interrupt and supervisory call interrupt. There is only one priority level for both since they are all exceptions.
(3) The next priority level is associated with external interrupts.
(4) Finally, I/O interrupts are of lowest priority in this hierarchy.

Interrupts arriving during machine check interrupt remain pending and are treated as follows:

(1) I/O interrupts are serviced first.
(2) External interrupts are serviced next.
(3) The program or supervisory call interrupts are serviced last.

12.5   Modern Interrupt Systems

Modern interrupt systems inherit from both PDP and IBM architectures. We examine this inheritance looking at two architectures: VAX-11/780 that sits at the basis of RISC machines, and MOTOROLA 6809 that sits at the basis of current PCs.

12.5.1   *Interrupt system in VAX-11/780*

This architecture generalizes and improves the interrupt mechanism provided in PDP-11 architecture. In this architecture there are four different processing modes: Kernel Mode (KM), Executive Mode (EM), Supervisory Mode (SM), and User Mode (UM). The processing mode can be changed by software using a privileged machine instruction called Change Mode. Each mode is characterized by its instruction set, its privileged registers, and its access rights to the memory area.

   An active process in this architecture is characterized by a Process Status Longword (PSL) composed of two 16-bit registers, $PSL_{0..31} = PSL_{0..15}, PSL_{16..31}$, described in section 9.7.3, referred to as Program Status Word and Processor Status Words, respectively. Program counter in this architecture is the general register R_{15}.

Interrupt agents in this architecture are I/O devices and are character-ized by Device Interrupt Vectors, the same as in PDP-11. However, VAX-11/780 provides 32 priority levels associated with 32 classes of interrupt agents. Interrupt Priority Level (IPL) is recorded in PSL[16..20]. Each inter-rupt level is associated with an interrupt handler and the bits PSL[16..20] of an interrupt handler contains its priority level. When an interrupt occurs it is granted only if $PSL[16..20]$ of the current process is smaller than the $IPL[16..20]$ of the interrupt handler of the interrupting agent.

There are 32 clusters of interrupts in VAX-11/780. The lowest priority, IPL_0 is assigned to the user processes. Its interrupt handler manipulates user requests. Priority levels $1 \leq i \leq 15$ are reserved exclusively for the operating system processes. The priority levels 16, 17, 18, 19 are associated with timers. I/O Devices interrupt at levels 20, 21, 22, and 23. The system clock interrupts at level 24. Finally, interrupt levels 25, 26, 27, 28, 29, 30, 31 are used for urgent processor conditions such as power failure.

I/O device interrupt agents are specified by Device Interrupt Vectors, $DIV = (DS, DB, NS, PC)$ as in PDP-11. $DIV.DS_7$ is ISR and $DIV.DS_6$ is ICR, thus interrupts can be enabled/disabled by program. Interrupts issued by other agents cannot be disabled. Some exceptions are enabled/disabled using PSL bits 4–7, i.e., program status word. There is no explicit IPR associated with the interrupt agents that are not devices. Priority of an interrupt agent is the IPL of its interrupt handler.

An interrupt vector is a double-word (i.e., a 64 bit word) that specifies the address of an interrupt handler on bits 0..31, and the conditions in which the interrupt handler is performed, on bits 31..63. The interrupt handler is executed on the interrupt stack (in the case of the external agents) or on the process stack (in the case of exceptions issued by the current process). When an interrupt handler starts processing its priority level in PSL can be raised. Some interrupt handlers treat events using writable control store microcode. In this case, the interrupt vector passes bits 2..5 as parameters to the microcode treating the event. The structure of the PC is in Figure 12.13. PC-s of interrupt handlers are longwords i.e., $PC_{0..1} = 00$. Hence, $PC_{0..1}$

31 30 29 28	27 26 25 24 23 22 21 20 19 18	17 16 15 14 13 12 11 10	9	8	7	6	5	4	3	2	1	0
Virtual address of interrupt handler								param			SM	

Fig. 12.13   Interrupt vector descriptor in VAX-11/780

is referred to as SM and is used by the interrupt system to record the conditions for the interrupt treating as shown below:

$$SM = \begin{cases} 00, & \text{if interrupt \& processor runs on interrupt stack;} \\ 01, & \text{if exception (IPL of its handler may be raised to 31;)} \\ 10, & \text{if event handled by writable control store microcode;} \\ 11, & \text{an interrupt vector with this code halts the machine.} \end{cases}$$

There are 128 interrupt vectors organized into an array called the System Control Block, SCB. The first 32 entries of SCB are exception vectors and the next 96 entries are interrupt vectors. Each I/O device level supports 16 devices. Interrupts are serviced on the interrupt stack, exceptions are serviced in process context on the process stack. Interrupts are serviced with the IPL of the interrupt agent, exceptions are serviced with the IPL of the process that initiates them. The interrupt signals that can be disabled remain pending while exceptions that can be disabled do not remain pending. Lower priority interrupts are queued behind higher priority interrupts.

Processor has a privileged base register, IBR, pointing to SCB. When interrupt i occurs the following actions are performed:

```
if (8*i+IBR)_{16..20} > (PSL)_{16..20}
   Save state on the stack;
   Fetch state and PC from (8*i + IBR);
   Treat interrupt;
   Restore state from stack;
else current process continues
   while interrupt remain pending
```

Most of the operations performed to switch the context from current process to the interrupt handler are hardware wired. Address of interrupt vector of interrupt i is $8 * i + IBR$.

Interrupt levels 1 to 15 are used as system calls issued by the procedures that belong to the operating system. They are manipulated by three privileged registers:

(1) Software Interrupt Request Register (SIRR) having a bit for every software priority level;
(2) Software Interrupt Summary Registeri (SISR) records an interrupt pending required by SIRR;

(3) Interrupt Priority Level Register (IPLR) is used to fetch or to set the IPL field in PSL.

The SIRR is used to request a software interrupt at the level i, $1 \leq i \leq 15$. This means that SIRR allows operating system to execute its components (functions/procedures) at 15 different priority levels. VAX-11/780 has the privileged instruction Move To Privileged Register (MTPR). MTPR i sets the bit i of the register SIRR, thus asking for an interrupt at the priority level i. For example, MTPR 15 sets the bit 15 of the register SIRR, asking to run a process at the interrupt level 15. During the instruction cycle, if bit i in SIRR is set the IPLR is fetched from $PSL_{16..20}$. Thus, if $IPLR \leq i$, an interrupt at the level i is initiated and, a routine defined as the interrupt handler for this level is activated. If $IPLR > i$, the interrupt requested by the previous operation remains pending in SISR.

12.5.2 *Interrupts in Motorola 6809*

Motorola 6809 is used here as model for the interrupt system in PCs. It is provided with three interrupt lines: Interrupt ReQuest line (IRQ), Fast Interrupt ReQuest line (FIRQ), Non-Maskable Interrupt request line (NMI). IRQ, FIRQ, and NMI differ from each other in their interrupt handler addresses, in how they are masked, and in the number of registers that are saved when such an interrupt occurs. Interrupt requests are identified by appropriate ISR-s. The ICR-s associated with ISR-s are given in the bits 4-7 of the Condition Code register, CC, Figure 12.14.

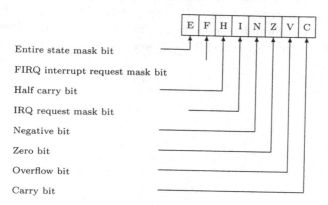

Fig. 12.14   Condition codes for Motorola 6809

12.5.2.1 *IRQ Interrupts*

If an IRQ interrupt is received the PSW is saved on the stack, CC[I] := 1 (i.e., disable IRQ interrupts) and fetch the NSR from a dedicated location (register). When the interrupt handler completes, it executes an Return From Interrupt, which performs the operations: restores the original value of the registers, CC[I] := 0 (i.e., enable interrupts on IRQ line) and restores the program counter of the interrupted process.

12.5.2.2 *FIRQ Interrupts*

FIRQ interrupt requests are treated similarly with IRQ interrupts, only faster. That is, only the PC and CC are saved on the stack and FIRQ interrupts are disabled, i.e., CC[F] := 1 is executed.

12.5.2.3 *NMI Interrupts*

The NMI interrupts are treated similarly to the IRQ and FIRQ interrupts. However, a program cannot disable the interrupts arriving on the NMI line. Thus, the NMI line provides the appropriate hardware support for real time applications.

12.5.3 *Modularizing interrupt system*

Processor cards may dedicate their pins as ISR-s. Hence, modular hardware allows different pins of a processor card to be assigned to different interrupt signals. This allows modular development of interrupt system (see Chapterb 7, Interrupt System in Linux) [Rusling (2002)]. That is, the same pin may be used as ISR for different agents in different architectures. However, the model of interrupt system discussed here does not undergo essential changes.

PART 4

Software Tools Supporting Program Development

Chapter 13

Problem Solving by Software Tools

CBPSP consist of rules that allow computer users to solve problems using computers. According to the services it provides, CBPSP is implemented by two classes of tools:

(1) Tools that manage computer resources and the events that arrive during program executions. These tools belong to the Execution Support Environment (ESP). They are organized as libraries of system functions that can be called by program execution process.

(2) Tools that allow computer user to map problems and problem solving algorithms into computer programs. These tools belongs to the Programming Support Environment (PSE). The execution of these tools is spawned by computer user using commands of a control language.

We examined the development of ESE tools in Part 3 of this book. Here we examine the design and evolution of PSE tools which are called System Programs (SP). More recent computer based problem solving methodology is identified with the process of program development. Therefore the collection of system programs are also called Problem Solving Environment. So here the acronym PSE is dually used. Collectively we refer to the ESE and PSE as software tools.

13.1 System Program Development and Use

Each program $P \in PSE$ solves a class of problems. For example, a C compiler compiles any C program. Therefore the development of a system program follows a well defined pattern that consists of:

- specify a class of problems;

- develop a solution algorithm for the problems of the class;
- map the solution algorithm into a system program;
- develop the control language command for system program use.

We assume here that the OS of the computer platform is provided with a Control Language (CL) and a Control Language Interpreter (CLI) that maps CL expressions into program running processes. Examples of a CL and CLI are a C-shell and the C-shell interpreter, respectively, in a Unix system. Once the system program is developed and implemented, in order to use it to solve a problem of the class we need to provide a parameterized specification of problems in the class. This of course requires us to develop a language that allows each problem of the class to be expressed as a valid expression of this language. For example, problem specification for a C compiler is "a file that contains a C program". The C compiler recognizes the problem it can solve by reading the C program from a file whose name ends in the suffix ".c". Problem specification for polynomial operations would be "a file that contains polynomials to operate on". It should be recognized by the polynomial system by its name suffix ".poly". For the system program use we need to design a command of the CL that calls the system program on input data to generate solutions. Example such a command is `cc -o f f.c` which calls C compiler to translate the C program in the file f.c into the executable program stored in the file `f`. Further, `f Input Output` is another control language command that calls the executable program `f` on the file "Input" as input and asks it to generate the result in the file "Output".

13.1.1   *Computer-based business*

Current software technology evolved to the stage where, for any class of problems, one searches for a system program that solves the problems of that class. Since the classes of problems are *problem domain specific* this means that software technology evolves toward a *computer service oriented business* where system programs are the exchange values. However, the missing stone in this evolution process is the lack of problem domain orientation of the CBPSP, which makes this business suitable for computer experts only. To join this business, domain experts of any problem domain, other than computer science, need either to get expertise in computer science, which stresses computer education to its limits, or to engage computer scientists to develop the system programs they need, which increases software complexity at a level where it threaten the existence of CBPSP itself [Horn (2001)]. The requirement of using command languages during CBPSP in order to make use of system programs makes the approach inconvenient. This inconvenience is somehow released by windowing systems where commands are represented by buttons that user needs to click. The buttons representing commands suppose to be reflective of the domain concepts handled by the software tools thus activated. But button clicking may lead to the loosing of the domain language, which may have more dramatic consequences. This is why there are voices of the originators of the CBPSP [Markoff (2012)] which ask for "Killing the Computer to Save It".

13.1.2 *System program requirements*

The major requirements for software tools are that they are efficient and convenient. These requirements are achieved through the mechanisms of sharing resources, ability to perform concurrently, ability to interact among them and with the computer user during problem solving process, and the support for component integration.

Software tools share computer resources (memory, processor, devices, information) which allow them to be efficiently used. For example, the same copy of a C compiler may be shared by all programmers developing C programs. To increase system performance software tools execute concurrently. For example, a compiler may run in parallel with an editor, and in parallel with various components of the operating system servicing current program execution. Software tools need to interact with each other and with the computer user, thus making problem solving process convenient. For example, compiler interacts with the RTE by asking it to perform I/O operations on its behalf. In addition, compiler interacts with the programmer by sending messages concerning correctness of the program it compiles. Shell interpreter receive user commands and send messages to the user about the behavior of the problem solving process. Tools T_1 and T_2 may be integrated in the sense that: *if T_1 provides a solution to a subproblem of problems solved by T_2 then T_1 should be used as a component of T_2*. So by integration, software tools make PSP efficient and convenient. Software architectures [Shaw and Garlan (1996)] discuss various integration patterns. For example, piping the output of a program into the input of another program is an example of such integration patterns.

13.1.3 *Software tool evolution toward cognitive tools*

Software tool evolution with problem domain is a more recent requirement spawned by the move to raise the cognitive power of the modern computers. The computation mechanism employed by a computer is encapsulated in the action Run explained in Chapter 9. So far the move towards raising the cognitive power of computers is mostly directed toward the evolving the action Run to simulate the human brain activity involved in the cognition process. This simulation requires the increase of the number of computer components to match the number of brains neurons, which further complicates the computer. In addition, because we don't really know how the neuron's electrical activity is transformed into constient cognition the experiments carried out so far [Pierce (2013)] lack the significance of the progress towards the goal.

There is however another solution to the problem of evolving the computer toward a cognitive tool, namely software tool evolution with problem domain. Software tools evolved so far as computer programs, through the mechanism of compatibility, independent of the problem domain they solve. The compatibility of a software tool T_2 (such as Fortran 10 compiler) with a previously developed tool T_1 (such as Fortran 2 compiler) means that T_2 needs to be designed such that it encapsulates all computation power used for the design of T_1 within the design of T_2. This is actually similar to the mechanism of evolving problem solving process within the human cognition. The difference results from the fact that the "compatibility" during human problem solving process is carried out through the natural language and software tool compatibility is carried out through computer languages. However, while human problem solving process is diversified by the nature of the problem domain (mathematical problems are solved using a mathematical language, chemistry problems are solved by a chemistry language, etc.) CBPSP is based on programming, provided as "a problem solving methodology that fits all problems". That is, the problem with software tool evolution by "compatibility" concerns the fact that tools T_1 and T_2 are programs designed to be used by computer educated people. Consequently, the compatibility approach evolves software tools with respect to the domain of computer programming. The compatibility approach do not evolve software tools with respect to the problem domain solved by the computer. Therefore the question to be answered now is: *can we apply compatibility approach to the evolution of software tools dedicated to an application domain, different from the computer science?* To answer this question we first observe that software tools developed so far are dedicated to the domain of computer programming. In other words, there are no domain dedicated software tools for domains other than computer science. But every prblem domain benefits of domain dedicated tools which domain experts use during their problem solving process. The evolution of these tools with problem domain is based on evolving humans cognition process through natural language. Therefore, the better solution to the problem of computer evolution toward a cognitive tool is to develop software evolution mechanisms with problem domain following the human cognition approach. Here we discuss this approach using the framework initiated by the Web-Based Problem Solving Process (WBPSP) [WBPSP].

Chapter 14

Web-Based Problem Solving Process

WBPSP is an extension of computer based problem solving process by developing software tools dedicated to problem domain experts. That is, during WBPSP, while solving a problem of the domain D, problem solver can use a Domain Algorithmic Language (DAL(D)), characteristic to the domain, instead of using a programming language. Looking back at the CBPSP, this means that problem solver executes problem solving algorithms using her own brain instead of converting them into programs to be executed by the computer. This can be done because with WBPSP the computer is used by problem solver as a "brain assistant" that perform the operations involved in the problem solving algorithm upon the problem solver requests. In other words, problem solver communicates with her computer using her natural language. But natural language evolves dynamically with problem domain and it is strongly ambiguous. This was the reason to interpose translators from domain language to the computer language, i.e., programming, in the problem solving process in the first place. However, looking carefully at this situation we observe that the problem lies in the requirement that programming languages be Turing complete. That is, programming languages have been developed as universal problem solving tools. On the other hand human oriented problem solving is domain characteristic. For a given problem domain (such as mathematics, physics, chemistry, engineering, business, etc.) problem solving algorithm uses a DAL, which is a fragment of natural language spoken by the problem domain experts. Domain algorithmic languages are learned by domain experts during their domain education process and their ambiguities are removed by the domain context. Therefore if a DAL is formally defined and if every concept employed by a DAL algorithm is associated with a computer artifact representing its computational meaning in the domain,

DAL expressions can be evaluated by problem solver using a computer in a similar way in which an arithmetic expression is evaluated using a calculator. Moreover, if the domain concept represented by a DAL algorithm that solves certain problem P is automatically associated with the computer program performing that algorithm as the concept's meaning, then DAL evolves with problem domain. Consequently the computer becomes a cognitive tool used by problem solver as a brain assistant during problem solving process.

Contrasting this approach of computer use during problem solving process with the computer use in the CBPSP we observe that while a programmer using a computer language manipulates computer concepts, a domain expert using DAL(D) manipulate domain's D concepts. Therefore the approach of using a computer as a brain assistant during problem solving process transforms the computer from a number crunching tool into a cognitive tool that is employed by its user as any other human developed tool.

Every domain D has a DAL, which is the fragment of natural language used by domain experts during their domain cognition process. As stated above, DAL's ambiguities are removed by the domain context. Usually DAL is developed on two layers: a basic layer defined by few primitive concepts that represent the DAL vocabulary, and a constructed layer which is defined by the collection of concepts developed by domain experts during the problem solving process. For example, natural numbers learned by students in their first grades are taken as the basic layer for the DAL that handle high school algebra, which is learned during student advanced classes. That is, DAL is naturally developed by the process of domain expert education. In other words, for every domain the domain experts learn this language during their education process, exactly as computer scientists learn computer languages during their education process. Consequently if a computer understands DAL(D) during a problem solving process, the computer manipulates domain D concepts instead of manipulating computer concepts.

The question now is what is the computing environment provided to the computer user using DAL during problem solving process? Since there is a potential infinite number of problem domains and every domain has its own DAL the computer is seamlessly shared by domain experts among them and by different problem domains. This is similarly to the Internet sharing, where everybody may have a laptop (or an iPad) connected to Internet and a browser allowing her to exchange information using the Interest. The difference is that in today Internet information sharing, the computer (server) provides documents to process while when computer is used as "brain assistant" in the problem solving process, the computer is required to perform computer artifacts associated with the concepts used by computer user during her problem solving process. Since different problem domains use different DAL-s during their problem solving process this means that computer is shared by both intra and inter domain computer users. While each DAL itself may be unambiguous as a fragment of natural language, and evolves with problem domain, all DAL-s are unified within natural language and thus make the natural language naturally ambiguous. Therefore, for disambiguation purpose, every domain needs to be provided with its own computing environment consisting of:

- A DAL used by problem solver to express her problem solving algorithms;
- A terminal employed by problem solver to send solution algorithms to the computer;
- A DAL interpreter that receives algorithms sent by problem user, performs these algorithms and, informs problem solver about the behavior of her algorithms.

Hence, there are no programming languages in this computing environments, there is no operating system and command languages, there is no windows and buttons to click. Just the natural language of the problem solver which she uses to dialog with her "brain assistant" during problem solving process. Does this means that programming as usual disappear? The answer is no, by the contrary, programming is done by computer experts in the "programming factory". Moreover, the brain assistant behaves like a computer. But instead of searching for the next "instruction" to execute in a program stored in computer memory it searches for the concept typed by the problem solver in her problem solving algorithm and executes the computer artifact associated with it. Where is this search carried on and how does this "brain assistant" differentiate between concepts that have the same names but different meaning, which natural language abound of? The answer to these questions reveals the open field of software development for non expert computer user, which consists of Computational Emancipation of Problem Domains, (CEAD).

14.1   Computational Emancipation of Problem Domains

CEAD is the process of developing the Domain Algorithmic Languages where problem domain is formally specified by a Domain Ontology (DO). Within a DO every domain concept is associated with a computer artifact representing its meaning. This formalizes a computer application domain in a similar manner with the mathematical formalization of the domain where concepts are associated with mathematical models that allows mathematicians to reason formally about domain properties. However, instead of associating concepts with mathematical models, within CEAD process concepts are associated with computer artifacts that represent their computational meaning in the domain. The development of these computer artifacts, their association with the domain concepts, and domain structuring using a domain ontology reveal a new interdisciplinary collaboration between domain experts, mathematicians, and computer scientists where:

- Domain experts develop the DAL-s;
- Mathematicians develop mathematical models that formalize the DAL concepts;
- Computer scientists develop computer artifacts representing DAL concept meaning.

For the basic level of the DAL this process is carried out by hand. As DAL evolves during problem solving process creating new concepts, DAL algorithms are associated with these new concepts automatically. Hence, the space where the "brain assistant" searches the meaning of the concepts it handles during problem solving process is the file holding the domain ontology. Different problem domains are represented by different domain ontologies. Therefore brain assistants of different problem solvers working on different domains are searching their concepts in different files, thus disambiguating the problem solving process. However, the implementation of the algorithms employed in a DO file are distributed on the Web and are referenced in the DO using Universal Resource Locators. Therefore WBPSP is actually a mechanism of distributed execution of algorithms on the Web.

14.2   Algorithm Execution During WBPSP

The answer to the question of how is the brain assistant executing computer artifacts associated with the domain concepts in the domain ontology is a little more elaborate. If the brain assistant is implemented as a computer platform, then in order to execute the computer artifacts associated with domain concepts, it requires the concepts to be associated with callable programs. That is, the file holding domain ontology is a collection of records of the form

```
<ConceptName, Program(ConceptName)>
```

However, if the brain assistant is implemented by a computer network, then the file holding domain ontology is a collection of records of the form

```
<ConceptName, URL(Program(ConceptName))>
```

Computer technology has already created tools [Horridge (2011)] that can be used to create and manipulate such files. Now, the brain assistant can be seen as a domain dedicated virtual machine that perform the following algorithm:

```
ConceptC = FirstDALConcept(DAL algorithm)
while (ConceptC is not End)
    Execute (ConceptC);
    ConceptC = Next(ConceptC, DAL algorithn);
Extract result + dysplay it to the user
```

The details of this brain assistant implementation are provided in the paper [Rus (2013)] whose URL is http://homepage.cs.uiowa.edu/~rus/myNewPPP.pdf.

The domain dedicated computer system thus developed is a collection of software tools that can be implemented in a cloud and problem solver can subscribe to the cloud system for her problem domain, exactly as any other cloud user. The main components of the resulting DAL system are:

- The file (better yet the database) that records the domain ontology which evolves with problem solving process;
- A Domain Dedicated Virtual Machine (DDVM) that implements the brain assistant described above. The language of this machine is standardized as a Software Architecture Description Language (SADL), [Rus and Curtis (2006)].
- DAL translator which maps DAL algorithms into programs executed on the Internet by the DDVM [Rus and Bui (2010)].

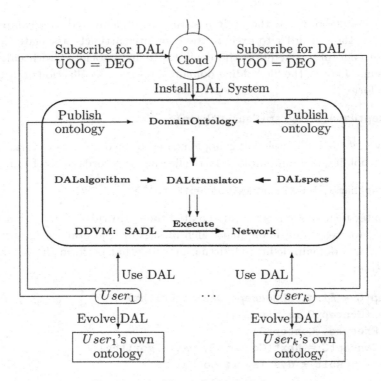

Fig. 14.1   Architecture of a DAL System

We have used the domain of arithmetic in order to test these ideas on the experimental model shown in Figure 14.1. Further, as shown in Figure 14.1, the user customizes the system to her personal use, evolving the problem domain she subscribed for with the concepts she learned and/or created during her own problem solving process. When the user decides to leave the system and cancel her subscription, the DAL System's manager may buy the knowledge developed by the user and update the domain, thus ensuring domain evolution with the concepts developed by the respective user. This ensures a domain evolution with the knowledge developed by problem solving process of all domain experts. A user doesn't need a computer in order to interact with the DAL System. An iPad or any other terminal which provides a two-way communication can be used in this purpose as described in Figure 14.2.

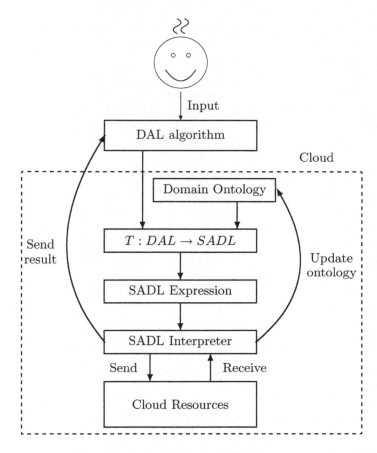

Fig. 14.2   Interacting with a DAL System

Chapter 15

Software Tool Development Illustration

Software tool design and implementation may be very complex. The best illustration of a software tool is the design and implementation of a translator. This is because we understand and use translators which are mappings $Translator : SL \rightarrow TL$ where SL is a languages called the Source Language, and TL is another language called the Target Language. If SL and TL are computer languages, depending upon their level of abstraction, the Translator is called a Compiler, an Interpreter, an Assembler, and/or a Loader/linker. The algorithm performing the mapping depends on our ability to structure SL and TL as mathematical abstractions. Further in this chapter we discuss the compiler implementation as a problem solved during WBPSP where the domain of expertise is Programming Languages. Hence, DAL for us is any programming language one would like to chose to express the compiler implementation algorithm. However, we hope this discussion to be a model for the Web-Based Problem Solving Process carried out for other problem domains.

15.1 Programming Language: The Concept

The usual textbook definition of a programming language is: *a Programming Language (PL) is a notation used to express computations carried out by computers.* However, there are three classes of people handling PL-s: language designers, who are people design languages; language implementers, who are programmers that design and implement translators; language users, who are programmers that use languages to solve problems by developing programs. Consequently people handling PL (designers, implementers, and users) may be different. Therefore, though they all manipulate the same PL, their understanding of that PL may be different. Consequence is that different implementations of a PL may be different.

15.1.1 *PL specification*

A PL is provided to its users as a notation defined by a collection of rules that allow one to construct well-formed expressions (programs) representing given computations. Example of such rules are those specifying C language programming. The definition of a programming language as a notation used to represent computations is adequate only for programmers. Language designers must answer such questions as: *what computations can one express with the given notation?* That is, language designer must provide a formal definition of the notation (language syntax and semantics). Language implementers must solve such problems as: *ensure that what programmer denotes is what machine executes!* That is, language implementer must also provide a formal relationship between semantics and syntax. Here we consider a PL a triple: $PL = \langle Semantics, Syntax, Semantics \leftrightarrow Syntax \rangle$ where:

(1) *Semantics*, further denoted by *Sem*, specifies the computations expressible by the language;
(2) *Syntax*, further denoted by *Syn*, specifies the notations used to express computations in *Sem*;
(3) The mapping $Sem \xrightarrow{\mathcal{L}} Syn$ specifies the rules that allow one to express computations $c \in Sem$ by notations $\mathcal{L}(c) \in Syn$; the mapping $Syn \xrightarrow{\mathcal{E}} Sem$ specifies the rules that allow one to evaluate notations $p \in Syn$ to computations $\mathcal{E}(p) \in Sem$.

For consistency reason the following constraints must me satisfied:

(1) $\forall c \in Sem(\mathcal{E}(\mathcal{L}(c)) = c)$. In plain English this says that for any computation c expressible through the language, the value of the expression of c must be c.
(2) $\forall p \in Syn(\mathcal{L}(\mathcal{E}(p)) = p)$. In plain English this says that for any expression p of the language, the expression of the computation represented by p must be p.

Conclusion is that since system programmers are language implementers, they need a definition of a PL that allows them to design and implement compilers $C : PL \to ML$ such that communication consistency is preserved.

Hence, the definition of a PL needs to include:

(1) A mechanism that allows program recognition as a syntactically valid construct of the PL. This implies a formal syntax.
(2) A mechanism that allows program generation as a semantically valid construct. This implies a formal semantic.
(3) The mappings $\mathcal{L} : Sem \mapsto Syn$ and $\mathcal{E} : Syn \mapsto Sem$ in the language definition $PL = \langle Sem, Syn, Sem \leftrightarrow Syn \rangle$, must be computable.
(4) The relationships $\forall c \in Sem\ (\mathcal{E}(\mathcal{L}(c)) = c)$ and $\forall p \in Syn\ (\mathcal{L}(\mathcal{E}(p)) = p)$ must be expressible by algorithms.

For example, considering C as a programming language we observe that:

(1) *C semantics* is the collection of computations that can be expressed as C language programs (not formally defined).
(2) *C syntax* is the collection of rules allowing us to write valid C programs. These rules are formally specified by BNF notation[Backus (1959)].
(3) *Learning C* is the collection of rules allowing C users to express valid computations in C semantics using appropriate notations in C syntax. These rules sit at the basis of learning C programming.
(4) *Evaluating C* is the collection of rules allowing programmers to evaluate C programs computing solutions they represent. These rules allow programmers to implement C compilers.

Assuming now that the concept of a programming language is well defined, we observe that the source and the target languages of a compiler are usually different. In addition, the source language is manipulated by human-programmers, while the target language is manipulated by the hardware-processor. Thus, human programmers and hardware processors communicate using translators.For example, C programmers implementing software tools use the C-language to express their programs. This implies that a C-compiler must be available and must ensure that processor performs the computations meant by the programmer in her universe of discourse. How is this possible?

15.1.2 *The language as a communication mechanism*

A general communication process implies two communicators, a **speaker** and a **hearer**, that exchange information using languages they speak. The general concept of a language used during a speaker and a hearer in a communication process is no different from the general concept of a programming language. Programming languages are particular only in the sense that their speakers are programmers that "speak programming languages" and their hearers are "machine processors" that perform computations implied by programmers during their communication. Therefore we use the general process of communication using languages to illustrate the major problems raised by language implementation.

Assume that the speaker speaks the language $L_1 = \langle Sem_1, Syn_1,$ $Sem_1 \leftrightarrow Syn_1 \rangle$ and the hearer speaks the language $L_2 = \langle Sem_2, Syn_2,$ $Sem_2 \leftrightarrow Syn_2 \rangle$. A communication between speaker and hearer is carried out by moving information on the following diagram of communication: $speaker \longrightarrow hearer \longrightarrow speaker \longrightarrow \dots$. Hence, the communication in a communication system implies a learning process that consists of:

(1) Speaker and hearer interact with their universe of discourse Sem_1 and Sem_2, respectively, thus generating knowledge k_1 and k_2 that represent the substance of their communication.

(2) To be subject of communication knowledge k_1 and k_2 must be represented as well-formed expressions of their languages, Syn_1 and Syn_2, respectively.

(3) If L_1 is different from L_2, in order to move information on the diagram of communication, translators $T_1 : Syn_1 \rightarrow Syn_2$ and $T_2 : Syn_2 \rightarrow Syn_1$ that preserve the knowledge k_1 and k_2, are required.

Knowledge Generation: the speaker interacts with her universe of discourse and generates knowledge expressions. For example, a C programmer speaker may asks a hearer (the processor of her computer) to generate the fifth prime number. Here we assume that the speaker knows that a number is prime iff it is divisible only with 1 and with itself. Since there are an infinite number of prime numbers the speaker uses $\mathcal{L}_1 : Sem_1 \rightarrow Syn_1$ to produce a prime number generator, say `primegen.c`. Then, the speaker gives `primegen.c` to the hearer saying: "use `primegen.c` to generate the fifth prime number".

Knowledge Evaluation: the hearer receives the knowledge from the speaker and evaluates it. In the example of generating a prime number, the processor of the computer representing the hearer translates the C language expression `primegen.c` into a valid expression of its machine language, $primeGenerator = T_1(primegen.c) \in Syn_2$. Then the processor uses $\mathcal{E}_2 : Syn_2 \rightarrow Sem_2$ to generate the prime number $p = primeGenerator(5) \in Sem_2$. Further the processor uses $\mathcal{L}_2 : Sem_2 \rightarrow Syn_2$

to generate the expression $\mathcal{L}_2(5) \in Syn_2$ (in our example '111') and gives it to the C programmer as the result. Notice that the C programmer receives the resulting $\mathcal{L}_2(5)$ (that is, 111) from the processor. The programmer needs to map $\mathcal{L}_2(5)$ into the expression $T_2(\mathcal{L}_2(5))$ in Syn_1 in order to be able to handle it. That is, since the speaker is a C programmer, she computes the value of the expression $(2^2 + 2^1 + 2^0)$ to get $7 \in Syn_1(L_1)$. In other words, speaker uses $\mathcal{E}_1 : Syn_1 \rightarrow Sem_1$ to map $T_2(\mathcal{L}_2(5))$ into the prime number 7 (seven), originally meant. The speaker and hearer can stop their communication process at will.

Conclusions:

(1) Language users use languages for interaction with their universe of discourse and for interaction with other communicators;
(2) The interaction with the universe of discourse is done by using the language learning function $\mathcal{L}$ to express knowledge (computing needs) as language constructs;
(3) The interaction with others communicators (machines) is done by using the language evaluation function $\mathcal{E}$ to evaluate language constructs to knowledge (their meaning).

During a communication process the expressions of one communicator's knowledge (say the speaker) are evaluated by the other communicator (say the hearer) using hearers evaluation mapping $\mathcal{E}$. This implies that communication is achieved by mapping one communicator's language expressions into valid expressions of the other communicator's language, such that the communication consistency is ensured. This means that the language use in any communication process implies translation!

15.1.3 *Translator definition and implementation*

A translator $T : L_1 \rightarrow L_2$ is a tuple $T = \langle H, C \rangle$, $H : Sem_1 \rightarrow Sem_2$, $C : Syn_1 \rightarrow Syn_2$ that makes commutative the diagram in Figure 15.1. A translators $T : L_1 \rightarrow L_2$ is implemented by embedding Sem_1 into Syn_2 thus facilitating the evaluation of L_1 elements as elements of L_2, as shown in Figure 15.2.

The rationale for this translation implementation results from the communication constraint: *speaker expressions are evaluated by hearer*. This is achieved by the following general process of translator implementation, which is no different from a general process of compiler implementation.

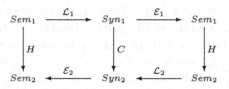

Fig. 15.1   Translator diagram

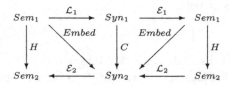

Fig. 15.2   Translator implementation diagram

(1) Semantics of L_1 is specified by representing it using the syntax of L_2.
(2) This ensures that for any well-formed expression w of L_1 there will be a well-formed expression w^T of L_2 which expresses the same meaning as w.
(3) Since w^T is an expression of L_2 it can be evaluated in L_2.

For example, consider communication between people speaking different languages.

Translator Correctness: if *Embed* is an isomorphic embedding of Sem_1 into Syn_2 then the tuple

$$H = Embed \circ \mathcal{E}_2, C = \mathcal{E}_1 \circ Embed$$

defines a correct translator $T : L_1 \to L_2$. The proof of this statement is in [Rus (2002); Van Wyk (2003)].

Translator Illustration: the implementation of a translator is a quite elaborated program. We will illustrate it here considering the simplest computer languages:

- The source language L_1 will be the assembly language of a computer platform, $AL = \langle AL_{sem}, AL_{syn}, Learn_{AL} : AL_{sem} \to AL_{syn} \rangle$.
- The target language L_2 will be the machine language of the same computer platform. $ML = \langle ML_{sem}, ML_{syn}, Learn_{ML} : ML_{sem} \to ML_{syn} \rangle$.

- (H, C) will be the assembler, that is, $H : AL_{sem} \rightarrow ML_{sem}$, $C : AL_{syn} \rightarrow ML_{syn}$, such that diagram in Figure 15.1 commutes.

The implementation of the assembler will be provided by the mappings: $H = Embed(AL_{sem}) \circ Eval(ML_{syn})$ and $C = Eval(AL_{syn}) \circ Embed(AL_{sem})$.

15.2 The Assembler

Informally, the assembler is the system program that maps assembly language programs into machine language programs. However, to design and implement an assembler we need a formal definition. This can be obtained by looking at the assembler as a translator $T : A \rightarrow M$, where $A = \langle A_{sem}, A_{syn}, A_{sem} \longleftrightarrow A_{syn} \rangle$ is the assembly language and, $M = \langle M_{sem}, M_{syn}, M_{sem} \longleftrightarrow M_{syn} \rangle$ is the machine language of the computer platform of interest. Now, since the assembler is a translator, assembler is defined as the tuple $T = (H, C)$ where: $H : A_{sem} \rightarrow M_{sem}$, $C : A_{syn} \rightarrow M_{syn}$ are such that the assembler diagram in Figure 15.3 is commutative. The diagram in Figure 15.13 is obtained from the translator

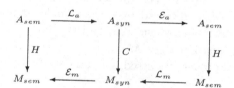

Fig. 15.3   Assembler diagram

diagram in Figure 15.1 by replacing L_1 with A and L_2 with M.

Following the procedure for translator implementation, the assembler $T : A \rightarrow M$ is implemented by embedding A_{sem} into M_{syn} thus facilitating the evaluation of A programs as M programs as shown in Figure 15.4.

Assembler is the software tool that provides the first level of abstraction of the physical machine. Therefore, the assembler is usually the first system program that needs to run on a new computer platform. It provides the framework for the implementation of the software tool hierarchy that transform the physical machine into the abstraction used by computer programmers. Thus, the assembler has a special role in the process of software design and implementation. Therefore, here we actually discuss an

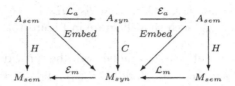

Fig. 15.4   Assembler implementation diagram

assembler generator which when fed with the machine language and the assembly language of a given machine is instantiated into the assembler of the respective machine. Feasibility of this approach for assembler implementation results from the fact that the assembly language of a machine M, $A = \langle A_{sem}, A_{syn}, A_{sem} \leftrightarrow A_{syn} \rangle$, and the machine language of the machine M, $M = \langle M_{sem}, M_{syn}, M_{sem} \leftrightarrow M_{syn} \rangle$, are related by the equality $A_{sem} = M_{sem}$. Hence, the semantic mapping $H : A_{sem} \rightarrow M_{sem}$ in the assembler definition is the identity mapping. Another consequence of the equality $A_{sem} = M_{sem}$ is that A_{syn} and M_{syn} are algebraic similar structures. Moreover, M_{syn} and A_{syn} are defined on three levels: lexical elements (also called generators), data and operation definition patterns, and program definition patterns. Again, since $A_{sem} = M_{sem}$, the mapping $Embed : A_{sem} \rightarrow M_{syn}$ required by the assembler definition is independent of the actual machine considered, and is obtained from the machine language learning function $\mathcal{L}_m : M_{sem} \rightarrow M_{syn}$. Hence, to implement an assembler by the approach discussed here one needs to:

(1) Develop the machine language $M = \langle M_{sem}, M_{syn}, M_{sem} \leftrightarrow M_{syn} \rangle$;
(2) Develop the assembly language, $A = \langle A_{sem}, A_{syn}, A_{sem} \leftrightarrow A_{syn} \rangle$;
(3) Instantiate the mapping $Embed()$ into $Embed(A_{sem}, M_{syn})$.

The embedding of the A_{sem} into M_{syn} is based on the assumption that A and M are similar algebraic structures and are both defined on three-layers hierarchy: (a) lexical elements, (b) operation patterns, and (c) program patterns, where:

(1) There is a finite number of lexical patterns of the assembly language and thus they can be specified by appropriate entries in the Lexical Table, (LexTab).
(2) A's operation patterns represent M's operations. They are defined by the appropriate entries in the Operation Table (OPTAB) specifying

assembly language operations in terms of the machine representation of their lexical elements stored in LexTab.

(3) A's programs represent machine language programs defined by binary patterns according to predefined standards resulting from the M's operation composition according to the machine architecture.

Example such tabular specification of the assembly language is the Class File Format of Java Virtual Machine (JVM). With this specification, the assembler generator discussed here is implemented by the three readings of the assembly language program:

(1) Reads an assembly language program statement by statement. Use the LexTab to identify the lexical elements composing each statement and remember their machine language representations in a Symbol Table (SymTab).

(2) Read again the assembly language program statement by statement. Use OPTAB to represent each statement as machine language code in terms of the machine representations of its lexical elements stored in SymTab. Remember the machine code representing assembly language statements in the Statement Table (StaTab).

(3) Read again the assembly language program statement by statement. Use StaTab to compose the machine language code representing the assembly statement into machine language programs according to patterns specified in the OPTAB.

Of course, using properties of the machine architecture, this general algorithm implementing an assembler generator can be simplified, as we shall see in the next. Further in this chapter we discus the machine language specification, assembly language specification, and assembler implementation. We will illustrate our discussion with Oolong, the assembly language of the JVL, and will use C language to develop the pseudocode of the assembler generator.

15.3 Machine Language Specification

The machine language of a computer system is defined by the tuple: $M = \langle M_{sem}, M_{syn}, M_{sem} \leftrightarrow M_{syn} \rangle$ where:

- M_{sem} stands for the machine language semantics;
- M_{syn} stands for the machine language syntax;
- $Learn_M : M_{sem} \to M_{syn}$ is the machine language learning relationship;

- $Eval_M : M_{syn} \to M_{sem}$ is the machine language program execution.

15.3.1 Machine language semantics

M_{sem} is specified as a Binary Computation System (BCS), $BCS = \langle\{0,1\}^*, Data, Operations\rangle$, where:

(1) *Data* are the binary patterns used for the codification of real data as machine representations;
(2) *Operations* are all machine operation codes (i.e., all operations performed by the control processor).

Notice that computations performed by M are expressed as sequences of machine operations and data called programs.

15.3.2 Machine language syntax

M_{syn} is specified by a three level hierarchical construction:

- **Level 0:** lexical objects (generators);
- **Level 1:** operation schemes (computation units representing machine instructions and data);
- **Level 2:** machine language program.

M_{syn} lexical objects are the collection of hardware recognized binary codes. Examples of such codes are opcodes, register numbers, addresses of memory locations, and immediate values. All other computation objects in M_{syn} are expressed in terms of these entities.

M_{syn} operation schemes are the machine language instruction and data words. For any given computer architecture, the machine language instruction words are defined by a fixed collection of parameterized patterns expressing machine operations in terms of operation and operand codes (see ISA discussed in the Chapter 5). Also, the machine language data words are defined by a fixed collection of parameterized patterns expressing machine language data as typed operand codes.

15.3.2.1 Data Representation Patterns

Each machine architecture has a finite set of parameterized patterns used to encode data as machine language elements. Examples of data representation pattern are fixed point and floating point data representation.

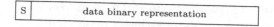

Fig. 15.5   Memory location holding fixed point data

A fixed point data is defined by the equality `data = sign value`, where sign is + or − and value is an integer. This is encoded into a memory location as shown in Figure 15.5. Here $S = 0$ if data value is positive and $S = 1$ if data value is negative. A floating point data is defined by the equality `data = sign mantissa * ` 10^E, where sign is + or −, mantissa is an integer, and E is a positive or negative exponent. This is encoded into a memory location as shown in Figure 15.6, where `Exponent` and `Mantissa`

S	Exponent	Mantissa

Fig. 15.6   Memory location holding floating point data

are binary representations of E and *mantissa*, respectively.

Observations:

- Data representation pattern are standardized by different organizations, such as IEEE, thus making easier the interaction between different computer architectures.
- Other data representation patterns, such as characters, decimal numbers, etc., may also be available.
- Data codification patterns are generated as binary values representable as `machine recognized codes` stored in memory locations.

15.3.2.2   *Instruction Representation Patterns*

Machine instructions are defined by a finite set of binary patterns to be stored in memory locations representing machine instructions. Machine instruction patterns are machine architecture specific. Here, we illustrate machine instruction patterns specific to three kinds of machine architecture: fixed-length instruction, multiple-length instructions, and variable-length instructions.

The fixed size instruction architecture is illustrated by Mix machine instruction pattern defined in Figure 15.7. Since Mix is a theoretical computer this pattern has only an illustration value. However, fixed length instruction patterns are used also by real machine, such as RISC computers. The characteristic of a computer architecture using fixed length instruction patterns is *faster instruction execution.*

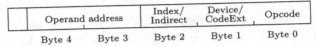

	Operand address	Index/ Indirect	Device/ CodeExt	Opcode
	Byte 4 Byte 3	Byte 2	Byte 1	Byte 0

Fig. 15.7   Mix machine instruction pattern

Multiple-length instruction architecture is illustrated by the IBM 360/370 architecture which uses four fixed patterns specifying instructions on 2 bytes, 4 bytes, and 6 bytes:

- **RR-pattern**: 2 bytes instructions performing operations of signature *Register* × *Register* → *Register*, encoded as shown in Figure 15.8.

Opcode	R1	R2

Fig. 15.8   RR instruction pattern

Interpretation: $0 \leq R1, R2 \leq 15$, R1 := R1 Opcode R2; R2 unchanged.
- **RX-instruction pattern:** four bytes instructions pattern encodes operations of signature *Register* × *Memory* → *Register* as shown in Figure 15.9.

Opcode	R	I	X	B	D

Fig. 15.9   RX instruction pattern

Interpretation: $0 \leq R \leq 15$, $0 \leq I \leq 15$, $0 \leq B \leq 7$, $X = 0$ when direct access, $X = 1$ when indirect access. Operation encoded is: $R = Opcode(R, ((D + (B + 8)) + I))$.
- **SI-instruction pattern:** four bytes instructions performing operations of signature *Immediate* × *Memory* → *Memory* as shown in Figure 15.10.

Interpretation: $0 \leq I - value \leq 2^{15} - 1$, $0 \leq B \leq 7$, $X = 0$ when direct access, $X = 1$ when indirect access. Operation thus encoded is: $D + (B + 8) = Opcode(I - value, (D + (B + 8)))$.

Opcode	I-value	X	B	D

Fig. 15.10   RX instruction pattern

- **SS-Instruction pattern:** encoding six bytes instructions performing variable length operations of signature $Memory \times Memory \rightarrow Memory$, as shown in Figure 15.11.

Opcode	Length	B1	D1	B2	D2

Fig. 15.11   SS instruction pattern

Interpretation: $\langle (B1 + 8) + D1; Length \rangle := Opcode(\langle (B1 + 8) + D1; Length \rangle, \langle (B2 + 8) + D2; Length \rangle)$

Variable length instruction architecture is illustrated by VAX-11/780 architecture where instructions are encoded on one variable-length pattern as shown in Figure 15.12.

Opcode	Operand 1	$\cdots$	Up to Operand 6

Fig. 15.12   VAX-11/780 instruction pattern

Interpretation: opcode is codified on one byte and specifies the operation and the number of operands. Each operand occupies two bytes and specifies an address expression in terms of lexical elements: register, memory location, immediate value, index, indirection.

15.3.3   *Machine language program*

A machine language program is a finite sequence of machine language instructions and data. Depending upon the execution environment, a program may have a variable size stack. However, note that any M_{syn} construct of level 2 (i.e., program) is expressed as a parameterized pattern in terms of constructs of level 1 (i.e., instructions and data). Figure 15.13 shows common ML program patterns.

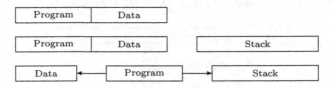

Fig. 15.13   Machine language program patterns

15.3.4   *Machine language learning function*

$Learn_M : M_{sem} \rightarrow M_{syn}$ is a collection of rules that show how to use codes of data and instructions to express machine language computations. Example of such rules is: *encode operations as instructions stored in adjacent and successive memory locations; do not mix instructions and data.* Other examples of $Learn_M$ rules are: rules for data codification, memory locations and register usage, machine language instruction and data generation, program and data storage in computer memory.

15.3.5   *Machine language evaluation function*

$Eval_M : M_{syn} \rightarrow M_{sem}$ is the machine language program evaluation. We use C language to provide a formal specification of the machine language program evaluation by simulating M_{syn} program execution. The assumptions are:

- Lexical elements (registers, memory locations, immediate values, modifiers (index, indirection)) are predefined codes given as constants for a given machine. They are stored in the LexTab.
- To simulate program evaluation we represent instruction and data patterns by the C language constructs called `InstructionPattern` and `DataPattern`, as seen below.

```
struct InstructionPattern
    {
    int             Opcode;
    struct OpdSpec Operand;
    struct ResSpec Result;
    };
```

```
struct DataPattern
    {
      int DataType;
      struct DataSpec data;
    };
```

where `Opcode` is in the LexTab and Operand and Result are address expressions specified by `OpSpec` and `ResSpec` respectively. Alsos, for the purpose of program evaluation we represent program pattern by a C structure, as seen below.

```
struct ProgramPattern
    {
      struct DataPattern   Data[MaxData];
      struct InstructionPattern Code[MaxCode];
    } Program;
```

Now the machine language program evaluation (or program execution) is simulated by the `EvalM()` C function.

```
EvalM(struct ProgramPattern *program)
    {
    struct InstructionPattern *PC; /* PC is program counter */
    PC = program;  /* program points to first instruction */
    while (PC.Opcode != Halt)
        {
          Evaluate(PC);
          PC = Next(PC);
        }
    }
```

Observations:

- The `Evaluate()` is architecture dependent and represents the function `Eval()` performed by the processor when the instruction having as the operation code the `Opcode` is discovered.
- Von Neumann architectures use a function *Next()* wired in the instruction cycle;
- Non Von Neumann architectures use a function *Next()* that may depend upon other relationships such as data availability.

For illustration purpose the target of the assembler discussed in this book should be a Virtual Machine (VM) that can be used to simulate the computation of any real machine. Java Virtual Machine (JVM) is such a machines. JVM (also known by compiler construction community as the P-machine)[Wilhelm and Maurer (1995)] was successfully used as the target in many projects on compiler design and implementation. Currently JVM is successfully used as an abstract machine simulating the computation performed by current real machines in Java language environments. Interpreters simulating the execution of JVM programs on real hardware are extensively implemented and accepted. Oolong[Engels (1999)] the assembly language of the JVM is freely available. Hence, applying our methodology for assembler constriction to JVM may provides a good educational experience.

15.4 JVM Specification

JVM is an abstract computer defined by the tuple $JVM = \langle Processor,$ $Program, ExecutionModel \rangle$. The *Processor* in this definition is an abstraction used to represent any concrete hardware. Hence, it should be a virtual computer and an implementation. Once this virtual computer is implemented on a particular computer platform all programs written for the virtual computer will run on that platform. This allows programmers to *write programs once* (for the virtual computer) and *run them anywhere*, (Java slogan). We follow JVM presentation in [Engels (1999)] to illustrate the concept of a machine language.

The virtual computer operates on an abstract memory handling *objects* rather than bits and bytes. That is, the virtual computer hides the complexities of a real hardware such as memory structure and addressing intricacies of instruction patterns, and program control and data flows.

JVM as a computer abstraction is defined by:

- The set of operations that it performs, called bytecodes.
- The structure of the program JVM can execute called the *Class File Format*, (CFF).
- The *Verification* algorithm that ensures the integrity of JVM program.

During program execution the JVM processor takes its instructions from the CFF. Operations performed by JVM and their operands are taken from a stack and their results are placed on the stack. Hence, address computation is not a problem. JVM operates on objects rather than operating on bits and bytes. The interpretation is the same for all instructions executed by JVM processor. JVM instructions are classified in 5 groups:

(1) Instructions whose operands are in top of the stack.
(2) Instructions for object allocation.
(3) Instructions for method invocation.
(4) Instruction for retrieving and modifying fields in the objects.
(5) Instructions for moving information between stack and objects.

Consider the following JVM code:

```
getstatic java/lang/System/out Ljava/io/PrintStream;
ldc "Hello, world"
invokevirtual java/io/PrintStream/println (Ljava/lang/String;)V
```

The meaning of this code is:

(1) Retrieve the value of `out` field in the class `java/lang/System` and push it on the stack; this is an object of the class `java/io/PrintStream`;
(2) Push the string constant `Hello, world` on the stack
(3) Invoke the method `println`, which is defined in the class `java/lang/PrintStream` and expects stack to contain an object of `java/lang/String` and a reference to `out`.

15.4.1   *Class file format*

Class File Format (CFF) represents a Java class as a stream of bytes. Java platform has methods for converting Java class files into classes in JVM. CFF is not necessarily a file, it can be stored in a database, across the network, as part of Java archive file, JAR, etc. CFF is standardized and is manipulated by the `ClassLoader`, which is part of Java platform. However, if one stores CFF in a nonstandard form then one needs to construct an appropriate `ClassLoader` to handle it.

15.4.2   *Verification algorithm*

The purpose of the verification algorithm is to ensures that JVM programs follow a set of rules that are designed to protect their integrity. The verification algorithm perform an abstract interpretation of CFF. If this fails the JVM program in the CFF is aborted.

15.4.3   *Java platform*

JVM performs fundamental computational tasks but it lacks features for doing computer-oriented things like graphics, Internet communications, etc. Java platform includes JVM and a collection of classes that are collected into the package `java`. Examples of such classes are: `java.applet`, `java.io`, `java.awt`, `java.security`, etc. The assumption is that JVM cannot function independent of Java platform. In other words JVM execution model assumes that Java platform contains `java.lang.Object`, `java.lang.ClassLoader`, `java.lang.String`, `java.lang.Class`. Note the dot-notation for Java and slash notation for JVM

15.4.4   *JVM architecture*

Architecturally JVM is divided into four conceptual data spaces:

- *Class area*, where the JVM program (CFF) is kept.
- *Java stack*, which keeps track of which methods have been called and the data associated with each method invocation.
- *Heap*, where objects are kept.
- *Native method stacks*, for supporting native methods.

15.4.4.1   *Class Area*

Stores the classes loaded into the system; each class is defined in terms of the properties: its superclasses, the list of interfaces (possibly empty), the list of fields, the list of methods and their implementations stored in the method area, the list of constants, stored in the constant pool. All properties of a class are immutable (i.e., are unchangeable).

15.4.4.2   *Class Descriptors*

Each field of a class is defined by a descriptor that shows the properties of the object occupying that field, such as the access rights and wether it is static or not. For nonstatic fields there is a copy in each object of the class; for static fields there is a single copy for the entire class of objects. Each method is defined by a descriptor that shows method type, access rights to the method, and method modifiers such as `abstract, static, etc.` An abstract method has no implementation; a non-abstract method has an implementation defined in terms of JVM instructions.

15.4.5 *JVM stack*

JVM operates on a stack of *stack frames*. A stack frame consists of three components:

(1) The operands of the operations performed by JVM. The operands are accessed by `push` and `pop` operations.
(2) The array of local variables. Local variables of a method are accessed by index.
(3) Frame data, which contains data to support constant pool resolution, normal method return, exception dispatch, and program counter PC that shows first instruction of the method.

15.4.6 *Execution model*

JVM program consists of a collection of methods. Program execution starts by pushing on the JVM stack the stack frame of the method `main()`. Each time a method is invoked a new stack frame is created and is pushed on the JVM stack. When a method terminates its stack frame is popped out, and control is given to the method that inveoked the terminating method. The JVM performs the loop:

```
while (PC.opcode != Halt)
    {
      Execute (PC);
      PC := Next(PC);
    }
```

The top frame of JVM stack shows the currently executing method and is called *active frame* (AF). Only the active frame can be used during JVM program execution. Each operation performed by JVM evaluates an expression whose operands are on the operand stacks and leave the result on the operand stack. When a method calls another method the PC of the caller is saved in the active frame. When callee completes the result is pushed on top of the operand stack and the caller is resumed using the PC from callee stack frame and caller array of local variables.

15.4.7 *The heap*

Each object is associated with a class (its type) in the class area and is stored in the heap. Each object has a number of slots for storing fields;

there is one slot for each nonstatic field in the class associated with the object. Each object has a number of slots storing methods that operate on that object; there is one method for each abstract method of the class associated with the object.

15.4.8　*Native method stacks*

Native methods are methods implemented using other languages than JVM. Native methods allow programmer to handle situations that cannot be handled completely by Java, such as interfacing with platform dependent features or legacy code. Native methods are executed using C-like stacks. Native methods do not exist on all JVM implementations; moreover, different JVM implementations may have different standards for native methods. The standard Java Native Interface, JNI, should be available for native method documentation.

15.4.9　*Garbage collection*

Each object consumes some memory from the heap. Eventually the memory allocated to JVM object is reclaimed. JVM reclaims object's memory automatically through a process called *garbage collection*. An object is ready to be garbage collected when it is no longer "alive". Rules that determining if an object is alive are:

(1) If there is a reference to the object on the stack then the object is alive;
(2) If there is a reference to the object in a local variable on the stack or in a static field, then the object is alive;
(3) If a field of an alive object contains a reference to the object then the object is alive;
(4) JVM may internally keep references to certain objects, for example to support native methods. These objects are alive.

15.4.10　*Verification process*

The verification process ensures that class files follow certain rules. Thus, it allows JVM to assume that a class has certain safety properties and to make optimizations based on this assumption. It also makes it possible to safely download Java applets from Internet. Java compiler generates correct code. However JVM programmer can bypass the restrictions. Verification algorithm ensures that this process is not bypassed. The verification process asks questions about CFF, such as:

- Is CFF a structurally valid class?
- Are all constant references correct?
- Are all instructions valid?
- Will stack and locals contain values of appropriate type?

15.5   JVM Language Syntax

Since JVM is a machine, its machine language is defined on a hierarchy of three levels: Lexicon, Constants and Instructions, and CFF.

- JVM Lexicon consists of byte codes, indices in CFF (integers), indices in the array of local variable (integers), constant tags.
- Constants and instructions (to be seen further).
- Class File Format (CFF) to be described further.

15.5.1   *JVM codes*

JVM uses Unicode character codes (rather than ASCCI or EBCDIC). The Unicode Consortium manages these codes. The Unicode was designed such that it can accommodate any known character set used by people's alphabets. Unicode Transformation Formats (UTF) UTF-8, UTF-16, UTF-32 are Unicode character representations on byte, 2-bytes (half-word), 4-bytes (word).

15.5.2   *Constant tags*

Byte representation of various JVM constants is specified by descriptors called *constant tags*. The specifications of these descriptors are in Table 15.1.

15.5.3   *The structure of CFF*

The JVM program pattern is called Class File Format (CFF). The CFF structure is used by JVM validation process. The first 4 bytes of CFF must contain the hex number **CA FE BA BE** which is used as the magic number telling the Validator that the data that follows is a JVM program, exactly as the suffix ".c" tells C compiler that a file whose name ends in ".c" contain a C program. Following the magic number are minor and major versions,

Table 15.1

Tag	Type	Format	Interpretation
1	UTF8	2+n	2 bytes encode n followed n bytes text
2	reserved		
3	Integer	4 bytes	Text of a signed integer
4	Float	4 bytes	Text of IEEE 754 floating-point number
5	Long	8 bytes	Text of long signed integer
6	Double	8 bytes	Text of IEEE 754 double-precision number
7	Class	2 bytes	Reference to class name, a UTF8 constant
8	String	2 bytes	Reference to string name, a UTF8 constant
9	FieldRef	4 bytes	2 indexes to consant pool: one showing the name and another showing the type
10	MethodRef	4 bytes	Same as FieldRef
11	IntMetRef	4 bytes	Same as FieldRef
12	NameAndType	4 bytes	2 bytes show name, next 2 show descriptor

each taking two bytes interpreted as a 16-bit unsigned: For example, JDK 1.0, 1.1: Major = 0X2D (45), Minor = 0X3(3); Java 2: Major: 0X2E(46); Minor: 0, if Major = 45 then Minor > 3. Figure 15.14 shows the structure of a CFF.

Magic#	Minor	Major	CnstPool	Class	Super	Fields	Interfaces	Methods	Attributes

Fig. 15.14   Structure of a properly formatted CFF

Each component of the CFF is prefixed by a count showing the number of entries contained in that component. In turns, each entry in the component is prefixed by a tag defining the manner in which this entry is interpreted by JVM. Thus, `ConstPool` is identified as the component that follows the Major and is prefiexed by a count showing the number of constants it contains. Each eantry in the `ConstPool` has the struture: `Tag Count String` where `Tag` defines the meaning of the `String` and `Count` is the size of the `String`. Class component is specified by the tag 7 and an index in the constant pool showing the class name as a string, and similarly superclasss; superclass component is identified by the tag value 8 and a two byte index at the superclass name in the constant pool. Interfaces are specieied by a count and each interface imethod is then specified by the tag 11 and two indicesd to constant pool, one showing the interface name and other showing its tyoe. Figure 15.15, an addaptation from [Engels (1999)], shows a fragment of the constant pool of the code:

```
.class Foo
.super Bar
.implements Baz

.field field1 LFoo;
.method isEven (I)Z
.end method
```

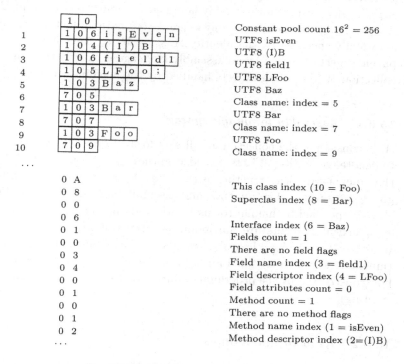

Fig. 15.15   Constant pool of a CFF

Most CFF sections begin with a count, which is a two-byte unsigned, followed by count instances of some pattern of bytes. Constant pool start with a count followed by as many constant patterns as it specifies. Each constant pattern consists of one byte tag and a number of bytes on which constant is written. The tag describes the kind of constant that follows and how many bytes does it take. If any tag is invalid or file ends before correct number of constants is found then CFF is rejected.

15.6   Assembly Language

The assembly languagei of a machine M is a tuple $A = \langle A_{sem}, A_{syn}, Learn_A : A_{sem} \leftrightarrow A_{syn} \rangle$ where A_{sem} stands for assembly language semantics, A_{syn} stands for assembly language syntax, $Learn_A : A_{sem} \rightarrow A_{syn}$ stands for assembly language learning function, and $Eval_A : A_{syn} \rightarrow A_{sem}$ stands for assembly language evaluation function. Since A_{sem} is formally specified by the identity $A_{sem} = M_{sem}$, the collection of computing objects handled by an assembly language is exactly the same as the collection of computing objects handled by the machine language.

15.6.1   *Assembly language syntax*

A_{syn} consists of the collection of all well formed symbolic constructs used to denote computing objects provided in the A_{sem}. Therefore the A_{syn} has the same hierarchical structure as the M_{syn}: lexical elements, assembly language constants and statements, and assembly language program. Further, A_{syn} is specified by human (or user) oriented mnemonic patterns. That is, A_{syn} lexical elements are mnemonic notations of M_{syn} lexical elements. In other words, A_{syn} lexical elements are: assembler specified symbols (mnemonics) which are fixed for a given assembler, and user specified symbols constructed by the programmer during assembly program development (writing).

15.6.2   *Kind of mnemonics*

According to their computational meaning the mnemonics are classified as:

- Mnemonics denoting machine operations, such as `add, sub, mul, load`, etc.;
- Mnemonics denoting pseudo operations (aslo called directivess) such as `def, ref, dc, dv, equ`, etc.;
- Mnemonics used to define and use macro operations, such as `macdef, macend, maccall`.

For the purpose of the assembler construction the mnemonics are represented here using C data structures:

- If mnemonics are strings of fixed length then their C representation could be:

```
char Mnemonic[MaxMnemLength];
```

where `MaxMnemLength` is the length of the longest string denoting a mnemonic;

- If mnemonics are strings of variable length then their C representation could be:

```
char *Mnemonic;
```

where `Mnemonic` is a pointer to a string representing the mnemonic.

15.6.3 *User defined symbols*

Usually, the programmer defined symbols during programming are:

(1) **Identifiers:** strings of characters which starts with a letter and contains letters, digits, and may be some other assembler defined symbols;
(2) **Numbers:** which are any decimal representation of integers or real numbers;
(3) **Literals:** strings whose values are their representations;
(4) **Expressions:** strings of identifiers, numbers, and literals separated by operators and parentheses;
(5) **Strings:** sequence of characters enclosed in special parentheses such as quotes " and ".

Programmer specified symbols are represented here by the C construct:

```
struct UserSpecSymb
    {
      int  Length;
      char Symbol[Length];
    };
```

The length of the symbol in characters is given by the integer `Length`. The symbol nature may be encapsulated within the program which recognizes it, or it my be provided by a descriptor associated with the symbol.

15.6.4 *Assembly language statements*

The assembly language statements are parameterized patterns constructed from lexical elements. The parameter components of such patterns are:

(1) Statement name called label – user defined ;
(2) Operation code, called mnemonic – assembler defined ;
(3) Operand, which is an expression – user defined;
(4) Comment, destined to programmers that may read the program.

The statement structures could be formally specified by the pattern:

```
Label  Opcode  Operand  Comment
```

where `Label`, `Opcode`, `Operand`, `Comment` are the components of the assembly statement. The statement representation by a C construct could be one of:

- *Fixed position pattern:* where parameter position determines its meaning;
- *Variable position patterns:* where a keyword is used to determine the component meaning.

For the purpose of statement recognition during assembler implementation, the statement specification must be formally provided. This can be done using the following BNF rules:

```
Statement = Label Mnemonic Operand Comment
Label    = String | empty
Mnemonic = String
Operand  = Expression {, Expression} | empty
Comment  = String | empty
```

The C representation of a fixed position pattern could be:

```
struct AssemblyStatement
     {
     char Label  [MaxLabLength];
     char Opcode [MaxMneLength];
     char Operand[MaxOpdLength];
     char Comment[MaxComLength];
     };
```

Notice that this representation waste space because it relies on maximum space reserved for each component. To prevent space wasting one can use a fixed size record representation of the assembly statement defined by:

(1) A symbol space where symbols making up statements are accumulated;
(2) A data structure holding pointers to the symbol space, Figure 15.16.

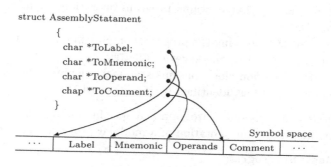

Fig. 15.16 Fixed fields statement representation

15.6.5 *Assembly language program*

An assembly language program is a sequence of assembly language statements. Formally, this can be defined by the following BNF notation:

AssemblyProgram = AssemblyStatement {,AssemblyStatement}

Depending upon assembler versatility, during the assembly process, the assembly language program can be represented by one of:

(1) An array of statement representation, such as

```
struct AssemblyStatement [Length];
```

where Length is the maximum number of assembly language statements composing the program.

(2) A more natural representation is a file defined by:

```
FILE *source, *fopen();
source = fopen (SourceProgram, "r");
```

15.6.6　*Program modularization*

Assembly language programs are modularized by sections of assembly language code identified by keywords. Common sections and keywords identifying them are:

- A program section that contains only data definitions, identified by the keyword DSECT;;
- A program section that contains program operations identified by the keyword PSECT;
- A program section showing the program contents in terms of the sections it contains, identified by the keyword CSECT;
- An interaction section that contains statement defining the interaction between other sections, identified by the keyword ISECT.

Hence, an assembly modular program is a specific package of one or more sections. C language representation of a modular program becomes:

```
struct AssemblyProgram
    {
    struct ContentSection     CSECT ContentsStatements;
    struct DataSection        DSECT DataStatements;
    struct ProcessingSection  PSECT ProcessingStatements;
    struct InteractionSection ISECT InteractionStatements;
    };
```

Facts:

(1) Object oriented (OO) assembly languages are a better choice for assembly language design;
(2) An OO assembly language program is a class that contains methods and fields and has ownerships and access properties. Note that methods of an OO assembly language program are simple assembly language sections.

Example OO assembly language is Oolong [Engels (1999)], the assembly language of JVM.

15.6.7　*Assembly language learning function*

$A_{Learn} : A_{sem} \rightarrow A_{syn}$ is the process that map machine language computations into their symbolic representations. This is intuitively visualized by the diagram in Figure 15.17.

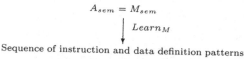

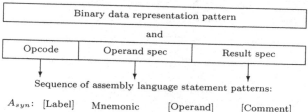

Fig. 15.17 The assembly language learning function

15.6.8 *Assembly language evaluation function*

For simulation purpose $Eval_A : A_{syn} \rightarrow A_{sem}$ is a mechanism for assembly language program evaluation implemented by C function EvalA:

```
EvalA(FILE *program)
    {struct AssemblyStatement *PC /* PC is program counter */
    program = fopen(AssemblyProgram, "r");
    PC = program;
    while (PC.Opcode != Halt)
        {Execute(PC);
        PC = Next(PC);
        }
    }
```

Contrasting $Eval_A$ and $Eval_M$ we observe that:

- Execute(PC) used by $Eval_M$ is wired in the hardware while Execute(PC) used in $Eval_A$ is a C funtions;
- Next(PC) used by $Eval_M$ is wired in the hardware while Next(PC) used in $Eval_A$ is a C funtions;

15.7 Assembler Implementation

The algorithm developed in Section 15.2 is visualized in Figure 15.18.

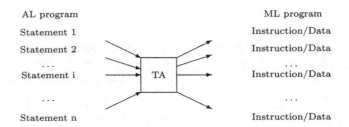

Fig. 15.18   The assembler algorithm

Using C language the Figure 15.18 can be represented as follows:

```
Assembler(FILE *ALP, FILE *MLP)
   {struct AssemblyStatement ALS_BUFFER, *APC;
    struct MachineStatement  MLS_BUFFER, *MPC;
    APC = read(ALP, ALS_BUFFER);
    MPC = &MLS_BUFFER;
    while (APC->Opcode != End)
        {map   (APC, MPC);
         write (MPC, MLP);
         APC = read(ALP, ALS_BUFFER);
         MPC = &MLS_BUFFER;
        }
    map (APC, MPC);
    write (MPC, MLP);
   }
```

The main assembler components are:

- *read()* reads program statements;
- *map()* maps assembly statements into instruction and data words; it is specified by the diagram in Figure 15.19;
- *write()* writes statement translation.

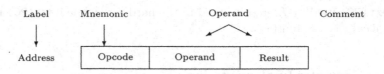

Fig. 15.19   Mapping assembly statements

15.7.1 *Generator translation*

Each generator class in the assembly language is mapped into binary code in machine language.

(1) Labels are mapped into addresses of memory locations that hold the elements they label;
(2) User defined symbols are mapped into addresses, registers, binary numbers, modifiers, as appropriate;
(3) Mnemonics are mapped into binary operation codes;
(4) Operands are mapped into address expressions of the form $AE(address, register, index, modifier, immediate)$;
(5) Comments are simply discarded.

15.7.2 *Statement translation*

Each assembly language statement is mapped into a sequence of one or more machine language instructions or data. For examples, using mnemonics dc (define constant), dv (define variable), add (add two entities), the assembler would process the section of assembly code:

```
dc 1234;
dv x;
add 1234, x
```

as follows:

- Partition the available memory into areas: constants, variables, code;
- Allocate the next free memory location from constants area, say Const(1234), to the constant 1234 and would stores the number 1234 in that location;
- Allocate the next free memory location from the variables area, say Var(x), to the variable x and would initialize that location to zero;
- Allocate the next free memory location from the code area to the statement add 1234, x and store in that location the machine instruction 1010 Const(1234),Var(x) where 1010 is presumably the binary code of the add operation.

15.7.3 *Program translation pattern*

Assembly language statement translations are assembled into a predefined machine language program pattern. CFF is an example of such pattern.

In conclusion, the assembler can be implemented by three readings of the assembly language program (called passes):

(1) **Pass 1:** translates all lexical elements (generators) and store their translations in appropriate tables;
(2) **Pass 2:** Uses generator translations generated by Pass 1 to translate all statements and stores their translations in appropriate tables;
(3) **Pass 3:** Assembles statement translations generated in Pass 2 into a machine language program according to the predefined machine language program pattern.

Example passes: consider $Oolong : OolongProgram \rightarrow CFF$, where CFF is the pattern:

```
Magic# Minor Major CnstPool Class Super Fields Interfaces Methods
Attributes
```

(1) **Pass 1:** maps Oolong program generators into appropriate constants specified by tags (descriptors);
(2) **Pass 2:** construct **CnstPool, Class, Superclass, Interfaces, Fields**, and **Method** representations. All are predefined patterns using index to CnstPool;
(3) **Pass 3:** assemble result of **Pass 2** into CFF.

Fact: JVM operates on stack! Consequently, there are no address expressions in JVM.

15.7.4 *Assembler optimization*

Assembly language programs are obtained by concatenating assembly language statements. Therefore program translation can be performed during Pass 2, i.e., the assembler can be implemented by:

(1) Pass 1: translate generators and store their translations into appropriate tables;
(2) Pass 2: translate statements and assemble their translations into the ML program according to given patterns.

15.7.5 *Data structures supporting assembler construction*

The data structures required by the assembler implementation are:

● OPTAB where the assembler defined elements (such as mnemonics) are stored;

- SYMTAB where user defined symbols are stored.

Notice, since assembler defined symbols are predefined, OPTAB is also a predefined data structure.

15.7.6 *The two pass assembler*

Pass 1: for each statement S:
translates S's generators and store their translations into the symbol table, SYMTAB.
Pass 2: for each statement S:

(1) Identifies the machine language pattern $M(S)$ holding the translation of S;
(2) Fill-out $M(S)$ with generator translations taken from SYMTAB;
(3) Assemble $M(S)$ into the ML program according to the ML program pattern.

Feasibility:

- A statement translation depends only on its generators which are in SYMTAB;
- ML program generation is determined by its instruction and data concatenation patterns;
- **Conclusion:** a two pass assembler is always feasible.

15.7.7 *One pass assembler*

If each statement of an assembly language program is expressed only in terms of symbols previously defined in the program then the assembler can be implemented in one pass. One pass assembler performs as follows:

For each statement S:

(1) Perform generator translation and store them in SYMTAB;
(2) Identify machine language statement pattern, $M(S)$, holding the translation of S;
(3) Fill-out $M(S)$ using SYMTAB. This is feasible because every statement is expressed only in terms of previously defined symbols;
(4) Assemble $M(S)$ accordingly.

15.7.8 *Data structures*

Data structures supporting assembler implementation are operation table (OPTAB), symbol table (SYMTAB), internal form of assembly statement (IFAS), File of Internal Form (FIF), and File of Object Generated (FOG), by the assembler.

OPTAB is the assembler predefined table that holds the mnemonics and their translations. Each mnemonic in OPTAB is however associated with the assembly language statement pattern holding it, its machine language translation pattern, and the two functions, `StmtMap` that recognizes the statement holding that mnemonic and translate it into the Internal Form of Assembly Statement (IFAS) by Pass 1, and `GenMap` that is called by Pass 2 to generate the machine code, when the IFAS holding that mnemonics is discovered. The OPTAB entry is shown in Figure 15.20. The mnemonics

Mnemonic	OpCode	$O|P|M|C$
Translation pattern		
$StmtMap : Statement \rightarrow IFAS$		
$GenMap : IFAS \rightarrow Translation\ pattern$		

Fig. 15.20   OPTAB entry

in OPTAB are classified as representing machine operations (O), pseudo-operations (P), macro definitions (M), and macrocalls (C). For an Oolong assembler the fields $O|P|M|C$ should be `ByteCode|Directive`.

The SYMTAB is the assembler constructed table that holds the translations of user defined symbols. A hash-table is usually the choice of SYMTAB implementation. We structure SYMTAB on two levels: a Type Definition Table (TDT), used as hash-kernel, and a Object Declared Table (ODT) used as overflow. TDT is predefined for a given assembly language and has a fixed size while ODT is a variable size table. Thus, for each entry in the table TDT there is a linked list of user declared symbols of the type specified by that entry in TDT.

For optimization purpose the assembler can use an Internal Form of the Assemble Statement (IFAS) thus preventing the second reading of the source text. The mnemonic is replaced in IFAS by a pointer to its entry in OPTAB, the label is represented by a pointer to its entry in SYMTAB, and operand expressions are mapped into postfix (or prefix) forms and their

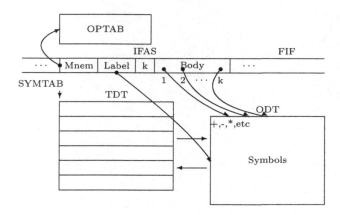

Fig. 15.21   Relationship between data structures

component symbols are pointers to their entries in SYMTAB or OPTAB. This IFAS structuring prevents Pass 2 of the assembler from reading the source or searching for various symbols composing the statements it processes.

The File of Internal Form (FIF) is created by Pass 1 and has as its records IFAS-s. The FIF is used to hold the internal form of the assembly program, and thus prevents two-readings of the source.

Finally, the machine language program generate by the assembler is stored in the File of Object Generated (FOG) by the assembler, which is CFF in case of JVM.

The relationship between the data structures supporting assembler implementation is shown in Figure 15.21.

Chapter 16

Software Tools for Correct Program Development

Programs are programming language expressions developed by people (programmers) who are experts on the syntax and the semantic rules defining the programming language they use. However, since program development is a human activity, according to the Latin proverb "errare humanum est", which translates in "to err is human", a program may contain errors. So, the problem faced by software developers becomes the development of tools that allow programmers to create correct programs during computer based problem solving process. For that the software developers need first to define the meaning of the expression "correct program". Since programs are algorithms expressed using programming languages, the program correctness becomes the correctness of the algorithms they represent. But irrespective whether we talk about the correctness of the algorithm or of the program, we need to remember that programs (or algorithms) are language expressions. And as language expressions they may contain two kind of errors: syntactic errors and semantic errors. Syntactic errors are violations of the language syntax during program development. Since language syntax is usually formally specified, syntax errors can be handled by the compiler. Semantic errors however are more difficult to handle.

Theoretically, semantic correctness of an algorithm is asserted saying that the algorithm is correct with respect to a specification. But a specification is also a language expression which is developed by a human and it can contain syntactical and semantical errors. Thus a correctness proof would have to be a mathematical proof, assuming both the algorithm and specification are given formally. In particular, correctness proof is expected to be the correctness assertion for a given program implementing the algorithm on a given machine. Further, the problem is discussed in the domain of logic, namely *Proof Theory* [Berwise (1978)]. Since here we discuss program correctness as a human activity during computer based problem solving process, we are concerned with the software tools which can be used to ensure that what a program is doing during its execution is what problem solver intended to do with the execution of her problem solving algorithm.

16.1 Syntax Correctness Tools

Syntactic correctness of programs developed using a programming language is checked by the compiler implementing that programming language. Hence, the major tool for syntax correctness proof is the compiler. Usually a compiler inputs the program and performs two tasks: first it recognizes the validity of the program with respect to the syntax rules defining the programming language, then the compiler maps the program into the language of the target machine, (hopefully) preserving the computational meaning of the source program. The first task is usually performed by regenerating the source program using the language specification rules while reading it from a file where the programmer has written it. The name of the file containing a program is dedicated to the programming language the programmer uses. The file dedication to the programming language is performed by a convention which asks to associate the programming language name with the name of the program, usually as a suffix of the file name used to store the program. Thus, a file named `fileName.Fortran` should contain a Fortran program, a file named `fileName.C` should contain a C program, etc. Further, a compiler $C : PL \rightarrow TargetM$ inputs the file `fileName.PL` and while reading the `fileName.PL` and looking at the grammar specifying the programming language PL, mimics the actions performed by the programmer while writing the program and thus regenerates the programs in the `fileName.PL` and represents it in an unambiguous form, usually an Abstract Syntax Tree (AST). The second task of the compiler consists of traversing the AST and mapping it into the language of the target machine `TargetM`. We have discussed the technicality of the compiler implementation in Chapter 15. Here we focus on the facilities compiler offers to the programming language user (the programmer) with respect to the creation of a correct program.

16.1.1 *Using the compile command*

A compiler that maps programs written in the programming language PL into the language of a target machine `TargetM` is a system program that is called by the interpreter of a Command Language of the form:

```
CompilerCompile Directives Input Output
```

where `Directives` are instructions given by the programmer to the compiler asking it to customize its work to the program written in the file `Input` and to generate the result in the file `Output`. The relationship between compiler, programming language, and the program is provided by using the naming convention as explained above. That is, the `Input` is a string that associates the source program name with the programming language name in the form `fileName.PL`. Using the `Directive`-s the programmer tells the compiler how to treat various events it may encounter during the compilation process. These events are determined by the facilities provided by the programming language to the programmer for easy program development. Examples of such facilities are:

(1) Separate compilation, which allows the programmer to develop her program by writing small pieces of code that can be separately compiled. Example is C compiler supporting separate compilation of C programs under Unix System [Bourne (1983)].

(2) Development of the source program `fileName.PL` on separate files that are included in the `fileName.PL` using an `include` macro-operation. See C language `#include` [Kernighan and Ritchie (1988)].

(3) Allowing the programmer to develop and use macro-operation. This implies a pre-processing of the source code to expand macro-operations and perform other tricks such as removing comments from the source code [Kernighan and Ritchie (1988)].

(4) Check the syntax of each of the separate code making up the program to see if programmer have obeyed the rules of the language.

(5) Convert the source program into assembly language.

(6) Convert the assembly language generated by the compiler into target machine code.

(7) Check whether the programmer has used things like functions and global variables in a consistent way. For example, if a non-existent name is used, compiler may complain.

(8) If the programmer wants to produce an executable from several source files, instruct the compiler how to fit them all together.

(9) Instruct the compiler to produce information for the system's run-time loader.

(10) Write the executable on the output file.

The compiling command should allow the programmer to tell the compiler how to treat each of the events determined by the facilities enumerate above.

If a syntax error is discovered during syntax-analysis (the first tasks performed by the compiler), the compiler could report it and then wait for the instruction from programmer telling it how to continue. The message compiler can send to the programmer informing her about a syntax error uses a specific convention, such as

```
LineNumber SyntaxError ''syntax rule violated''
```

where `LineNumber` is the line number is the source file `fileName.PL` where the error has been detected and the `syntax rule violated` is an indication telling the programmer which grammar rule has been violated during the program development. The information carried out by this message should be enough such that the programmer could correct the application of the "syntax rule" at the `LineNumber` and then tell the compiler to continue. Therefore, the command calling the interpreter that activates the compiler should be a necessary tool for syntax correctness. For example, `gcc file.c` tells the GNU C compiler to compile the program in the file `file.c` and returns the first syntax error discovered in that program. But, for efficiency reason [Aho *et al.* (January 1, 1986)], compilers are instructed to go ahead and discover all the syntax error in the file they process and report all of them such that the programmer can eliminate all the syntax error of the program. The problem is that in order to let the compiler proceed ahead when a syntax error is discovered, compiler must patch the program text at the erroneous place with some text which may introduce other syntax errors. That is, one syntax error may propagate in the program and thus not all errors reported by the compiler may be programmer's error. Another problems faced by the compiler with regard to the syntax check is determined by the incomplete information generated by the short-cuts allowed by by the programming language. Example of such short cuts are the defaults used in various language constructs, such as function declarations in C and `return()` statement [Kernighan and Ritchie (1988)]. These defaults may be accepted by the compiler but the code it would generate is not guaranteed correct. Therefore, when such defaults are discovered the compiler must warn the programmer that a potential semantic error may be encountered. How can all these situations be managed by the interpreter of the compile command?

The solution to these problems is usually given by providing working "directive" on the compile command. To distinguish these directives from other parameters of the command line they are given by names prefixed by a special character such as "-". Thus the command line of the compiler is an expression of the form.

```
CompilerCompile -Option_1 ... -Option_k fileName.PL targetM
```

where -Option_1, -Option_2, ..., -Option_k are directives given by the programmer to the compiler. The directives are usually processed in several steps, each of which being possible done by a separate program. Almost all this detail in compile command processing is hidden from the programmer thus making the compile command a call to a front end that manages calling all the programs implementing the options with the right arguments. For example, the main options for the GNU C compiler command gcc fileName.c are [GCC Compiler Command]:

- No-option command. That is, % gcc fileName.c tells the compiler to compile fileName.c, performing silently all the steps above. If the source program is developed on more than on file, say fileName1.c, fileName2.c, etc., then the command should include all of them, as in % gcc fileName1.c fileName2.c etc.. Note that the syntax analysis perform just syntax analysis. It does not check for any logical mistakes the programmer may have made.

- By default gcc compiler outputs the target program into the file a.out. To change this default the option -o fileName may be used, which tells the compiler to output the target code generated into the file fileNames instead. Thus, with % gcc fileName.c the executable is a.out; with % gcc -o executableName fileName.c the executable is executableName

- To tell the gcc compiler that no target should be generated the option -c needs to be used. This is useful for toy programs where the programmer just want to check the syntax. Thus, the command % gcc -c fileName.c will produce an object file (not an executable) called fileName.o. This can be later linked together with other object files, generated by separately compiling other C programs, into an executable.

- The option -g tells the compiler to collect debugging information. Thus, using the command % gcc -g -o executable fileName.c the compiler would generate debugging information relating the source program fileName.c with the executable program in the file executable. This information allows the program `fileName.c` to be run by the programmer under the control of a debugger in the *debugging mode*, that is, stepwise. The debugger is a program that can use this information to show the source code as the programmer steps through the program. The disadvantage is that all this extra information makes the program much bigger. Normally, a programmer would use -g option while she is developing a program. When the program is debugged, i.e., it performs as expected by the programmer, then the programmer compile a release version without -g option.

- The option -O (notes, capital O) tells the compiler to create an optimized version of the executable. The compiler performs various clever tricks to try to produce an executable that runs faster than normal. The programmer can add a number after the -O to specify a higher level of optimization, but this often exposes bugs in the compiler's optimizer. Thus, the command `% gcc -O -o executable fileName.c` will produce an optimized version of the executable program in the file `executable`.

- To force the `gcc` compiler to tell the programmer all syntax errors and all warnings it encounters the programmer should use the -Wall directive. This enables the compiler to produce all the warnings which the authors of the compiler believe are worthwhile.

- The directive -ANSI turn off most, but not all, of the non-ANSI C features provided by gcc. Despite the name, it does not guarantee strictly that source will comply to the standard.

- The directive -pedantic turns off all non-ANSI C features. Without this directive gcc allows the programmer to use some of its non-standard extensions to the standard. Some of these are very useful, but will not generate *portable code*, that is, code that will work with any C compiler on any system. In conclusion, the command `% gcc -Wall -ANSI -pedantic -o fileName fileName.c` will produce an executable program in the the the file `fileName` after checking `fileName.c` for compliance with the standard C syntax.

- The directive -library specifies a function library called `library` to be used at link time. The common example of `library` use is when compiling a program that uses some of the mathematical functions in C. Socket packages used for Internet programming [Stevens *et al.* (2004)], and shared memory and controlling parallel program interaction provided with IPC under Unix V [Gray (1998)] are other examples of program packages that require the usage of special libraries. Hence, the command `% gcc -o fileName fileName.c -lm` allows the program `fileName.c` to use mathematical funtions provided in the library `libm.a`.

16.2 Tools for Correct Semantic Program Development

Semantic correctness of programs is a rich topic in theoretical computer science. But the abundance of software tools developed to help individual programmers create semantically correct programs do not match this richness. This is probable the consequence of the human cognition process involved in correct program creation. It is difficult to create (if at all possible) tools that would customize the process of checking program correctness to the thinking of every individual programmer while writing a particular program. We are not talking here about the software testing business [Software Testing] which abound in tools provided to check the quality of the software products manipulated by the software business. Here we are talking about the system software tools offered to the individual programmers that allow them to check whether what the machine is doing while running their programs is what they expected it to do. Contrasting such software tools with the tool involved in software testing we observe that while traditional software testing tools can be implemented at any-time in the software development process and may be independent of the programming language used by programmer and operating system that controls the target machine, the system software tools used for checking the semantic correctness of the programs belong to the program development process and depend upon the programming language used by the programmer and the operating system controlling the computer on which the program is designed to run. The two most common such tools are program testing-packages and program debuggers.

16.2.1 *Program testing packages*

Programs are expressions of computations while computations they represent are dynamic processes which evolve in time and depend on the data on which they operate. The modeling of the computation expressed by a program is done using temporal logic [Manna and Pnueli (1992)]. The diversity of data on which a program is executed generates a diversity of passes the computation it represents may evolve. Computation tree logic (CTL) is a branching-time logic used to model computations performed by a programs and the model checkers [Clarke *et al.* (1986)] are the software tools that can be used to check the correctness of the computation performed by a program. Unfortunately, model checkers are not common software tools provided by current program development environments. However, we envision model checkers as ideal software tools for domain based problem solving process [Rus (2012)] described in Chapter 14.

Hence, while currently there is little one can do theoretically about the program expression with regard to the dynamic process it represents, one can feed the process with data that would help the programmer to trace all passes on which the computation can evolve. A data set that can be used to trace the computation evolution represented by a program is called a program testing package . Since every program is an expression of a specific computation there is little systematic help one can offer with respect to the program testing package construction. The inspiration should come from the structure of the computation expressed by the program and the language constructs that express the computation evolution on different passes. Branching and looping constructs offered by the programming language are usually essential for that purpose.

16.2.2 *Program debuggers*

Debuggers are software tools that are designed to take as data executable programs and run them under the control of the programmer. Hence, the debugger reads the executable program instruction by instruction and executes that instruction. Upon instruction termination, depending upon the events generated by the computation, the debugger may read and execute next instruction or tell the programmer about the events discovered. That is, every instruction executed by the debugger may generate an interrupt (a trap) and the decision to continue the execution is let to the trap handler which performs under the control of the debugger's user. A program executed by the debugger is also said to be executed in *trapping mode*. Hence, the debugger is a kind of virtual monitor. Therefore, in order to develop a debugger on a given architecture that architecture must satisfy the Popek and Goldberg conditions for virtualization [Popek and Goldberg (1974)]. With respect to the debugging process the debugger must be provided with a front-end that consists of a Command Language Interpreter that allows the user to control the debugger according to conditions satisfied by the executable program performed by the debugger. The best known debuggers are:

- GNU Debuggers (GDB) [GDB] called GDB and named gdb, is the standard debugger for the GNU operating system. However, it is a portable debugger that runs on many Unix-like systems and works for many programming languages, including Ada, C, C++, Objective-C, Free Pascal, Fortran, Java[1] and partially others.

- Intel Debuggers [IDB] IDB, a symbolic source code debugger used to debug C++ and Fortran programs, to disassemble and examine machine code and examine machine register values, and debug multi-threaded applications running on Linux OS. A GUI and command-line interface are available on host systems running Linux OS.
- Lesson Learned DataBase (LLDB) Debugger [LLDB] a next generation, high-performance debugger, built as a set of reusable components which leverage existing libraries in the larger LLVM Project, such as the Clang expression parser and LLVM disassembler. LLDB is the default debugger in Xcode on Mac OS X and supports debugging C, Objective-C and C++ on the desktop and iOS devices and simulators.
- Microsoft Visual Studio Debugger [MSDN] provides complete support for debugging Windows Store Apps that run on all versions of Microsoft Visual Studio.
- Valgrind[Valgrind] a programming tool for memory debugging, memory leak detection, and profiling. Originally Valgrind was designed as a memory debugging tool for Linux on x86. However, it has evolved to a generic framework for creating dynamic analysis tools such as checkers and profilers. Valgrind is used by Linux-based projects [Valgrind] and works on Mac OS X.
- WinDbg, [WinDbg] a multipurpose debugger for Microsoft Windows, distributed on the web by Microsoft. It is used to debug user mode applications, drivers, and the operating system itself in kernel mode.
- Java Development Tools (JDT)[JDTDebug] JDTDebug, consisting of several plug-ins that support the running and debugging of Java code.

Further we illustrate the GNU debugger used for the debugging of C language programs.

16.3   Steps Towards Correct C Program Development

There are four steps in the process of a correct C program development:

(1) Write the program on a file whose name is ".c" terminated. This is how the C compiler recognize its input as being a file that contain a C program.

(2) Remove all syntax-errors from the program. For that one needs to compile program using the command **gcc myFirstC.c**. All syntax-errors discovered by the C compiler in the program written in the file **myFirstC.c** are reported as messages on the screen of one's terminal. The form of these messages is:

myFirst.c:line# error: text of the syntax error in line#

The programmer needs to read these error messages and change the line-numbers of the file **myFirst.c** thus reported such that the resulting program conforms to the syntax of C language. However, remember that syntax-error discovered by the compiler may propagate in the program and therefore the error location in the source program compiler reports may not be right. While compiler tries to discover all syntax error contained in a program it changes the source program such that it can progress further with program analysis. These changes allows the compiler to proceed with source program analysis, but they also may generate fictional errors and thus, the error location in the source program is not usually correct. Programmer needs to understand the text she has written and the syntax error which the text may contain. There is no tool that may help the programmer with this process. The programmer must understand C language syntax to carry out this activity.

(3) Remove all the warnings the C compiler sends to the programmer concerning her program. Warnings are similar to syntax errors and the compiler sends them to the programmer following the same mechanism as syntax errors. But warnings are not syntax errors. Warnings are compiler's limitation in treating some legal conditions. For example, if the **main()** function in the C program contains no **return()** (which is not required) the C compiler may tell the programmer that control reaches end of that function. Warnings are reported by the compiler in the similar way with the syntax errors and are intermixed with syntax-errors using messages of the form:

myFile.c:line# warning: text of the warning in line#

A program that generates warnings may well execute correctly but the C compiler cannot guarantee that this will happen. Therefore, in order to use the debugger to create a semantically correct program, a C program must be syntactically correct. Hence, the programmer needs to eliminate all syntax errors and warnings the C compiler finds in the program. But the C compiler does not automatically generates all warnings that may exists in a program. Hence, in order to force the C compiler to report all warnings it discovers in the program and then to eliminate them, one must call the C compiler with the option -Wall on. For example, to force the C compiler to report all warnings it discovers in the program written in the file myFirstC.c one must call the compiler with the command gcc -Wall myFirstC.c. Again, there is no tool that may help the programmer with the process of removing the warnings from a C program. To remove the warnings reported by the C compiler one needs to understand the meaning of the C language construct the compiler complains about and to fix its syntax accordingly.

(4) Make sure that the computation the programmer wants to implement is actually implemented by the program. For that the programmer needs to execute the code generated by the compiler on battery-of-testes that cover all cases of control-flow in the program. However, due to the dynamic nature of the computation a program expresses, it is difficult (if at all possible) to develop a complete battery of tests that could guarantee the semantic correctness of the program. Therefore the programmer needs to check the correctness of the computation her program expresses executing the program step-wise, under a debugger. This activity is called *debugging* the program. Every programming language is supposed to provide a tool called debugger that allows the programmer to run the program stepwise, statement-by-statement if necessary, while examining the values of the variables involved in the statements that are executed in one step. To use this tool the programmer needs to have an executable program, i.e., a program on which compiler reports no syntax errors. In addition, the debugger relies on the information collected by the compiler during code-generation in order to do its job. The compiler collects this information if the user asks it to do so. The user asks the compiler to collect debugging information using an appropriate option on the compilation command. The C language program development under Linux system use *Gnu compilers*. To tell the Gnu C compiler to collect debugging information the programmer must use the -g option on the compiling command. That is, the programmer must call the Gnu compiler using the command gcc -g file.c. Then the programmer must tell the debugger to execute her program. For that, the debugger must first be started using the appropriate command, such as gdb, if a.out is the executable run

by the debugger, or `gdb executable` if `executable` is the file containing the program run be the debugger. Once the debugger is started on a program it needs to be restarted after various events checked by the programmer. The command that GDB uses in this respect is `run executable` or `run executable Input Output` where `Input` and `Output` are the Input and Output files of the `executable`.

In conclusion, use the following steps in order to develop a correct C program:

(1) Write the program in the file `file.c` and compile it with the command `gcc -Wall file.c`. If syntactic errors or warnings are reported, the programmer must fix them. The programmer needs to repeat this step until no syntax errors or warnings are reported by the compiler.
(2) Compile the program with the command `gcc -g file.c`. The use of the option "-g" tells the compiler to collect debugging information.
(3) Run the program under the debugger as explained below.

16.3.1   *Using the GDB debugger*

The purpose of a debugger, such as GDB, is to allow the programmer to see what is going on "inside" the program while the program is executed or what was the program doing at the moment when it crashed.

GDB can do four main kinds of things (plus other secondary things in support of these four) to help programmer catch semantic errors (also called bugs) in the program:

(1) Start the program, specifying anything that might affect its behavior.
(2) Make the program stop on specified conditions.
(3) Examine what has happened, when the program has stopped.
(4) Change things in the program, so the programmer can experiment with correcting the effects of one bug and go on to learn about another.

One can use the GDB to debug programs written in C, C++, Fortran, and Modula-2. To use GDB the programmer needs to compile the program by the command:

    `gcc -g program.c`, which creates the executable `a.out`, or
`gcc -g -o program program.c`, which create the executable `program`.

These commands tell the compiler to collect debugging information.

16.3.2 *Running the program under GDB*

GDB user can start the debugger with no arguments or options by tying the command gdb. In this case the assumption is that the executable running under debugger is a.out. The most usual way to start GDB is however with one argument or two, specifying an executable program and possible the a core file generated by a previous program crush. For example:

```
gdb /* the debugger executes the file a.out */
gdb program /* the debugger executes the file program */
gdb program core /* core is a previous memory image of program */
```

In addition, the user can also specify a process ID if she want to debug a running process. For example, gdb program 1234 would attach GDB to process 1234 (unless the programmer also have a file named 1234; GDB does check for a core file first).

16.3.3 *Frequently used commands*

Here are some of the most frequently needed GDB commands:

- run [arg-list] make the debugger run the executable program using the arg-list, if specified.
  Example: run text1 text2 restarts the debugger running the program specified by the command gdb executable where the executable uses the arguments text1 and text2.
- break [file:]line sets a break-point at the statement recorded on the line line in the file file, if specified.
  Example: break file.c:28 or break 28 would set a break-point at the statement recorded on the line 28 of the file file.c.
- break [file:]func sets a break-point at the statement calling the function func in the file file.c, if specified.
  Example: break test.c:func or break func sets a break-point at the entry in the function func in the program test.c.
- bt backtracks the program when it stops, that is, display the program stack when the program stops.
- print expr evaluate the expression expr and print the result.
  Example: print i would print the value of the variable i.
- continue or c tells the debugger to continue the running of the program (after it was stopped, for example, at a break-point).

- `next` tells the debugger to execute the next source program line (after stopping). Note, it steps over any function call in the line.
- `edit [file:]function` tells the debugger to look at the program line where it is presently stopped.
- `list [file:]function` tells the debugger to type the text of the program in the vicinity of where it is presently stopped.
- `step` tells the debugger to execute next program line (after stopping). Note, it steps into any function call in the line.
- `help [name]` tells the debugger to show information about GDB command `name`, or general information about using GDB.
- `quit` tells the debugger to exit. That is, one exits from GDB by `quit`.

PART 5
Computer Operation by Problem Solving Process

Chapter 17

Using First Computers to Solve Problems

The problem solving methodology using a computer is a process that evolves on the following steps:

(1) Formulate the problem;
(2) Formalize the problem;
(3) Develop an algorithm that solves the problem;
(4) Program the algorithm (i.e., encode the algorithm as a valid program of a programming language available on the computer);
(5) Compile the program thus obtained;
(6) Load and link the compiled program;
(7) Run the program;
(8) Use the results in the universe of discourse.

The use of the first man-made computer for problem solving was performed by the programmer and is summarized in Figure 17.1

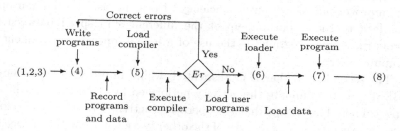

Fig. 17.1 The first operating system

The assumption here is that a minimal set of problem-solving tools required by this process are available. Hence, the numbers on the diagram in Figure 17.1 represent problem-solving steps and the text represents programmer's actions carried out during transition between steps. The agents involved in this process are: the human problem solver (i,e, the programmer), I/O devices, and the processor. The programmer formulates the problem, and writes and corrects programs, prepares data on information carriers, loads info carriers into I/O devices, and pushes buttons to initiate execution of various tools. The I/O devices read and write info carriers working under the control of the programmer. The processor executes predefined system and user programs stored on info carriers or in computer's memory.

Major issues faced by problem solving process is the efficiency and convenience of computer use by the problem solver. The computer is a complex and very expensive human-made tool. The difference in speed between the three agents involved in problem-solving is the main source of inefficiency in computer exploitation. To increase computer efficiency, procedures to reduce the difference in speed among the three agents operating the computer, needed to be developed. The first idea to increase the efficiency was to improve the speed of the slowest agent, the human programmer.

Programmer's activities which could be speeded up are the mechanical operations, i.e., the information carrier preparation, device loading, and button pushing. Consequently, a computer service was created where specially trained persons would operate the hardware system. The person trained to operate a hardware system was called a system operator. That is, first operating system was a human operator.

The nature of the three agents involved in CBPSP using the first man-made computer is different. So, how good can the human operator be for the improvement of computer efficiency? Does the use of a human operator lead to the smoothing up of the differences in speed between the agents running a program? Is the use of a human operator convenient for computer user?

The second idea, that if implemented, would improve the efficiency of CBPSP was to eliminate the activity performed by the slowest agent, the programmer. This means that the operator's activity of running a program must be executed by one or both of the other two agents, the I/O device and processor. This solution could be implemented by creating an automaton to execute the operator's task. Originally this automaton was implemented by a program called a *monitor*, or a *supervisory program*, or an *executive program*.

The tasks of the automated operator are performed by a set of routines which interact with each other in a well-defined way to operate the hardware system. To be implemented this set of routines requires first the formalization of the job performed by human operator. Remember, the first step of CBPSP is the problem formalization step! Historically, a computing system that consists of programs which perform the task of operating a hardware system was also called an *operating system*.

The job of a computer operator was to *run programs*. Data on which the operator acts are info carriers, I/O devices, and control panel buttons. The transformation steps undergone by a program run by the operator are performed by executable programs initiated by the operator. In order to be executed by a program, operator's activity must be formalized and represented by a data structure. Data representation of the operator's activity was called a job. Hence, operating system inputs jobs and performs the actions of running the programs specified by these jobs.

17.1 Job Formalization

There are two classes of operations executed by the operator while running a program: load devices with information carriers and push buttons to initiate program execution. The loading of devices with information carriers must be executed by the human operator. However, this can be done in parallel and asynchronously with the actions performed by operating system. If the locations and parameters of the programs to be executed are available, the initiation of program execution can be performed by the operating system.

Terminology we use further is *anonymous*. The term *operating system* was coined later, in 1960-s! Due to the abundance of names used for the automated computer operator, such as *monitor, supervisory, executive*, etc., by different computer manufacturers, we use here the term *control program* (CP).

17.2 Control Program

Data manipulated by computer operator in early 1960 were punched-cards. Hence, job-data representation used to record operators actions was a package of punched-cards. In order to be performed by the CP, the actions performed by the human operator must be encoded on punched-cards and must be mixed with the data to be processed by the programs initiated by the CP. Consequently, a CP reads packages of punched-cards and performs actions encoded on them. While the operator can continuously batch jobs together at one end of a job package, the CP can continuously process the batched jobs at the other end.

Hence, the formalization of computer operator's job requires: a Job Data Structure (JDS), representing the objects handled by the human operator, and a control program which operates on the JDS and executes the same operations as a human operator would do. However, JDS consists of card packages which contains cards on which two types of information is recorded: control records to be processed by CP, and data records, to be processed by programs initiated by CP. That is, control records represent commands sent to the CP while the data records represent data to be processed by the programs initiated by CP. Since jobs are batched one after another, to locate a JDS in a batch of jobs, two specific control records are necessary: a *JOB* control record, delimiting a job begin, and an *EOJ* control record, delimiting the end of the job.

Formally, a JDS consists of a sequence of information records having the following structure:

(1) First record is `JOB`, which delimits the beginning of a job in a batch of jobs.
(2) Last record is `EOJ`, which delimits the end of a job in a batch of jobs.
(3) Between `JOB` and `EOJ` there are control records to be processed by CP and data records to be processed by the programs initiated by CP.

The control and data records of a job are organized on the information carrier of the same device, (punched-card or punched-tape readers). To distinguish among them, a field on the information carrier and a special character, later called the *prompt*, was recorded in this field. Since punched cards were originally used to record JDS, the first column of the card and one of the characters $, %, >, /, also called control characters, were used as *prompt* to distinguish control records in the JDS. For simulation purpose, JDS could be represented in C by an array of `InfoRec` as described below:

```
struct InfoRec
       {
       char ControlChar;
       char Information[79];
       } JDS[MaxLength];
```

An example of a job data structure follows:

```
JDS[0] = $JOB Parameters;
JDS[1] = $Step_1 of the Job;
JDS[2] = Data for Step_1;
        . . .
JDS[k] = $ Step_n of the Job;
JDS[k+1] = Data for Step_n;
        . . .
JDS[n] = $EOJ Parameters;
```

The control records in a JDS encode programs run by the CP such as compilers, loaders, linkers, user programs, and their parameters, such as program name, programmer name, program priority, program running time, etc. These programs gradually transform the user program from its high-level source into its machine executable form. The length of a JDS depends on how many steps and how much data are involved in the particular job in the JDS. A batch of jobs can be organized into a JobFile, as seen below:

```
$JOB John's program
$Language Pascal
$PascalCompiler
Pascal program
$Target John's binary
$Linker
John's binary
$Target
John's executable
$Run John executable, 10minutes
John's binary
$PrintResults
Printer
$EOJ John's program
$JOB Peter's program
$Language Fortran
$FortranCompiler
Fortran program
$Target
Peter's binary
$Run Peter's binary. 5 minutes
```

```
$PrintResults
Printer
$EOJ Peter's program
$EOF
```

17.3 Communication Protocol

CP and programs initiated by CP share the `JobFile` by the rules:

(1) CP processes control records while the programs encoded on the control records and initiated by the CP process data records.
(2) The interaction CP ↔ programs initiated by CP consists of:

    (a) If a control record is read by the user program it returns control to the CP to interpret it;
    (b) If a data record is read by CP an error message is transmitted to the operator batching jobs in `JobFile`.

(3) The first record in the job is a control record.

The requirement that data for a user program be read from the `JobFile` can be relaxed. Nevertheless, this protocol of communication remains rather restrictive. To evolve this system, thus improving the efficiency of the CBPSP, we need to know how to relax the requirement mentioned above, and why is this protocol of communication restrictive. The restrictions provided in the communication protocol result from the sequential nature of the JDS and from the fact that JDS is shared between CP, programs initiated by CP, and human operator constructing JDS and batching them in the job file.

    The control records used within a JDS evolved towards the abstraction called *the job control language*. They are still in use today, metamorphosed into system program calls to the system programs given in the programming support environment. Example of such a call is the command `gcc options file.c` in Unix environment and and the `C compiler icon` in a window system.

17.4 The Design of CP

CP operates on a `JobFile` and performs:

(1) Read an information record (e.g., a punched card);

(2) If a control record is read, interpret it; if interpretation fails, abort the job and send a message to the operator;

(3) If a data record is read, send a JDS error message indicating that the communication protocol has been violated;

(4) User programs initiated by CP return control to the CP.

The environment of the CP is shown in Figure 17.2.

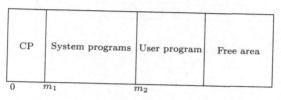

Fig. 17.2 CP's computing environments

Program execution in this environment is specified by the following action:

Perform::

    ProcessJobs(JobFile) || BatchJobs(JobFile)

ProcessJobs embodies the actions performed by the processor and devices on the JobFile; BatchJobs embodies the actions performed by the human operator while constructing and batching jobs at the end of the JobFile. The implementation of this CP is shown in Figure 17.3. The C pseudocode expressing the algorithm in Figure 17.3 follows:

```
ControlProgram(FILE *JobFile)
   {struct InfoRec{char CC; char Info[Length]}REC;
   boolean Found = false; REC = read(JobFile);
   while (REC.CC != EOF)
         {if (REC.CC == '$')
             {Found = search(REC.Info);
              if (Found) initiate(REC.Info);
              else{Err:SystemProgram nonexistent;flush(JobFile);}
             }
          else{Err:Control record expected;flush(JobFile);}
          Found = false; REC = read(JobFile);
         }
   }
```

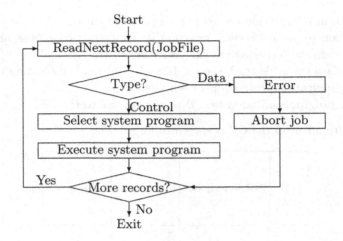

Fig. 17.3   Control program

The operator, CP, and I/O devices interact by the following protocol:

(1) Operator constructs JDS-s and batches them into *JobFile*.
(2) CP processes JDS-s from the *JobFile* observing the rules:

- Control records are processed by the control program;
- Data records are processed by the programs initiated by CP.

(3) If the protocol at (2) is violated:

- a JDS error results;
- the job generating the error is aborted;
- the next job in *JobFile* is processed.

To evaluate the goodness of this methodology for CBPSP one needs to answer such questions as:

(1) Is CP algorithm correct? That is, does it simulate the activity of the human operator running a program?
(2) Is CP algorithm reliable? That is, is it error tolerant?
(3) Is the CP algorithm efficient and convenient? How is this program started and how is it halted? How does this program evolve with problem domain?

Note that if JDS is correctly constructed then CP is correct. However, attempts to deal with the issues raised by questions (1), (2), (3) above led to the modern operating systems.

Chapter 18

Batch Operating System

The computing environment of CP allows two types of programs to coexist in main memory: system programs, that perform actions initiated by CP, and user programs, that perform user computations. They must cooperate while executing a job. However, while performing their functions these programs perform destructive operations, such as `read(JobFile)` which can replace the contents of a memory area with the information red from the JobFile, thus destroying information stored in computer memory. The destruction of information would be a consequence of user programs and system programs violating their interaction protocol. For example, a user program may input a data record into a buffer that covers a portion of a system program memory area. A system program may input a control record into a buffer that covers a portion of a user program memory area. How can we prevent such situations?

Since `read(JobFile)` must be executed by both CP and the user program, a first solution would be to make it unique. If `read(JobFile)` is unique, it can be designed and implemented to execute correctly. Can this ensure computation security? For an answer to this question we should be able to answer other important questions, such as: Do both the CP and the user program have their own copy of the function `read(JobFile)` or do they share the same copy? When each has a copy how can this copy be authenticated? When one copy is shared how can one enforce its usage? Who should be the owner of the shared copy of `read(JobFile)` function?

18.1 Hardware Provisions for Reliability

A simple solution to the problems raised by these questions is neither easy nor obvious. To solve these problems special hardware and software was necessary. To enforce the communication protocol in a CP environment new hardware must be invented. The goals of the new hardware is to ensure the reliability of the CP ↔ User Program communication protocol. This could be obtained by assigning a *mode* to the process of program execution. Then, CP process executes with a mode called the *system mode* and the user process executes with another mode called the *user mode*. The new hardware should ensure that computer resources, such as processor instructions, access to memory, devices, info, etc., available to processes running while performing in system mode are different from those available to processes executing in user mode. Further, the execution of destructive operations, such as doIO(), should be available only while process perform in system mode. In addition, the new hardware should not allow a user program to execute in system mode and should facilitate mode switch from user to system and vice-versa. We call this *hardware provisions for reliability* and it consists of a one bit register called Mode Bit (MB) and an Interrupt Mechanism (IM). The MB is defined as follows:

- MB splits the instruction set into two disjoint groups: *privileged instructions* and *non-privileged instructions*, such that: *InstructionSet* = *Privileged* ∪ *Nonprivileged* and *Privileged* ∩ *Nonprivileged* = ∅.
- Instruction execution is defined by MB by:

$$MB = \begin{cases} 1, & \text{system-mode, all instructions can be executed;} \\ 0, & \text{user-mode, only non-privileged instructions can be executed.} \end{cases}$$

So, by design conventions when MB = 0 only non-privileged instructions are executed. Then, if doIO()-s are privileged they cannot be executed by user programs. However, when MB = 1 all instructions can be executed, that is, doIO() can be executed by CP on behalf of user processes, as service requests. Moreover, instructions operating on MB, such as Set Mode Bit, are privileged.

The IM is defined by the equation:

$$\text{if}(\text{MB} = 0 \land \text{Opcode} \in \text{Privileged}) \text{ Interrupt};$$

The actions performed by the processor when this interrupt signal is received are:

(1) Save PSW of the current program into a dedicated location, say OldPSW;
(2) Switch the mode bit to privileged, i.e., perform MB := 1;
(3) Fetch PSW from a dedicated location, say NewPSW.

Consequently, if I/O instructions are privileged the user is forced to ask their execution as services from CP. The responsibility for transferring the control back to the user program, once a service is performed, rests with the control program.

18.2 Software Provisions for Reliability

In order to use the hardware provision for reliability to implement a reliable CP one needs to employ a "system call operation", whose mnemonic is SC, which switches the MB and thus allows the system to perform privileged operation. In addition, we also need a data structure that accommodates all services provided by the CP. Examples of such a data structure is the *Service Table* in Figure 18.1. Then a program that receives the control after interrupt does:

(1) Save the entire state of the processor, if necessary;
(2) Use OldPSW to search for the requested service; if found activate it, otherwise abort the program and return to CP.

Each of the programs providing services to the user returns control to a system program called `scheduler/dispatcher`, which restores the system state before service request and continues user program execution.

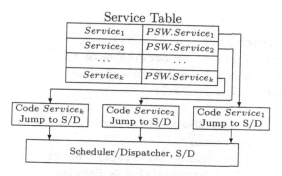

Fig. 18.1 Services provided by CP to user programs

In order to simulate this implementation of a CP we may use the following conventions:

- Service calls can be simulated by instructions expressed by the following C structure:

```
typedef int (* func)();
struct ServiceCall
      {
      char CODE = 'SC' /* SC is an opcode */
      func Service;    /* Function performing the service */
      int  ServiceParameters;
      };
```

- When an interrupt generated by a service call occurs, PC points to a `ServiceCall` instruction which is saved in `OldPSW`.
- For simulation purpose `OldPSW` and `NewPSW` may be described by the following C structure:

```
struct PSW.Record
      {
      int State;
      struct ServiceCall *PC;
      }OldPSW, NewPSW;
```

Service implementation is performed by the following treat event algorithm:

```
#define MaxNumber /* Nrumber of services provided by CP */
TreatEvent()
  {
  struct ServiceEntry
        {func Service; /* Service name */
         struct PSW.Record ServicePSW;
         }Service[MaxNumber];
  int i = 0;
  char *event = OldPSW->PC->Service;
  while  (i < MaxNumber)
        if (strcmp(event, Service[i]->Service) != 0) i=i+1;
        else  PSW = Service[i].PSW.Service;
  Error: No such service is provided by the system;
  Abort Program; PSW = CP.PSW (PSW of the control program);
  }
```

The `TreatEvent()` function either returns an error and abort the program that initiated it, or initiates a service function that calls scheduler/dispatcher upon its termination.

18.3   Batch Operating System

The control program discussed in this section was called the Batch Operating System (BOS). The flow of control in a BOS is defined as follows:

(1) Start the computer with MB = 1;
(2) BOS reads next record of JDS, select next program to execute, load it, change mode, i.e., perform MB := 0, and transfer control to the selected program.
(3) The user programs use SC to call BOS to perform services. The calling mechanism switches the operation mode, i.e., performs MB := 1.

The user programs operate under BOS as follows:

- When a program needs a service it issues a "system call" to perform it.
- The BOS performs the requested service and then returns control to the program which requested that service.
- When a program terminates, it transfers control back to BOS by another system call, thus performing $MB := 1$.
- BOS determines what follows; flow of control in BOS is shown in Figure 18.2.

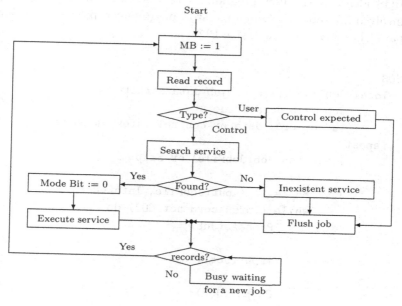

Fig. 18.2   Batch operating system

C pseudo-code of this BOS is:

```
BatchSystem(FILE *JobFile)
{
 char Found, MB = 1;
 struct InfoRec REC = read(JobFile);
 while (REC.CC != EOF)
     {if (REC.CC == '$')
         {Found = search(REC.Info);
           if (Found) { MB = 0; initiate(REC.Info)}
           else {Err: nonexistent system program; flush(JobFile);}
         }
       else {Err: control record expected; flush(JobFile);}
       MB = 1; REC = read(JobFile);
     }
}
```

The assumption here is that $ is the control character (i.e., the prompt).

18.4 Solving Problems with BOS

BOS identifies the user program using a service call. The three agents involved in problem solving (operator, programmer, processor) perform in parallel as shown by the action BOS:

```
BOS::
  local JobFile: file of job data structures,
        Job: job data structure,
        InfoRecord: data or control information record;
  repeat
          1_1:Batch(Job,JobFile) or Skip: 1_1^
                ||
          1_2: MB := 1; Input(JobFile, InfoRecord);
               while (InfoRecord not EOJ) do
                   Process(Job);
                      or
                   Input(Job);
                      or
                   Output(Job);
```

```
              or
          Skip ;
      1_2^
  forever
```

Observations:

(1) Human operator and the control processor are explicitly shown in this action.

(2) Programmer is hidden in the actions performed by Batch(). That is, when the control-record discovered by Batch() represents a program (user of the system) that program execution represents the programmer who developed it.

(3) I/O operations are explicitly shown because they are performed by BOS on behalf of the program requesting them.

How reliable is a BOS? To answer this questions one need to answer the following questions before:

(1) Does the interaction among the BOS components ensure its reliability?

(2) Is the system protected against malicious actions of its users?

(3) Are system users protected against malicious actions of other users?

(4) Are system users protected against malicious actions of the system?

Chapter 19

Problem of Protection

The mode bit and the interrupt mechanism are used to enforce a controlled communication between the BOS and the programs initiated by BOS, (among which the user program is). They cannot provide protection against malicious actions that the agents that share the computer can exercise against each other.

19.1 Scenario for BOS Violation

A sample of the system memory configuration required by the BOS is shown in Figure 19.1. A sample of a user memory configuration is given

oldPSW	PSW of interrupted program	
newPSW	state	*goto Event*
	. . .	
Event	Treat Event	
Service	*request$_1$*	*goto Service$_1$*
Table	*request$_2$*	*goto Service$_2$*
BOS: MB=1	. . .	
	request$_n$	*goto Service$_k$*
Service$_1$	*Program$_1$*	
Service$_2$	*Program$_2$*	
	. . .	
Service$_k$	*Program$_k$*	
	Other programs	

Fig. 19.1 BOS: system memory area

281

in Figure 19.2. The reliability of the system relies on restricting the user program to use only non-privileged operations. This can be violated by a skillful programmer, as seen in Figure 19.2.

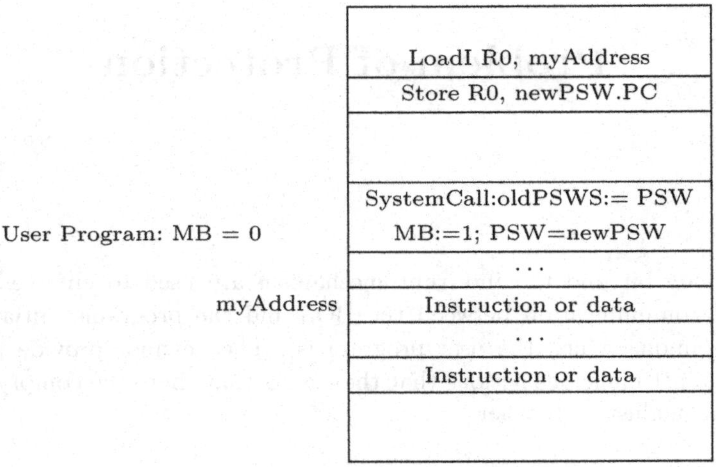

LoadI R0, myAddress
Store R0, newPSW.PC
SystemCall:oldPSWS:= PSW MB:=1; PSW=newPSW
. . .
Instruction or data
. . .
Instruction or data

User Program: MB = 0

myAddress

Fig. 19.2   Scenario for BOS violation

Notice that before issuing a system call the user program performed: newPSW.PC := myAddress. That is, knowing the address of the dedicated memory location that contain the newPSW, the skillful programmer can replace the address of the program that receive the control after the Interrupt with the address myAddress in the area of his own program. Thus, when the user program issues a system call, which usually transfers the control to TreatEvent procedure, the control is transferred to the memory location myAddress with the MB = 1. Consequently, at this point the user program can use privileged and non-privileged instructions because MB = 1. How could we prevent this?

19.2   Provisions for Memory Protection

If user program could be prevented to change the contents of the dedicated memory location newPSW the scenario for BOS violation could not be performed. More general, if memory allocated to a program is protected from interference by other programs then the program is protected against malicious actions from other programs. However, notice that the program is not protected against its own malicious actions! Thus, the first solution to the problem of protection is provided by protecting the memory occupied by the operating system.

The implementation of this solution to the problem of protection requires a new piece of hardware in the control processor, namely a Protection Key (PK) register, defined by:

$$PK = \begin{cases} 1, & \text{if program can access entire memory;} \\ 0, & \text{if program can access only its own memory.} \end{cases}$$

The assumption is that operations on PK are privileged, i.e., are allowed only when MB = 1. Since BOS can executes PK := 1 when it starts it has access to the entire memory. On the other hand, the user program is started by BOS with PK = 0 and MB = 0. Thus, the user program cannot change PK because operations on PK are privileged. Moreover, since PK = 0 the user program is prevented from accessing the memory area occupied by the operating system. Hence, skillful programmers cannot perform the operation `Store R0 newPSW.PC` because `newPSW.PC` is in system memory area.

19.3 A Flexible Solution for Memory Protection

Computer memory is shared among many different programs that may require different kinds of access to it. For example, a program may require to `read` a portion of memory, another program may require to `write` on a portion of memory, and yet another program may require to do both `read`, `write` operations on memory. Therefore, we need a more flexible solution to the memory protection problem. To increase flexibility, PK must allow more than two memory areas to be protected, and different kind of access to different memory areas it protects.

The implementation of the more flexible memory protection mechanism was used by IBM 360/370 and consists of the following:

(1) Split memory into blocks of fixed size. IBM uses memory segments of size 2K.
(2) Associate each memory block with a register called the Access Key (AK). The collection of all AK registers used by a given architecture can be implemented by a dedicated memory area called Protection Memory (PM).

(3) PK register (in PSW) and $AK[i]$ in PM define the type of access allowed on the memory block $Bl[i]$ associated with $AK[i]$.

For example, assume that a computer system has a memory of 128K bytes, denoted $Memory = Byte[0..127K]$. This memory can be seen as composed of 64 blocks of size 2K. That is, $Memory = Bl[0..63]$, where addresses in $Bl[i]$ are: $2K*i, 2K*i+1, \ldots, 2K*i+2K-1$, $i = 0, 1, \ldots, 63$. To protect this memory we would need 64 access keys, say $AK[0..63]$ where $AK[i] \overset{Protects}{\longrightarrow} Bl[i]$, $i = 0, 1, \ldots, 63$. An $AK[i]$ implemented by a 3 bit register would allow read, write, execute, on the associated page. Thus, a PM of size 64*3 bits would suffices. The value of $AK[i]$ can be defined as follows:

$$AK[i] = \begin{cases} 0, & \text{if no read or write is allowed on } Bl[i]; \\ 1, & \text{if only read is allowed on } Bl[i]; \\ 2, & \text{if only write is allowed on } Bl[i]; \\ 3, & \text{if both read and write are allowed on } Bl[i]. \end{cases}$$

The values of $AK[i]$ can also be bit-wise interpreted. For example, bit 1 can be interpreted as read, bit 2 as write, and bit 3 as execute.

To control the operations on memory using PM approach, assume that PK register is in PSW and operations on PK are privileged. When a program performs operations on $Bl[i]$, PK is loaded with an information which matches the access key $AK[i]$. Operations on $Bl[i]$ are allowed only if PK matches $AK[i]$, $i = 0, 1, \ldots, 63$. Relationship between PK and AK are shown in the Figure 19.3.

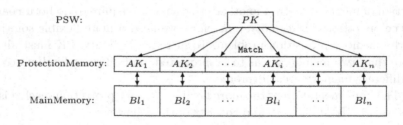

Fig. 19.3   Relationship between AK and PK

Thus, when a reference at a memory location in block Bl_i is attempted the following test is performed:

```
if PK matches AK_i grant access else interrupt;
```

19.3.1 *Matching PK and AK in IBM-360/370*

In IBM-360/370 PK is a 4 bit register, $PK = PSW[8..11]$, and memory is split into 128 blocks of size 2K called segments. Thus, a byte $AK[i]$ can be used to protect two segments: $Segment[i]$ is protected by $AK[i]_{0..3}$ and $Segment[i+1]$ is protected by $AK[i]_{4..7}$; Consequence, a PM of 64 bytes can protect a memory of 256K bytes. The relation between PK and AK is in Figure 19.4. The following test is executed during memory access cycle:

PK	AK		Read	Write
$PK = 0$	$AK = any$		Yes	Yes
$PK \neq 0$	$AK \neq 0$	$AK = 0$	Yes	Yes
		$AK = PK$	Yes	Yes
		$AK \neq PK$	$if\ AK = 1\ then\ Yes$	No
			$if\ AK \neq 1\ then\ No$	No

Fig. 19.4   IBM memory protection

```
if (PSW.PK matches Memory.AK)
  GrantAccess;
else
  Interrupt: Memory Violation;
```

This solution is still inflexible and rather complex! Protection mechanism works on physical locations while programs may employ location abstractions. In addition, the `matching` operator is fixed within the computer architecture.

19.4   Virtual Memory

PDP-11 implemented memory protection by limit registers. The executing process is provided with two registers, a lower bound, LB, and an upper bound, UB. When process execution starts, LB and UB are loaded with lower bound and upper bound of memory allocated to the program. At each memory references at an address a this is granted only if $LB \leq a \leq UB$. This protection mechanism evolved into what is today called *virtual memory* which provides today solution to the problem of protection.

The physical memory of the computer is split into a number of *memory frames*, say $Frame_0, Frame_1, \ldots, Frame_n$, where each frame has a fixed size, say $size(Frame) = 2^k$, for a given k. For example, if $size(Frame) = 2^{10}$ and $n = 2^{10}$ them the computer has a physical memory of 2^{20}, i.e., 1M, split into 2^{10} physical frames. On the other hand, programs use virtual memory. Each program uses as much virtual memory as it needs. The virtual memory is split into memory pages, where the size of a memory page is the same as the size of the physical memory frame. Hence, a program of size 100K developed in a virtual memory of page size 2^{10} would use 100 pages, say $Page_0, Page_1, \ldots, Page_{99}$. Every program address is a tuple $(Page_i, D)$, $0 \le D < 2^{10}$. Relationship between the program and physical memory is defined by a Program Page Table (PPT), whose entries are tuples of the form $(Page_i, Location_i)$ where $Location_i$ shows the physical address of the $Page_i$. This allows a program to be partially loaded in physical memory and also to be spread within memory frames which are not necessarily adjacent, thus avoiding memory fragmentation. For example, the 100 page program in the example above could all be generated on a disk having a PPT[99] (in main memory or on the disk), where each PPT[i], $i = 0, 1, \ldots 99$ could be a tuple (i:w, $Address_i$), $i = 0, 1, \ldots, 99$ and $w = 0$ if $Address_i$ is a disk address and $w = 1$ if $Address_i$ is a memory frame address. Program execution consists of a procedure that loads in main memory the PPT and few pages in the available page frames, appropriately updating the PPT-entries. Then, when an address $Addr = Page_i \oplus D$ is used during program execution, the physical address accessed is $PPT[i]Location_i \oplus D$ if $w = 1$ or a *page fault interrupt* if $w = 0$. If a page fault interrupt is issued, the program is suspended until the page referenced is loaded in main memory. Notice that since pages and page frames the same size and the size is suppose to be a power of 2 the $\oplus$ is a bit concatenation operator. So, the cost of this solution to memory implementation is an indirection through the PPT.

19.4.1 *Program generation*

Program is generated by compiler using a relative address space that starts with address zero and continues as necessary, say n. Program address space is paged, i.e., $Program = page_0 \, page_1 \ldots page_p$, $p = n/size(Frame) + 1$. Compiler (loader/linker) packages the program thus generated into the $PPT[0..p]$ setting $PPT[i] = (i : 0, diskADR_i)$ where $diskADR_i$ is the disk address of program page i.

19.4.2 *Program execution*

At execution time PPT and few pages of the program (including the page containing the program start address) are loaded in memory. PPT is updated, i.e., $PPT(i) = \langle AK_i, i : w, Location_i \rangle$ where AK_i shows the access rights to program page i. At each memory reference at an address a, a is split into page number + displacement, i.e., $a = i \oplus D$ and:

(1) if $PPT[i].w = 1$ and PK *matches* AK_i, access is granted;
(2) if $PPT[i].w = 1$ and $PK\neg$ *matches* AK_i, memory violation is generated;
(3) if $PPT[i].w = 0$, page fault Interrupt is generated.

Notice that this increases execution time with at least one indirection at each memory access. A faster solution is necessary.

19.5 Associative Memory

Associative memory consists of a small number of very-fast registers that can be searched by content-association. One associative register can store three numbers interpreted as:

(1) Program Page Number (PN);
(2) Memory Frame Number (FN);
(3) Access Key (AK) to the program page number PN.

Associative memory is searched by *content-association* rather than by index. Hence, the decision whether a page is in main memory or on disk is much faster. Note that search by association means searching a pattern in parallel in all registers that belong to the associative memory.

19.5.1 *Using associative memory*

At compile time a program is associated with a PPT which shows where the pages composing the program are and what kind of access is allowed on the page. At execution time the operating system allocates a few page frames to the program and loads PPT and few program pages into these frames, while updating the associative memory accordingly. When a program accesses the address $a = k.pageSize + D$ in the page k the real address accessed is $FM \oplus D$ where FM is the frame number where page k is loaded. Operating system uses AK in associative memory to record access rights at that page and statistics about the memory frame usages. This allows more informed decisions that optimize memory management. The associative memory is also known as the *Translation Lookaside Buffer* (TLB).

19.5.2 *Combined solution*

PPT may be large while associative memory is small. Therefore to improve efficiency, a combined solution is needed. In the combined solution, the system maintains a complete PPT and a small associative memory. Active pages are loaded in the associative registers. Appropriate statistics in the associative registers allow operating system to manipulate PPT and to optimize memory management at program execution time.

Memory allocated to the program is no longer a large block of physical memory. Program is scattered among available frames. Access keys to a memory frame are a few bits in the associative registers that record access rights and statistics. Only the last page of the program may be incomplete. Therefore memory fragmentation is reduced to the internal-fragmentation. Operating system can collect statistics of memory frame usage and thus can optimize memory usage. Program can be speeded-up by appropriate swap-in and swap-out strategies.

Pages and page frames are units of physical resources allocated to the program. Hence, this solution to protection problem though flexible does not protect the computing objects composing the program, such as procedures and data, rather it still protects memory resources allocated to the program. Various components (procedures, functions, data) of a program may not necessarily require an integer number of pages and page frames. Hence, memory waste results due to internal fragmentation. Hence, the following question arise: *could we design protection mechanisms that would protect memory allocated to program components rather than protecting memory partitions (segments, frame, etc)?*

19.6   Protect Procedure's Memory

A more refined solution to the problem of protection can be obtained by associating the concept of access with the logical units of the program, such as procedures and data segments. Hence, instead of protecting the memory blocks allocated to a program one can develop mechanisms to protect the memory allocated to the procedures and data composing the program. Every active program unit (such as a procedure) may be associated with a list of program units (procedures and data) which it can try to access, and every program unit may be provided with some access rights to its memory area which it exports to other program units. Hence, the program logical units allowed in memory at a given time can be layered on rings or levels of protection, defined as follows:

- $Level_0$ is made up of the procedures which have no access restrictions to other procedures.
- $Level_i$, $i > 0$, is made up of the procedures which have controlled access rights to the memory allocated to the procedures in $level_j$, $j < i$, but have no access restrictions to memory areas allocated to the procedures and data on the levels $j \geq i$.

This solution to the memory protection was suggested by Multics project[Graham (1968); Organick (1972)], where the procedures in memory are structured as shown in Figure 19.5.

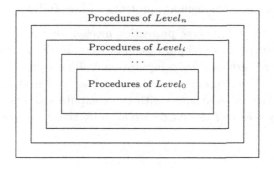

Fig. 19.5 Protection rings in Multics

The implementation of Multics protection rings requires a new piece of hardware, and was experienced on the machine GE645. Namely, to accommodate Multics rings the program counter of the machine GE645 is extended such that it can record a pair of indices (i, j) attached as the protection rings (i, j) of the executing procedure. If the current procedure belongs to level k, and protection ring in PC is (i, j) then its access to another program logical unit is defined by the test:

```
if (i <= k <= j)
  GrantAccess;
else
  Interrupt;
```

The VAX-11/780 computer simplified the protection rings used in Multics to just four levels: *kernel* > *executive* > *supervisor* > *user*. Bits (22,23) in the PSW are used to specify the protection level of the currently running procedure. Bits (20,21) of the PSW specify the protection level of the previous procedure run by the system.

Summarizing, we notice that the mechanisms used for reliability and protection consists of:

(1) Registers that control the communication between system processes and user processes by forcing user processes to request some computations as services provided by system process. Example is the mode bit that splits the instruction set into privileged and non-privileged.

(2) Registers that control the access to the memory occupied by a process, preventing the active process to access memory areas occupied by other processes. Example such registers are: PK in PSW and AK in protection memory as used by IBM, limit registers used by PDP, virtual (one-level) memory, associative memory, protection rings (GE645, VAX-11/780)

However, notice that these protection mechanisms complicate the hardware and do not protect computational objects. Rather, these mechanisms protect the hardware used by computational objects present in the system at a given time. Therefore, the question whether we can develop protection mechanisms that are associated with the computation objects we want to protect, independent of the hardware used by these computation objects, is still unanswered.

19.7   A Software Strategy for Protection

The software strategy for protection associates access with the computation objects themselves (procedures and data) instead of memory area occupied by them. For that the following questions must be answered: How can we uniquely identify a computing object irrespective of the hardware it uses? What should be the structure of a computation object such that it can be protected by software means? What is the impact of these questions on the computation objects used in Unix operating system?

First, from the viewpoint of their access, computing objects which share the resources of a computer system can be classified as processes and segments. Processes are computing objects that can exercise access to other computing objects. Segments are computing objects that can be accessed by other computing objects. Note that processes can both access other computer objects and be accessed by other computing objects. Hence, processes and segments are not disjoint. Computing objects that can exercise access to other objects are further called *processes* and computing objects that can be accessed by a process are called simply *objects*. Since a process can be accessed by another process, all processes are objects. However, not all objects are processes.

19.7.1 *Identifying computing objects*

Computing objects are abstractions that have owners. Therefore computing objects could be identified by the names their owner associate with them. So, the mechanism for computing object identification in a shared computing system is similar to the mechanism used by post office to identify the objects it manipulates. In other words, computer users are uniquely identified by the computer system. Then, for identification purpose we can extend the name of a computing object with the name of its owner.

Name extension allows multiple objects to be identified by the same name and multiple names to identify the same object. This is a procedure already used by computer technology. For example using the suffix .c, C compiler identifies any file that may contain a C program. The implementation of this approach for computer object identification follows:

(1) Each computer platform has two classes of users: *operating system*, that controls the system and provides services, and **computer users**, serviced by the operating system.
(2) Each computer user is identified by an information record in the system. The operating system is represented by system-managers which are called *super-users*.
(3) The computation objects owned by each computer user are standardized as *files* and are organized on an appropriate data structure (usually a tree) maintained by the operating system as the *file system*.

Consequently each computing object is identified by the node it occupies in the file system tree. That is, the computing object xxx of the user yyy on a computer platform CCC is identified by:

(1) The Uniform Resource Locator (URL) identifies the CCC in the computer network.

(2) The node yyy is uniquely identified by the file system of the computer CCC.

(3) The node xxx is uniquely identified by the application using it in the subtree rooted at yyy in the file system of the computer CCC.

19.7.2   *Accessing objects*

The property whereby OBJ_1 is allowed to access OBJ_2 is called a *capability of OBJ_1 for OBJ_2*. Therefore, in order for OBJ_1 to access OBJ_2, the following must happen:

- OBJ_1 must have OBJ_2 on its capability list.
- OBJ_2 must allow the access requested by OBJ_1.

Hence, each computing object (be it a simple object or a process) in the system consists of the following three components:

(1) A list of capabilities (CL) specifying the objects which this object can access.

(2) A list of access rights (AR) specifying the type of access that this object allows other objects to perform on it.

(3) The object itself, (BODY).

Thus, each computing object is defined by a triple $OBJ = \langle CL, AR, BODY \rangle$. When OBJ_1 tries to access OBJ_2 the following checks are performed:

(1) Check whether $OBJ_2 \in CL(OBJ_1)$, i.e., check if OBJ_2 is on the list of capabilities associated with OBJ_1. If not, access is denied.

(2) If $OBJ_2 \in CL(OBJ_1)$ check whether $OBJ_1.access \in AR(OBJ_2)$, i.e., check if the access action requested by OBJ_1 is on the access rights list of object OBJ_2. If so, the access is allowed. Otherwise the access is denied.

19.7.3   *Theoretical implementation*

Computing objects in the system at a given time can be maintained in a data structure called the access matrix (AM) [Lampson (1985)]. Lines of AM are labeled by processes and columns are labeled by objects. The access matrix element $AM(i, j)$ records the capability list of process i and the access rights of object j. Hence, when process i tries to access the object j the tests $j \in AM(i,j).CL$ and $i \in AM(i,j).AR$ are performed. If they are both true the access is granted, otherwise the access is denied. Figure 19.6 shows the access matrix implementation of the protection software.

	$Object_1$	$Object_2$	...	$Object_i$	...	$Object_n$
$Process_1$	AM(1,1)	AM(1,2)	...	AM(1,i)	...	AM(1,n)
$Process_2$	AM(2,1)	AM(2,2)	...	AM(2,i)	...	AM(2,n)
...	...	...	...	...	...	...
$Process_j$	AM(j,1)	AM(j,2)	...	AM(j,i)	...	AM(j,n)
...	...	...	...	...	...	...
$Process_m$	AM(m,1)	AM(m,2)	...	AM(m,i)	...	AM(m,n)

Fig. 19.6   Access matrix implementation of protection software

19.8   Practical Implementation

For a given system, the access matrix is sparse. So, if we interpret lines as processes and columns as files then we can implement it by associating every line (process) with the list of files it can access, (CL), and associating each column (file) with the list of operations that can be performed on it, (AR). Since each process is represented by a file it becomes a tuple $\langle CL, AR, Body \rangle$. Hence, the access cam be checked by the file-system.

Access matrix representation of a computer security model lacks visualization. A graph representation would provide visibility[Tygar and Wing (1987)] The motivating example from [Tygar and Wing (1987)] is in Figure 19.7. Note that as in any enterprise, employees have read access

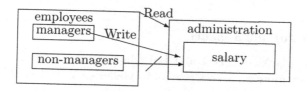

Fig. 19.7   A motivating example for visibility

to all administrative files, some managers have access to salary files, and non-managers have no access to salary files. This modeling of the access matrix can be transformed into a graph language using the following conventions for visual entities:

(1) Boxes: □ represent groups of objects named by box-labels. In turn, a box can contain other boxes, i.e., groups of objects can be classified in subgroups. That is, boxes can be composed and typed. Types constructors are: Nil, Atom, Array, Record, Union, User-defined.
(2) Positive arrow $\square A \to \square B$ indicate that all objects in box A have access to all objects in box B. When arrow starts inside the box it means "some objects, not all". When arrows ends inside a box it means "to some objects, not all".
(3) Negative arrow: $\square A \not\to \square B$ indicates that no object in A has access to objects in B.
(4) Arrows may be labeled by the name of access they provide/forbid.

These elements allow us to design a visual model of security by operations on pictures. The common such operations are:

(1) *Merge:* coalesce two boxes into a new box containing them; access rights do not change.
(2) *Partition:* splits a box into two boxes (inverse of *Merge*); access rights are unchanged.
(3) *Grouping:* arrows displaying some objects not all can be grouped into a box representing the source objects, or a box representing the target objects.
(4) *Flattening:* is the inverse of *Grouping*.

Ambiguity may arise due to negative arrows and group intersections. However, an algorithm that determine ambiguities in a picture allows us to remove ambiguity.

19.8.1 *Bell-LaPadula model*

The BellLaPadula Model [Bell and LaPadula (1996)] is a state machine model used for enforcing access control in government and military applications, used to define the *confinement problem*. Confinement problem addresses the prevention of information leaking and is the base for the US Department of Defense standards and consists of:

(1) All system users and system files are classified by their security restrictions from 1 to n;

(2) Users with security level i are allowed to read files with security classifications j, $j \leq i$;

(3) Users with security level i are allowed to write (modify) files with security classification j, $j \geq i$.

For example, the security classification could be: top-secret, secret, public. A user with security level *secret* can read *top-secrete* and *secrete* files and can modify *secret* and *public* files. Visual expression of Bell-LaPadula model is in Figure 19.8, where S stands for secrecy, W stands for write, and R stands for read.

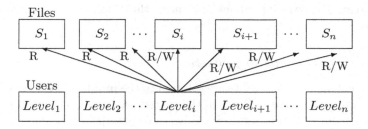

Fig. 19.8   Bell-LaPadula model of security

19.8.2   *Unix implementation of protection*

Objects in Unix are files. Each file has an *owner*, a *group*, and *other* as the file's capability list. Each file provides to its owner, group, other, the access rights *read, write, execute*. The three octal digits associated with each file are used to implement this mechanism of protection, i.e., a file is specified by: `fileName [rwx][rwx][rwx]` where access $r, w, x = 0|1$.

File creation in Unix is performed using two three octal digits masks: cmask (creation mask) and umask (user mask). Default values for cmask and umask are set by system administrator. Usually the values are cmask = 777 for executable files and directories, and cmask = 666 for text files. On the other hand umask = 022. The bits associated with a file at its creation time are cmask - umask. Thus, at creation time the access rights at the directory files in Unix are rwx for owner, r_x for group, r_x for other, and the access rights to the text files are rw_ for owner, r_ _ for group, r_ _ for other. However, the umask can be changed by the command: umask xxx, $0 \leq x \leq 7$.

File rights can be checked by the command: `ls -l fileName`. In addition, file rights can be changed by the command: `chmod Mode fileName`, where `Mode` is a regular expression defined by the pattern `Mode=[u|g|o][+|-][r|w|x]`. Other file informations can be obtained in a buffer whose address is buf, by using the functions: `int stat(const char *path, struct stat *buf)`, `int lstat(const char *path, struct stat *buf)`, and `int fstat(FILE *fd, struct stat *buf)`. These functions and the data structure `struct stat` used as their argument are described in the library `sys/stat.h`. Note that the functions `stat()` and `lstat()` are similar. However, when `path` is a symbolic link `lstat()` returns info about link entry while `stat()` returns info about the file.

19.8.3 *Conclusions to protection*

Access matrix provides a software solution to the problem of controlling the access rights to various objects in the system. A complete implementation of this software solution is too expensive to be practically feasible. However, this model of protection has a strong theoretical interest: *it allows formal reasoning about protection*. The feasibility of this solution is facilitated by capability based architectures such as Plessey 250, CAP, IBM System/38, and Intel iAPX 432. Unix solution is a good approximation.

Chapter 20

Timing Program Execution

Timing program execution is particularly important to avoid the infinite looping of a program, thus preventing the denial of service aspect of system security. It is of equal interest when computation time becomes a shared resource of the computer platforms as required by real-time applications and time-sharing systems. Timing program execution requires a new architectural change which consists of providing hardware support for clocks and appropriate software support to manipulate these clocks. Hardware support for timing program execution consists of two kind of time measuring gadgets called clocks and timers. Clock registers (CLK) are used to time instruction execution and Timer registers (TMR) are used to time program execution. Clocks and timers behave similarly, they interrupt computation after each time unit they can measure.

Clocks and timers are implemented by fast registers that are automatically incremented or decremented by the instruction execution hardware. They are designed such that they overflow or underflow after a number of increments or decrements that can be performed during the time unit they measure. Clocks and timers differ in the mechanisms (interrupt handlers) that treat the interruptions they generate. Clock interrupts are manipulated by the hardware performing the instruction execution. Timer interrupts are manipulated by the software that manages process state-transition diagram.

20.1 Hardware Support

Hardware support for a clock is a register in the control processor called here the *clock*. As long as the power is on, the clock is incremented by the hardware *at the rate of the electrical impulses*. When clock overflows, an interrupt is generated. The clock interrupt is automatically treated by the hardware circuitry which decrements (or increments) a special purpose register of the processor, called a *timer*, and reset the clock register to zero.

The size of the clock register allows the measurement of the time slice between two clock interrupts. This time slice is called a *tick* or a *clock* and it is a characteristic of the hardware. The clock register is manipulated only by the hardware.

The hardware support for the timer consists of one or more special purpose registers dedicated to the timing process. Timer registers are available to the program as any other general purpose register. In contrast with the clock, when a timer register overflows it generates an interrupt which is treated by an interrupt handler in the software and is used to time program execution.

Each instruction is designed to be executed by the hardware during an integer number of independent steps. Each such step takes at most one clock to complete. The number of steps (or clocks) each instruction takes to execute is a constant that depends only on the instruction and the hardware which performs it. To time instruction execution, one can set the number of clocks required by every instruction in a predefined read-only array called TICKS and let the code of the operation be an index in this array. Then TICKS[opcode] is the number of clocks hardware needs to execute the operation designated by `opcode`. Thus, by setting CLK to the value of TICKS[opcode] when the instruction execution starts and by decrementing the CLK after each `clock` time slice, the CLK underflows precisely when the instruction execution time is over. However, the interrupts generated by CLK are standardly treated by the hardware by incrementing or decrementing the timer TMR and reseting CLK to zero.

20.2   Software Support

Software support for timing program execution consists of routines in the operating system that treat the interrupts generated by TMR and instructions that allow programmer to manipulate TMR. A minimal set of such instructions is:

```
Set TMR, C /* loads TMR with the  constant C */
Read R, TMR /* Store the contents of TMR into register R*/
Increment TMR, C /* increments TMR with a constant */
Decrement TMR, C /* decrements TMR with a constant */
```

Figure 20.1 shows the timing mechanism using CLK and TMR.

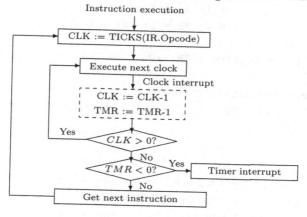

Fig. 20.1   Timing instruction execution

This can be simulated by the C pseudocode:

```
boolean InstructionExecution (struct InstructionWord IR)
 {int CLK = TICKS[IR.Opcode];
  while (CLK > 0)
       {ExecuteNextClock(IR.Opcode);
        /* A clock interrupt occurs */
        CLK = CLK - 1;
        TMR = TMR - 1;
        }
  if (TMR < 0) return(true);
  else return(false);
 }
```

The timing of program execution can thus be simulated by the C pseudocode:

```
ProgramExecution(struct InstructionWord PC)
   {Set TMR, ''TimeSlice'';
    boolean interrupt = false;
    struct InstructionWord IR = *PC;
    while (IR.Opcode != Halt)
         {interrupt = InstructionExecution(IR);
```

```
          if (interrupt == true)
            /* Time-out interrupt */
            {oldPSW = PSW; MB = 1; PSW = PSW(TimeInterrupt);}
          else
            {PC = Next(PC); IR:=*PC;} /* Get next instruction */
          }
      /* Program-termination interrupt */
      {oldPSW = PSW;  MB = 1; PSW = PSW(ProgramTermination);}
      }
```

Facts:

(1) TimeSlice is an integer representing the number of clocks the program will execute before generating a time interrupt.

(2) For BOS, TimeSlice is provided by the control-card (record) RUN that requires program execution. For example, $ RUN ExecTime:6 minutes asks the BOS to run the program for 6 minutes.

(3) While interpreting RUN, BOS converts the ExecTime into the number of clocks it represents and stores it into the TMR, just before initiating the program.

For example, assume that system clock is $1\,\mu s$ and a program needs to be run for at least 6 minutes. The operating system computes the number of clocks in 6 minutes. Since the number of clocks in 6 minutes is 6 * 60 * 1,000,0000 = 360,000,000. The operating system stores 360,000,000 in the TMR. After 360,000,000 clocks from its start, the program either terminates or generates a timer-interrupt.

20.2.1 *Related terms*

The *clock speed* (also called clock rate) is the speed at which a microprocessor executes instructions. For example, Intel 80286 microprocessor requires 20 cycles to multiply two numbers, Intel 80486 performs the same calculation in one clock tick. Therefore, Intel 80486 is 20 times faster than Intel 80286. The *clock tick* is the smallest unit of time recognized by a device. For example, PC's clock ticks runs at 66 MHz. This means that there are 66 million clock ticks (or cycles) per second. Since modern CPUs run much faster (up to 3 GHz), the CPU can execute several instructions in a single clock tick. The *system time* is the number of ticks that have transpired since some arbitrary starting date, called the epoch. For example, the Unix system time is the number of seconds elapsed since the start of the Unix epoch at 1 January 1970 00:00:00 UT. Windows NT system time is the number of ticks since 1 January 1601 00:00:00 UT (Gregorian calendar) but returns current time in milliseconds.

In conclusion, the clock register CLK is used to time instruction execution and the timer register TMR is used to time program executions. Prior to powering up a computer the number of ticks required by every instruction are stored in the TICKS array and let the instruction opcodes be indices into this array. Prior to starting program execution the operating system loads the TMR with the number of clocks representing the slice of time that program execution is allowed to hold the processor. When time stored in TMR elapses, the timer generates an interrupt. The operating system treats this interrupt accordingly.

20.2.2 *Conclusions on reliability*

Mode Bit (MB) and Interrupt Mechanism (IM) constrain the program to use only non-privileged instructions. This enforces the *protocol of communication*. Protection Memory (PM) and Protection Key (PK) constrain the program to use only the memory allocated to it by the operating system. This enforces *protection*. Capability List (CL) and Access Rights (AR) constrain the program to access only computation objects provided in CL using only access-functions provided in the AR list of the accessed object. This enforces *information security*. Clock register (CLK) in the processor and the timer register (TMR) constrain the program to execute only a given amount of time. This eliminates one aspect of *service denial*.

20.3 Computer System Abstraction

Now, a computer system can be seen as consisting of three subsystems: *hardware system*, *user system*, and *software system* which performs as follows:

- Hardware system performs computation tasks on behalf of its users.
- User system allows computer users to define the computations performed by the hardware.
- Software system controls the interaction between hardware system and user system.

The architecture confines the hardware system to behave like an open system with exit gates to the software system, interacting asynchronously

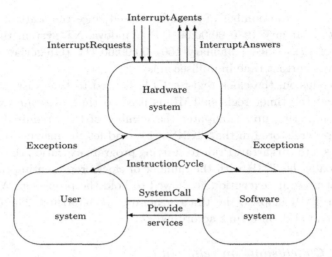

Fig. 20.2   Computer system

with its environment and synchronously with the computations it performs. The asynchronous interaction is achieved by the interrupt mechanism. The synchronous interaction is achieved by the exception mechanism. The software systems controls the system interactions with its environment and its users by receiving and treating interrupts and exceptions, Figure 20.2.

Chapter 21

Efficiency of Batch Operating Systems

BOS has been developed as an automaton that controls the operation of a computing system consisting of: an operator batching jobs at one end of a JobFile, a computer which processes jobs from the other end of the JobFile, and devices that perform I/O operations encoded in the records of that JobFile. BOS evolved by automating the procedure performed by a human operator controlling the system while answering such questions as: *is this automaton correct?* and *is this automaton reliable?*. However, since computer is an expensive tool used by humans during problem solving process, questions such as: *is this automaton efficient?*, *is this automaton convenient?*, and *does this automaton evolve with problem domains?*, need also be answered.

21.1 Overlapping Activities

BOS was developed as a solution to the problem of overlapping the activities performed by human operator, on the one hand, with the activities performed by I/O devices, processor, and memory, on the other hand, while operating the computer system during problem solving process. To obtain maximum efficiency, each of the agents involved in problem-solving should work with its entire capacity. This can be obtained if an operating system can be designed that allows all the agents involved in problem-solving to work in parallel and independent of each other. Using the language of actions, BOS should be an automaton that perform the following solve action:

```
Solve::
    local JobFile: file of Jobs,
```

```
        Job1, Job2, Job3: job data structures;
repeat
   Operator: Batch(Job1,JobFile) or Skip :^Operatpr
      ||
   Processopr: Process(Job2, JobFile) or Skip :^Processor
      ||
   IOdevice: DoIO(Job3, JobFile) or Skip :^IOdevice
forever
```

To expose the difference between BOS as developed so far and a system performing `Solve` action we reproduce here BOS action:

```
BOS::
  local JobFile: file of job data structures,
        Job: job data structure,
        Record: data or control information record;
  repeat
    Operator Batch(Job,JobFile) or Skip:^Operator
       ||
    Processor: MB := 1; Innput(Record, JobFile);
        while (Record not EOJ) do
          Process(Job) or Input(JobData) or
          Output(JobResults) or Skip:^Processor;
  forever
```

Now we can observe that with BOS action there is no overlapping between processor and I/O devices. Processor performs either program instructions in *user mode* or I/O instructions in *system mode*. With `Solve` action however, while processor performs machine instructions I/O devices perform at the same time I/O operations. Moreover, I/O operations performed by I/O devices could be on behalf of the current program executed by the processor, called *overlapping* mode, or they could be on behalf of another program, called *concurrent* mode. The overlapping and concurrency are different operating modes. Due to sequential nature of job processing one cannot design concurrent systems using a JobFile!.

21.2   Measuring System Performance

By definition system performance is defined by the formula $Performance = \frac{ProcessorTime}{TotalTime}\%$ where $ProcessorTime$ is the time spent by the processor performing actual operations on the current job and *Total-Time* is the total time spent by the processor on the current Job. When I/O operations are initiated processor must wait for I/O operation completion before continuing program execution. Increase in efficiency can be obtained if we can control the processor to perform in parallel with the I/O devices rather than waiting for I/O operations completion. The implementation of this idea requires new hardware that would allow the processor to poll the devices asking whether they are free to operate, or that would allow the I/O devices to interrupt the processor when they are free to operate. This hardware has allowed us to evolve BOS such that actions *Batch()*, *Process()*, and *DoIO()* perform in parallel. Since *Batch()* action is already independent of the other two actions we need to look here only at the actions *Process()* and *DoIO()*. Figure 21.1 allows us to evaluate the performance when *Process()* and *DoIO()* perform serial.

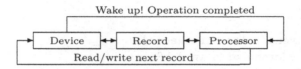

Fig. 21.1   Processor←⟶I/O device serial activity

In this scenario the processor sends an instruction to the device, and while the device reads/writes, processor is idle. When the device terminates, processor performs and device is idle. So, the C expression of this scenario is:

```
SerialActivity()
    {
    while (MoreRecords in JobFile)
        {Start I/O operation;
            while (Device busy)
                ; /* Processor is idle */
        Process record;
            while (Processor busy)
                ; /* Device is idle */
        }
    }
```

If the time spent by the device processing one record is T and time spent by the processor processing one record is t *(note, $T \gg t$)* then the Total Time (TT) required to process a sequence of n records is $TT = n \times (T + t)$ and performance of the system is $P = \frac{t}{T+t}$. Since $T \gg t$ processor is idle most of the time, and system performance is close to zero.

In the scenario that overlap the *Process()* and *DoIO()* activities the processor starts the device to get next data record. While the device works, the processor is idle. When device terminates, processor starts the device for the next data record and then in parallel processes the data that has already arrived instead of waiting for the next data record to arrive. During overlapping activity the processor and I/O devices communicate by one or both of the mechanisms: processor polling I/O devices or I/O devices sending interrupt signals to the processor. The C expression of the overlap scenario is:

```
Overlap ()
   {
     Start read/write FirstRecord;
     while (MoreRecords in JobFile)
         {
           while (Device busy)
              ;  /* Processor is idle */
           Start read/write NextRecord;
           Process PreviousRecord; /* Proceed concurrently */
         }
     Process LastRecord;
   }
```

The time required to process n records in this scenario is $n \times T + t$. Since $T \gg t$, the TotalTime, is $TT \approx nT$. Hence, the system performance is $P = \frac{t}{T}\%$ Comparing the two expressions $SerialPerformance = \frac{t}{T+t}\%$ and $OverlapPerformance = \frac{t}{T}\%$ we conclude that the gain in performance is almost negligible. While system performance can be further increased by various buffering systems [Bic and Shaw (2003)] that overlap Read, Write, Execute operations, the sequential nature of JobFile does not support the true parallel processing as required by the `Solve()` action. Therefore we will continue to look at the BOS evolution that concerns the changing of the JobFile.

21.3 Off-Line Operation

The first idea that would allow further increase in performance would be to replace the slow devices (card reader, card puncher, etc.) used to organize JobFile with faster devices such as disks, tapes, drums. The first significant evolution of BOS following this idea was obtained by mapping the Job-File off-line on tape which is then mounted on Tape Reader/Writer by the human operator, thus obtaining the Tape Operating System (TOS), whose action is shown in Figure 21.2.

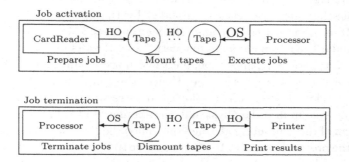

Fig. 21.2 Off-line job processing

Here OS stands for operating system and HO stands for human operator. That is, a TOS is a BOS which uses a magnetic tape as data carrier for the JobFile operating the system by the rules:

(1) Operator prepares JOBs as usually and maps them off-line on magnetic tapes (MT) which are then mounted on an MT unit.
(2) TOS reads and processes jobs from a magnetic tape and writes results onto a magnetic tape.
(3) At job termination the operator dismounts tape and print results off-line.

Notice, since MT units are much faster than CRs, increase in efficiency is expected. The implementation of this idea requires the development of special I/O devices like card readers, line printers, etc., with the facility to input/output directly onto magnetic tapes. However, this idea evolved to a new computer configuration consisting of:

(1) A main computer, performing data processing;

(2) Small computers acting as satellites preparing data for the main computer.

This job processing mode evolved further to today distributed systems.

The advantages TOS system is that the main computer is no longer constrained by the speed of slow devices. It is however, constrained by the speed of magnetic tape unit. But no changes are needed in the user programs running on the usual BOS in order to run them on the TOS. I/O operations are performed by virtual devices that read/write their info records from/on magnetic tapes. That is, as user programs execute I/O operations by requesting them as services provided by the operating system, data comes from a virtual card reader, (paper tape, etc.) which are organized and standardized on a common magnetic tape. Results are printed using a virtual card puncher (paper tape, etc.) which are organized and standardized on a common magnetic tape. Hence, the concept of a *logical device* is thus developed. Programs use logical devices which are mapped by the operating system into the physical devices connected to the system. This is the origin of the computing abstractions called the *file*, and of the I/Odevice use by the protocol: `open(File,Device)`, `doIO()`, `close(File,Device)`. The logical device employed in the user's program evolved into the concept of a file (external file). The physical device used by the system to perform I/O operations evolved to the concept of a device file (internal file). The operating system binds the external file used in the user program to an internal file in the system. This evolved into the file system as a component of the operating system.

Major limitations of the TOS result from the the sequential nature of the tape, which does not allow the system to get direct access to various jobs waiting in the job file. Hence, while a job performs I/O operations the processor can perform in parallel only computations of the same job, that is, processor cannot move ahead to execute computations of another job. Therefore the I/O operations of one job cannot be performed in parallel with the processing operations of another job.

21.4 Disk Operating System

A JobFile organized on a disk allows the system direct access to the jobs in a job files. Implementation of this idea results in Disk Operating System (DOS) where:

(1) JDS recorded on cards are sent from cards onto the disk.
(2) Each job has a Job Summary (JS) in computer memory.
(3) The location of job data structure on disk is recorded in JS.

Thus, the advances provided by DOS are:

(1) I/O operations of a job can be overlapped with processing operations of another job.
(2) I/O operations can be performed in parallel with processing operations, irrespective of the job they belong to.
(3) While a job is processed, its I/O requests are satisfied by reading/writing a disk. Similarly, its output requests can be written to a disk.
(4) When a job is completed its actual output can be printed.

The manner of the computer operation described above defines a job processing mode called *Simultaneous Peripheral Operation On-Line* (SPOOLING) depicted in Figure 21.3.

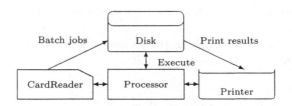

Fig. 21.3   Spooling operation

The advantages of DOS are:

(1) The spooling operation uses a disk as a very large buffer.
(2) Spooling is however capable of overlapping I/O operations for one job with processor operations for another job. This is the result of having direct access to the disk image of JDS.
(3) The program which accumulates JDS-s in a job pool on disk is called an *InSpooler*. The program which prints the data accumulated into another pool is called an *OutSpooler*.

The SPOOLING was first implemented at the Houston Computation Center of NASA under the name Houston Automatic Spooling Program (HASP) system [IBM (1971)].

21.5   Multiprogramming System

The operation mode which overlaps processor activity for one job with the I/O operations requested by other jobs was called *multiprogramming*. Data structures that support multiprogramming are the JDS kept on disk, directly accessible, and the JS, kept in main memory in a Job Summary Table (JST). The JS summarizes the computing activity supplied to the system and allows direct access to the job on disk. A scheduling algorithm can schedule for execution various jobs in the JST according to a given policy (not necessarily FIFO). Since jobs represent computer users and they are scheduled for execution according to criteria that compare computer users among them, the computer user becomes a new computing abstraction. She needs to be codified and recorded in the system. To qualify for computer usage, the computer user need to be identified as a legal user of the computer. Therefore, computer users are represented by data-records consisting of their unique-names, resource requirements, priorities, jobs submitted, etc. Thus, users are recorded in a user directory maintained by the system. The user directory allows the system to validate the user rights to submit jobs for execution and provides a billing mechanism.

Common information held in the JS can be structured in a record that can be specified as a C structure as follows:

```
struct JSentry
     {struct DirectoryEntry *User;
      char *JobName;
      int  State;
      int  Priority;
      int  DiskAddress;
      int  MemoryAddress;
      int  RunningTime;
      int  StartTime;
      int  TerminateTime;
     };
```

Common information in user directory entry can be specified by the following C structure:

```
struct DirectoryEntry
     {char *UserName;
      char *AccountNumber;
```

```
char *PassWord;
int  ProcessorTime;
int  I/O Time;
int  OtherResources;
}UserDirectory[MaxNumber];
```

Graphic the JST is shown in the Figure 21.4.

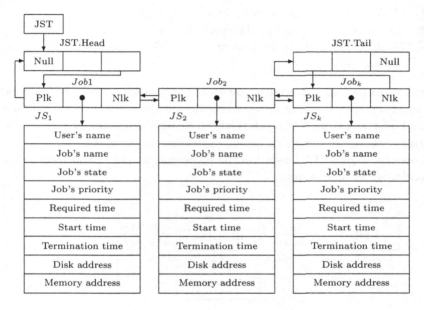

Fig. 21.4   JST used by multiprogramming system

The implementation of a multiprogramming systems maintains two job pools on the disk, called here *InPool* and *OutPool* respectively, and a job summary table in main memory. Job arrival to the computer is manipulated by a subsystem called *InSpooler* and Job departure from the computer is manipulated by a subsystem called *OutSpooler*. Job running by the computer is manipulated by yet another subsystem called *Job Scheduler*.

At job arrival time the InSpooler creates a JS representing the jobs, link JS into the JST, and send the job itself into the InPool on disk.

When a Job terminates the OutSpooler takes care of its departure from the system. It sends the job's results in the OutPool, frees the disk area occupied by the job in the InPool and OutPool, and update the JST accordingly by deleting the JS of departed job.

Job scheduler performs job transition from InPool to the memory when job's turn to execution comes (long-term scheduling). It also performs job scheduling for execution of the jobs already in memory (short-time scheduling) and job transition from memory to the OutPool when job terminates, or from memory into the InPool, when its memory resources are required for other purposes (long-time scheduling). Consequently, for the implementation purpose the JST is maintained in three linked lists:

(1) The InList which accumulates JSs of new jobs arriving in the system;
(2) The OutList which accumulates JSs of jobs waiting for termination;
(3) The ReadyList which accumulates JSs of jobs in main memory waiting for execution.

InList, OutList, and ReadyList are managed by a *long-term* scheduler and a *short-term* scheduler. Long-term scheduler performs transitions: InList→ ReadyList and ReadyList→ OutList. Short-term scheduler performs transitions between running jobs on the processor, i.e., ReadyList $\xleftrightarrow{switchCntext}$ Processor. Figure 21.5 illustrates the processing manner performed by the multiprogramming system.

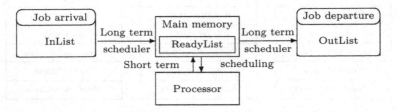

Fig. 21.5   Job processing by multiprogramming system

Scheduling criteria used by a multiprogramming system perform such optimizations as: maximize processor utilization time, maximize throughput of the system (i.e., maximize the number of jobs completed), minimize turnaround time for each job (i.e., minimize the time between job arrival and job departure), minimize the waiting time in the ReadyList. Scheduling algorithms that can implement these criteria are

- First In First Out (FIFO), where the first job arrived is first job serviced.
- Shortest Job First (SJF), where job requiring smallest time is serviced first.
- Priority scheduler, where the highest priority job is serviced first.

- Round-robin scheduler, where each job is run for given time-slice after which processor is preempted and, if not completed, the job is rescheduled.

These algorithms can be implemented as preemptive or non-preemptive.

21.5.1 *Efficiency*

As long as there is some job to execute processor is not idle. Therefore, multiprogramming system should maintain a high performance of computer utilization. However, when too many jobs compete for processor, this competition can degrade computer performance because the processor becomes busy switching from one queue to another and from one job in a queue to another, in the detriment of user computations. This is called *threshold state*. To avoid this state statistic information is needed correlating the number of jobs in the three scheduling queues. That is, to maintain a high performance, the multiprogramming system needs to make efficient use of the processor and I/O devices. The number of jobs present in the system at a given time is called the multiprogramming degree. If multiprogramming degree is too large, the efficiency of the system is decreased rather than increased.

Chapter 22

Convenience of the BOS

Computer based problem solving process evolved the BOS to perform the action:

```
Solve::
   local JobFile: file of Jobs,
         Job1, Job2, Job3: job data structures;
   repeat
      Operator: Batch(Job1,JobFile) or Skip :^Operator
         ||
      Processor: Process(Job2, JobFile) or Skip :^Processor
         ||
      IOdevice: DoIO(Job3, JobFile) or Skip :^IOdevice
   forever
```

This action is implemented by the multiprogramming systems which while preserving the correctness and reliability of BOS also maintains a high efficiency of computer utilization. Since the system became a commercial object, to make it user-desirable it also needs to be convenient to its users.

The characteristic of BOS is the lack of interaction between computer users and processes performing their jobs under the control of the operating system. Jobs are prepared, submitted to the system, and their results appear at some later time. During submission and processing stages there is no relation between jobs and their owners. Interaction between a job and its user would enable the user to direct computations performed by the system according to the progress of transformation steps undergone by the source program toward its execution, and according to the behavior of the programmed algorithm during its execution. Consequently, user

315

interaction with her job processing processes would lead to more convenient system usage.

22.1 Interactive Systems

An operating system which provides on-line communication between users and their job processing processes is called the *interactive system*. An interactive system is characterized by the set of instructions users can give either to the operating system or directly to processes executing their programs during their job processing. This entails the cooperation between operating system and computer user during computer based problem solving process. The implementation of this cooperation requires the input of an interactive system to be the keyboard of a terminal device (not the JobFile) and the output to be a printer or the screen of a display terminal. The user uses the terminal device to send commands to the system or to processes performing her computations, and the system uses the printer (or terminal's screen) to send messages informing the user about the behavior of her computations.

Notice that with an interactive system JobFile is abandoned! The job data structure is replaced by a program written by the user in a Job Control Language (JCL) that instructs the system about the transformation steps required by her job during computer-based problem solving process. The commands of this program define the job steps to be executed by the operating system. Program execution is explicitly requested using a JCL command. The job processing is initiated by the user from the input terminal using a command in the JCL. Example JCL is a Unix shell. Using C-shell language and % as the prompt, we can illustrate the interactive job processing by the following commands:

(1) The shell command that allows the user to write a C program in the file `myFirst.c` could be: `% vi myFirst.c`. Performing this command the system opens the file `myFirst.c` and the user type the C program as contents of this file.

(2) The shell command asking the C compiler to compile the program written in `myFirst.c` could be: `% cc -Wall -o myFirstProgram myFirst.c`.

(3) The shell command asking the system to execute the program `myFirstProgram` could be: `% myFirstProgram input1 input2 ....`

The results are generated on an output specified by the input arguments or by a file descriptor used in `myFirst.c`. This manner of interaction evolved from typed control language commands to clicking window icons. However, the interaction by clicking buttons does not change the essence of communication. It only changes the mechanism of communication. The design and the implementation of an interactive system remain the same. Due to human-nature, clicking icons (probable) increases user convenience. But employing the button clicking the user may loses the advantage of communication abstraction provided by the language.

22.2 Functionality of an Interactive System

With an interactive system jobs arrive continuously from user's terminal. The JDS, maintained on disk by the multiprogramming system, is replaced by a continuous stream of commands. When the operating system finishes treating one command it seeks the next command from the same input. This is exactly like with BOS operation which seeks the next control record from the same card reader or equivalent input device. The data processed by a user's command do not necessarily follows the command. They can come from files specified by the command arguments. The protocol of interaction between the computer user, the system, and I/O devices is defined by the following rules:

- **The user:** gives a command, via an I/O device, to the interactive system and waits for the answer.
- **The system:** receives the command, analyzes it, and executes it. Then, system answers by sending a prompt to the output terminal, signaling the completion of the command.
- **The IOdevice:** performs I/O activity of the running programs (system or user) while programs themselves my be suspended.

Fact: with an interactive system user decides the next command to be given, conforming to the behavior of problem-solving algorithm and to the system's answer.

22.2.1 *Computing environment*

The computing environment of an interactive system consists of:

- A Job Control Language, example C-shell;

- An interpreter that reads, analyzes, and interprets JCL commands sent by the user;
- An interactive text editor that allows the user to enter the program and its data. Example such editors are emacs, vi, vim, pico, etc. Since Microsoft word is a document development it cannot be used as a component of an interactive system.
- An interactive debugger that assists the user with program debugging. Example interactive debuggers are dbx and gdb.

Note that with a window-system, commands are replaced by the menu in a window-bar. Hence, the interpreter receives the commands associated with the icons in the menu. There is no need for a JCL. But the *user* ⟷ *system* communication is limited by the number of icons in the menu. Example of such a system is Microsoft Windows-XP. Here we focus on JCL based interactive systems.

22.2.2 *Interactive system implementation*

The hardware that facilitated the implementation of interactive systems was the development of input/output terminals that can be used by both the system and the user. The user sends commands to the system via such terminal asking it to perform certain computations. The system sends messages back to the user reporting about the behavior of computations thus initiated. The user can interrupt the system from the terminal whenever necessary. The terminal is provided with a cursor holding the place of next character of the current command. A prompt on its initial position indicates that the system is ready to receive a command. When user types the first character of a command, a user interrupt occurs. System treats this interrupt by initiating a program that reads the command. When user types end-of-command symbol the device initiates a device interrupt. The system treats this interrupt by initiating a program that executes the command. When program executing the user command terminates, the system sends a prompt to the terminal thus returning control to the user. For convenience reason whatever a user types on the input (the keyboard) is echoed on the system output (the screen).

The software support for the implementation of an interactive system include:

- A command language and its interpreter;

- A ReadCommand() function that is activated when a user interrupt is received;
- A PrintPrompt function that is activated by the system when a computation is completed;
- A collection of executable programs that can be executed by the system on behalf of the user. User's programs are in this collection. The interpreter searches this collection when a device interrupt is received signaling that a command has been entered.

The C pseudocode implementing an interactive system is in Figure 22.1.

```
InteractiveSystem()
   {char prompt[Size1], Buffer[Size2]; boolean  check;
   while (true) /* Repeat forever */
       {wait (UserInterrupt);
       ReadCommand (Buffer); check = CheckCorrectness(Buffer);
       if (check)
          {check = SearchCommand(Collection,Buffer);
          if (check)
             {check = ExecuteCommand;
             if (check) prompt = ''OK'';
             else prompt = ''Err: Program error'';
             }
          else prompt = ''Err': Nonexistent function'';
          }
       else prompt = ''Err: Incorrect command'';
       print (prompt); /* Answer to user */
       }
   }
```

Fig. 22.1   Interactive system implementation

Computing environment of an interactive system uses the same mechanisms as BOS: system programs and system calls. However, while the BOS initiates system programs automatically during JOB processing, independent of job behavior, the interactive system initiates system programs only in response to the commands received from users. The mechanism of the system call is used in the same way by both batch and interactive systems. Since there is a continuous interaction between the system and the computer user during job processing the interactive system achieves the goal of user convenience. Moreover, with an interactive system the debugging can be done dynamically by a continuous interaction between programmers and their executing programs.

The major disadvantage of an interacting system as specified above results from its lack of efficiency. The processing speed of a computer controlled by this interactive system is reduced to the speed of the user asking the system to execute commands. Question to be answered now is: could we transform these disadvantages into an advantage by allowing many users to share the system's time?

22.3   Time-Sharing Systems

TSS combines the multiprogramming system, which provides high performance of processor utilization, with the interactive system, which provides user convenience. With such a system, the processor's time becomes a resource shared between all the users of the system. Consequently, TSS is like a multiprogramming systems: a pool of jobs are accessed by the system and are scheduled for execution according to given criteria. However, unlike the multiprogramming systems, job-transformation steps are manipulated by job's owner from a terminal provided by the system to its user. Each user sits at her own terminal and has access to one or more programs in computer memory. Execution of one program is a transaction. Since user's transactions are assumed to be short, only a small portion of the processor's time is needed for each user. Therefore, the processor can be switched among users, who, in effect, share the processor's time.

22.4   TSS Implementation

The `ReadCommand(Buffer)` operation performed by the interactive system on behalf of one user can be executed by TSS in parallel with the `ExecuteCommand(Command)` operation performed on behalf of another user. This can be implemented by TSS using the interrupt mechanism and processing mode defined by MB exactly as multiprogramming BOS implemented the I/O operation execution of one job in parallel with processing operations of another job. Hence, users of a TSS are given impression that each of them use a dedicated computer while they are actually operating on a shared machine. Communication protocol that sit at the basis of TSS is:

- Each user sends commands to the system, using `ReadCommand` `(Buffer)`;
- The system receives user's commands and accumulate them in a command waiting queue;
- The system operates on the command waiting queue and interprets the commands stored there in an order determined by a scheduler, such as FIFO.

Hence, the implementation of TSS is based on the fact that each computer user has her own terminal that can be used to send commands to and to receive messages from the system. The commands are received and are processed by the TSS as done by the interactive system. However, all users can type and send commands to the system simultaneously, and in addition, while a user types a command, the system may execute other commands and moreover, I/O devices may perform I/O activity of yet other programs. Consequently, the TSS consists of three concurrent processes:

(1) `GetCommand`: a process that initiates the `ReadCommand(Buffer)` function to read the next command sent by a user sitting at her own terminal.

(2) `QueueCommand`: a process that sends the commands typed by the users into a command queue.

(3) `ExecuteCommand`: a process that manages the command queue, i.e., updates it and executes the next command in the command queue.

Processes `GetCommand, QueueCommand, ExecuteCommand` perform in parallel while sharing resources. `GetCommand` and `QueueCommand` share the input buffer where a command is read. `QueueCommand` and `ExecuteCommand` share the queue where commands are accumulated. Therefore the expression of TSS in the action-language is:

```
TSS ::
    inout CommandBufer,CommandQueue;
    L0: repeat
          GetCommand (CommandBuffer);
            ||
          QueueCommand(CommandBuffer,CommandQueue);
            ||
          ExecuteCommand(CommandQueue);
        forever: ^L0
```

Hence, TSS is similar to Solve actions. However, || within Solve is an *interleaving* operation while within TSS it is a *parallel* operation.

22.5 Synchronization and Sharing

Each of the three process components of a TSS needs to synchronize its actions with the actions of other components while operating on shared resources. This synchronization and sharing must preserve the consistency of TSS operation. Therefore the implementation of TSS requires a *lock data type* that can be used to enforce the order of TSS component operation while preserving the consistency of resources they share. The lock data type used to implement concurrent process has been introduced by Edsger Dijkstra [Bic and Shaw (2003)] under the name **semaphore**. Here we redefine the semaphore as a data type whose values are natural numbers and is supported by the three atomic operations: **Set**, **Signal**, and **Wait**. That is, a variable S of type semaphore can take values in the set $\mathcal{N} = \{0, 1, 2, \ldots\}$. The semaphore operations on the variable S are defined by:

(1) For $v \in \mathcal{N}$, $Set(S, v)$ is an atomic operation that performs $S := v$. Note, v may be a value that can be obtained by the evaluation of an appropriate expression.
(2) $Signal(S)$ is an atomic operation that performs $S := S + 1$.
(3) $Wait(S)$ is an atomic operations that performs $S := S - 1$. However, if $S = 0$, $Wait(S)$ imply waiting until $S > 0$ because $0 - 1 \notin \mathcal{N}$.

Now, two processes P1 and P2 can use a semaphore S to synchronize their actions to perform in the order $P_1 \to P_2$ by the following code:

```
Semaphore S; Set(S,0);
P1::
    repeat forever
        ComputeBefore; Signal(S); ComputeAfter
P2::
    repeat forever
        ComputBefore; Wait(S); ComputeAfter
P1 || P2
```

Since S is set to 0, P2 cannot proceeds past Wait(S) operation until P1 executes Signal(S). Thus, P2 waits for P1. The processes P1 and P2 can share a resource R, such as a buffer, by executing their operations on R in mutual exclusion, i.e., only one process operates on R at a time. Process P1 and P2 can use a semaphore S to share a resource R in mutual exclusion performing the code:

```
Semaphore S; Set(S,1); resource R;
P1::
    reaped
        Compute1;Wait(S) Operate1(R) Signal(S);Compute2
    forever
P2::
    repeat
        Compute1;Wait(S) Operate2(R) Signal(S);Compute2
    forever
P1 || P2
```

The code performed by a process while sharing a resource in mutual exclusion with another process is called a *critical section*. A critical sections is correctly implemented only if the semaphore protecting it is in initialized to 1. For example, the code `Wait(S); Operate1(R); Signal(S)` is a correct critical section in process P1 because $Set(S, 1)$ is performed outside the code of process P1. Similarly, `Wait(S); Operate2(R); Signal(S)` is a correct critical section in process P2 for the same reason. Consequently during the parallel process $P1||P2$, P1 and P2 share correctly the resource R.

22.6 Synchronization and Sharing in TSS

The three main processes composing a time-sharing system synchronize their actions by the following protocol:

(1) `GetCommand()` waits for a user to send a command and **signals** the QueueCommand() when a command arrives;
(2) `QueueCommand()` waits for the `GetCommand()` to finish reading a command and then sends that command into the CommandQueue and **signals** the `ExecuteCommand()` telling that a command is available for execution;
(3) `ExecuteCommand()` waits for the `QueueCommand()` to send a command in the CommandQueue and **signals** the user when the execution of her command completes.

Note that all users can send commands in a `CommandBuffer`, thus this must be done in CS. Similarly, all commands wait for execution in the CommandQueue, so operations on CommandQueue must also be in CS.

The three semaphores used to implement the synchronization in TSS are: `User`, `Device`, `Processor`. Since they implement the synchronization between the three agents involved, they are initialized in the global part of TSS as follows:

```
Set(User,0);
Set(Device,0);
Set(Processor, 0);
```

During TSS operation the three main processes composing the system share the `CommandBuffer`, where a command is read, and the `CommandQueue`, where commands wait for execution. The operations on the `CommandBuffer` are performed in a critical section protected by the semaphore `Buffer`. The operations on the `CommandQueue` are performed in a critical section protected by the semaphore `Queue`. Since the semaphores `Buffer` and `Queue` are used to implement critical sections, they are initialized in the global area of TSS as follows:

```
Set(Buffer, 1);
Set(Queue, 1);
```

Thus, the operations on `CommandBuffer` are performed in the following critical section:

```
Wait(Buffer};
Operate on the CommandBuffer;
Signal(Buffer);
```

The operations on the `CommandQueue` are performed in the following critical section:

```
Wait(Queue};
Operate on the CommandQueue;
Signal(Queue);
```

Processes `GetCommand()` and `QueueCommand()` share the `CommandBuffer` where the command is read, as seen in Figure 22.2. Processes `QueueCommand()` and `ExecuteCommand()` share the `CommandQueue` where the user commands are waiting for executions, as seen in Figure 22.3.

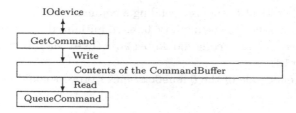

Fig. 22.2   Sharing the CommandBuffer

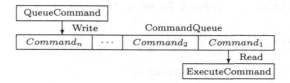

Fig. 22.3   Sharing the CommandQueue

22.6.1   *Implementation of a TSS*

The C pseudocode of the GetCommand() process could be:

```
GetCommand()
    {extern semaphore User, Device, Buffer;
     extern char CommandBuffer[Size];
     boolean check;
     while (true) /* Repeat forever */
         {
          Wait (User);
              {
               identify user;
               Wait(Buffer);
               ReadCommand (CommandBuffer);
               check = CheckCorrectness(CommandBuffer);
               Signal(Buffer);
               if (check) Signal (Device);
               else "Message: bad command; discard buffer";
              }
         }
    }
```

The action that identify the user sending a command must be performed in critical section! That is, a semaphore `UserId` initialized by `Set(UserId,1)` needs to be used and the code should be: `Wait(UserId); identify user; Signal(UserId);`.

The C pseudocode of the `QueueCommand()` process could be:

```
QueueCommand()
    {extern semaphore Device, Processor, Queue;
     extern char *CommandQueue, DeviceBuffer[Size];
     while (true) /* Repeat forever */
          {
           wait (Device);
               {
                identify device;
                Wait(Queue);
                append (DeviceBuffer, CommandQueue);
                signal (Queue);
                }
             Signal(Processor)
          }
    }
```

The action that identify the device sending a command to command queue must be performed in critical section! That is, a semaphore `DeviceId` initialized by `Set(DeviceId,1)` needs to be used and the code should be: `Wait(DeviceId); identify device; Signal(DeviceId);`

The C pseudocode of the `ExecuteCommand()` process could be:

```
ExecuteCommand()
  {extern queue CommandQueue; semaphore Processor, Queue;
   char Prompt[Size1], NextCommand[Size2]; boolean check;
   while (true)  /* Repeat forever */
        {Wait (Processor);
         Wait(Queue);
         NextCommand = GetNext(CommandQueue);
         Signal(Queue);
         check = SearchCommand(NextCommand);
```

```
    if (check)
      {check = Execute(NextCommand);
       if (check) Prompt = ''OK'';
       else Prompt = ''Err: Program error'';
      }
    else Prompt = ''Err: Nonexistent function'';
    PrintPrompt;
   }
 }
```

The action that print the **Prompt** answering the user command must be performed in critical section! That is, a semaphore **PromptId** initialized by Set(PromptId,1) needs to be used and the code should be:

```
Wait(PromptId);
        Print Prompt;
Signal(PromptId);
```

22.6.2 *TSS operation*

User initiate a user interrupt when she hits the first key of the terminal keyboard. The GetCommand process identifies the user who sent the interrupt and initiates the I/O program to read the next command line. I/O program reading a command initiates a device interrupt when end of command is typed. The program that treats this interrupt signals the QueueCommand() process to move the command to the command queue. When QueueCommand() process terminates it tells ExecuteCommand() process that a new command has arrived in the CommandQueue. Thus, TSSaction is:

```
TSSaction::
    inout DeviceBuffer, CommandQueue;
    repeat
      GetCommand(User,DeviceBuffer);
         ||
      QueueCommand(DeviceBuffer,CommandQueue);
         ||
      ExecuteCommand(CommandQueue, Processor);
    forever
```

GetCommand(), QueueCommand() and ExecuteCommand() are three independent processes that perform in parallel overlapping user, processor, device actions. They share buffers and ensure that all computer users are fairly treated. This is done by appropriate scheduling of the ExecuteCommand(). Most of the today operating systems are both time-sharing and batch multiprogramming.

Chapter 23

Real-Time Systems

A real-time system is a computing system that interacts in real-time with its environment. Real-time systems are used as control devices in dedicated applications. Examples such applications are surgical operations, aircraft control, industrial plant control, embedded-devices in house-hold appliances, etc. Software systems which control these applications are real-time systems also called control devices.

Fact: a real-time system is constrained by the time period in which *it must react* to the events that arrive from its environment.

23.1 Real-Time Constraints

Time period between environment signaling the system and system generating changes in the control device of the application is called the *real-time constraint*. To ensure the safety of the application, system reaction time must be within precise limits. The violation of real-time constraints may result in catastrophic results.

The implementation of a real-time system must be supported by appropriate hardware and software that allow control devices to send and receive signals to and from the environment. The operating system which supports real-time applications must ensure by its *interrupt response time* (see IRT defined in Section 12.3) that real-time constraints of the application will be satisfied.

Hardware support for real-time applications consists of: a real time clock that sends interrupt signals at a given rate, a collection of sensors that bring signals from the environment to the system and from the system to the environment, converters which perform such mappings as *Analog* $\longleftrightarrow$ *Digital* signals and an appropriate interrupt mechanism.

To further discuss the real-time systems we assume that the `time-interval unit` (TIU) at which the real time clock sends interrupt signals to the real-time application has the value 1. This value depends only upon the application. That is, TIU of the application (such as a second) is characteristic to the application and is the smallest time interval representing the real-time constraint of an application component. Examples TIU-s for various applications are:

- For surgical applications TIU = 1 second. Rationale is that the system monitors patient's pulse with the goal of maintaining it at 1 pulse/second.
- For an atomic plant controller TIU = 1/100 seconds. Rationale is that it takes 1/100 seconds for the atomic plant walls to change temperature with 10 Celsius degrees.
- For a flight controller TIU = 1/10 seconds. Rationale is that it takes 1/10 seconds for the flying object to change direction in order to avoid an obstacle.

The values of TIU-s used above are hypothetical and have nothing to do with the real-time systems controlling such applications.

Software support for real-time applications consists of: the interrupt handlers which process the interrupts generated by the signals sent by the real-time clock and by the sensors, a real-time scheduler that schedules for execution each process which composes the application so that the real time constraint of the application is satisfied, and a collection of processes that perform the task of the application. These are started-up by the real-time scheduler at given time-intervals.

Fact: for a given real-time application, there is one process for each physical device which sends or receives signals to or from the environment.

23.2   Component Integration

The mechanism used here for real-time system component integration is a time-table, TT [Brinch-Hansen (1977)], which includes all processes in the real-time system and specifies the wake-up time interval for each process controlled by the real-time scheduler. Each entry in TT specifies:

- The name of a process, `Name`;
- The address of its code, `Address`;

- The time passed since the process associated with this entry was last activated, called `Time`;
- The wake-up time called `Delay`, which is the period between two successive activations.

The wake-up time of each process in TT must be an integer number of TIU-s of the application.

To implement the time constraints of the application we assume that the real time clock sends interrupts signals at a constant rate intervals called clocks. Example of a clock is one microsecond. A number of clock interrupts makeup the time interrupt unit (TIU) of the application. Hence, to ensure that the application meets its real-time constraints, the state of each process must be checked after each time interrupt unit.

23.3 Scheduling

The real-time clock interrupt handler measures the TIU of the application. Thus, when a TIU elapses the real-time clock signals the scheduler. The real-time scheduler checks the elapsed time of processes in TT and restarts all those that must be executed in the next time interval in order to observe the time constraints of the application. Graphic image of a real-time application is in Figure 23.1.

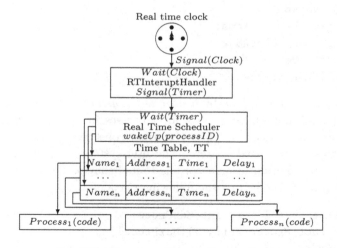

Fig. 23.1 Structure of a real-time application

The C language sketch of a real-time interrupt handler is:

```
int ClockInterval = 0,
    RealTime = "time-interrupt unit of application";
semaphore Timer; Set(Timer,0);
RealTimeInterruptHandler()
   {if (ClockInterval < RealTime)
      ClockInterval++;
    else
      {ClockInterval = 0;
       Signal (Timer);
      }
   }
```

23.4   Time-Table Scheduling Policy

Assume that each process must be rescheduled for execution after a given constant time interval called Delay. The Delay of a process depends upon the task performed by the process and can be changed by the user of the application. In addition, the Delay must be an integer number of time-interrupt units of the application. C language expression of a TT entry:

```
typedef int (*process());
struct ProcessEntry
      {char *ProcessName;
       process  FuncAddr;
       int   Delay, Time;
      }TT[MaxProcs];
```

System initialization is done by a *user* ⟷ *system* interaction interface. During this interaction Delay-s of all processes in TT are initialized at given values determined by their real time constraints and the Time of all processes is initialized at zero. The user-system interaction interface allows system re-initialization according to its behavior. Now, the real-time scheduler can be sketched by the following C code:

```
extern semaphore Timer; int MaxProcs;
      struct ProcessEntry TT[MaxProcs];
RealTimeScheduler()
   {
```

```
int i;
while (true)
    {Wait (Timer);
        {for (i = 0; i<MaxProcs; i++)
            {if (TT[i].Time<TT[i].Delay)
              TT[i].Time++;
            else
              {awake(TT[i].Address);
              TT[i].Time = 0;
              }
            }
        }
    }
}
```

All processes in the time table can be awakened concurrently at a given time. If they share variables, mutual exclusion on these variables must be ensured by the code of the real time process.

Bibliography

Abstract Systems (2010). Abstract systems theory, `http://www.encyclo pediaofmath.org/index.php/Abstract_Systems_Theory`.

Aho, A., Sethi, R. and Ullman, J. (January 1, 1986). *Compilers: Principles, Techniques, and Tools* (Addison Wesley).

Backus, J. (1959). The syntax and semantics of the proposed international algebraic language of the Zurich ACM-gamm conference. in *Proceedings of the International Conference on Information Processing. UNESCO.*, p. 125132.

Bell, D. and LaPadula, L. (1996). Secure computer systems: Mathematical foundation `http://www.albany.edu/acc/courses/ia/classics/bellla padula1.pdf`.

Berwise, J. (ed.) (1978). *Handbook of Mathematical Logic* (North–Holland).

Bic, L. F. and Shaw, A. C. (2003). *Operating Systems Principles* (Prentice Hall).

Blass, A. and Gurevich, Y. (2013). Abstract Hilbertian deductive systems `http://research.microsoft.com/en-us/um/people/gurevich/opera/204.pdf`.

Bourne, S. (1983). *The Unix System* (Addison–Wesley).

Brinch-Hansen, P. (1977). *The Architecture of Concurrent Programs* (Prentice-Hall).

Checkland, P. B. (1998). *Systems Thinking, Systems Practice* (John Wiley & Sons Ltd.).

Checkland, P. B. and Scholes, J. (1990). *Soft Systems Methodology in Action* (John Wiley & Sons Ltd.).

Clarke, E., Emerson, E. and Sistla, A. (1986). Automatic verification of finite-state concurrent systems using temporal logic specifications, *ACM Transactions on Programming Languages and Systems* **8**, 2, pp. 244–263.

Donovan, J. (1972). *Systems Programming* (McGraw-Hill Book Company).

Enderton, H. (1977). *Elements of Set Theory* (Academic Press).

Engels, J. (1999). *Programming for the Java Virtual Machine* (Addison Wesley).

GCC Compiler Command (2014). Option summary – using the gnu compiler collection (gcc), `https://gcc.gnu.org/.../gccOption--Summary.ht`.

GDB (2014). The GNU project debugger, www.gnu.org/s/gdb.

Googheart, B. and Cox, J. (1994). *The Magic Garden Explained* (Prentice Hally).

Graham, B. (1968). Protection in an information processing utility, *Communications of the ACM* **11**, 5, pp. 306–312.

Gray, J. S. (1998). *Interprocess Communications in UNIX*, 2nd edn. (Prentice–Hall).

Hopcroft, J. and Ullman, J. (1979). *Introduction to Automata Theory, Languages, and Computation* (Addison-Wesley, Reading, MA).

Horn, P. (2001). *Autonomic Computing: IBM's Perspective on the State of the Information Technology* `http://www.research.IBM.com/autonomic/manifesto`.

Horridge, M. (2011). Protègè-OWL tutorial `http://owl.cs.manchester.ac.uk/tutorials/protegeowltutorial/`.

IBM (1971). *The HASP System, HASP* —— (IBM).

IBM (1992). *RISC System/6000^{TM} POWERstation and POWERserver*, 2nd edn. (IBM SA23-2643-01).

IDB (2014). Intel debugger user's and reference guides, `https://software.intel.com/en-us/articles/idb-linux`.

JDTDebug (2014). JDT Ddebug – Help – Eclipse help.eclipse.org/projects/eclipse. jdt.debug

Kernighan, B. W. and Ritchie, R. D. (1988). *The C Programming Language*, 2nd edn. (Prentice Hall).

Knuth, D. E. (1968). *The Art of Computer Programming*, Vol. 1 (Addision-Wesley).

Lampson, B. W. (1985). Protection, *ACM Operating System Reviews* **19**, 5, pp. 13–24.

Landin, P. (1966). The next 700 programming languages, *Communications of the ACM* **9**, 3, pp. 157–166.

Levy, H. and Eckhouse, R. (1980). *Computer Programming and Architecture* (Digital Press).

LLDB (2014). LLDB homepage, lldb.livm.org.

Malcev, A. (1970). *Algorithms and Recursive Functions* (Wolters–Nordhoff Publishers, Groningen).

Manna, Z. and Pnueli, A. (1992). *The Temporal Logic of Reactive and Concurrent Systems: Specification* (Springer-Verlag New-York, Inc.).

Markoff, J. (2012). Killing the computer to save it *New York Times, 30 October*

Markov, A. A. and Nagorny, N. (1988). *The Theory of Algorithms* (Springer).

Minsky, M. (1967). *Computation: Finite and Infinite Machines* (Prentice-Hall., Inc. NJ.).

MSDN (2014). Debugging in visual studio – MSDN – Microsoft, MSDN.microsoft.com/en-us/.

Nagel, E. and Hofstadter, D. (2008). *Gödel's Proof* (NYU Press).

Organick, E. (1972). *The Multics System: An Examination of its Structure* (MIT Press, Cambridge, MA.).

Peterson, J. (1978). *Computer Organization and Assembly Language Programming* (Academic Press).

Pierce, R. (2013). Watson and the future of cognitive computing *ACM TechNews, Monday August 5*.

Polya, G. (1957). *How To Solve It*, 2nd edn. (Princeton University Press).

Popek, G. and Goldberg, R. (1974). Formal requirements for virtualizable third generation architectures, *Communications of the A.C.M.* **17**, 7, pp. 412–421.

Rus, T. (2002). A unified language processing methodology, *Theoretical Computer Science* **281**, 1–2.

Rus, T. (2012). Computer integration within problem solving process, homepage. cs.uiowa.edu/~rus/.

Rus, T. (2013). Computational emancipation of problem domains, homepage. cs.uiowa.edu/~rus/.

Rus, T. and Bui, C. (2010). Software development for non-expert computer users, in *Proceedings of the International Conference on Cloud Computing and Virtualization* (Management University, Singapore), pp. 200–207.

Rus, T. and Curtis, D. (2006). Application driven software development, in *International Conference on Software Engineering Advances, Proceedings* (Tahiti), p. 32.

Rus, T. and Rus, D. (1993). *Systems Methodology for Software* (World Scientific).

Rusling, D. A. (2002). *The Linux Kernel* (David A. Rusling).

Schanin, D. (1986). The design and development of a very high speed bus — the encore multimax Nanobus, in *ACM'86 Proceedings of 1986 ACM Fall joint computer conference* (IEEE Computer Society Pres, Los Alamitos, CA, USA), pp. 410–418.

Shaw, M. and Garlan, D. (1996). *Software Architecture: Perspective on an Emerging Discipline* (Prentice Hall).

Sipser, M. (2006). *Introduction to the Theory of Computation*, 2nd edn. (Thomson Course Technology).

Smith, J. and Noir, R. (2005). *Virtual Machines* (Morgan-Kaufmann).

Software Testing (2014). Software testing — wikipedia, the free encyclopedia, en.wikipedia.org/wiki/Software_testing.

Stevens, W., Fenner, B. and Rudoff, A. M. (2004). *UNIX Network Programming* (Addison–Wesley).

Systems Methodology (2013). Soft systems methodology. en.wikipedia.org/wiki/Soft_systems_methodology.

Takeuti, G. and Zaring, W. (1971). *Introduction to Axiomatic Set Theory* (Springer-Verlag).

Tygar, J. and Wing, J. (1987). Visual specification of security constraints, in *The IEEE Workshop on Visual Languages* (IEEE Press, New York, Linköping, Sweden, August 19–21), p. unknown.

Valgrind (2014). Valgrind — wikipedia, the free encyclopedia.

Van Wyk, E. (2003). Specification languages in alebgraic compilers, *Theoretical Computer Science* **231**, 3, pp. 351–385.

WBPSP (2012). A 2020 compouter user, homepage.cs.uiowa.edu/~rus/2020 user.pdf.

Wilhelm, R. and Maurer, D. (1995). *Compiler Design* (Addison–Wesley).

Wilson, B. (1990). *Systems: Concepts, Methodologies and Applications* (John Wiley & Sons Ltd.).

WinDbg (2014). Windbg — wikipedia, the free encyclopedia.

Index